Desmond Seward was born in Paris a
College, Cambridge. He is one of Britain
ans and the author of twenty-nine books

Other titles in the series

Forthcoming

Naples,
A Traveller's Reader
Edited and introduced
by Desmond Seward

———

ROBINSON

ROBINSON
First published in the UK in 1984 as *Naples: A Traveller's Companion* by Constable and Co. Ltd

This edition published in 2018 by Robinson

10 9 8 7 6 5 4 3 2 1

ISBN: 978-1-47214-230-6

Typeset in Whitman by Hewer Text UK Ltd, Edinburgh
Printed and bound in Great Britain by CPI Group (UK) Ltd, Croydon CR0 4YY

Papers used by Robinson are from well-managed forests and other responsible sources.

MIX
Paper from
responsible sources
FSC
www.fsc.org   FSC® C104740

Robinson
An imprint of
Little, Brown Book Group
Carmelite House
50 Victoria Embankment
London EC4Y 0DZ

An Hachette UK Company
www.hachette.co.uk

www.littlebrown.co.uk

For

HRH Prince Ferdinand of The Two Sicilies, Duke of Castro

Contents

THE ANGEVIN CHURCHES: SANTA CHIARA, SAN LORENZO MAGGIORE, SANTA MARIA DONNAREGINA, SAN GIOVANNI A CARBONARA AND THE INCORONATA

ARAGONESE AND VICEREGAL CHURCHES: SANTA
ANNA DEI LOMBARDI, SAN DOMENICO MAGGIORE,
SAN GIACOMO DEGLI SPAGNUOLI, THE CERTOSA
DI SAN MARTINO AND THE GESÙ NUOVO

THE PALAZZO REALE (ROYAL PALACE)

THE TEATRO SAN CARLO

VIA TOLEDO AND THE PALACE OF CAPODIMONTE

THE APPROACHES TO NAPLES
THE PALACE OF CASERTA

THE PALACE OF PORTICI

VESUVIUS AND POMPEII

LIFE, CUSTOMS AND MORALS IN NAPLES

Acknowledgements

My first debt is to H.E. Don Achille de Lorenzo for his memorable hospitality at Naples. It was a privilege to have the encouragement of one who knows so well the history and traditions of his own beloved city. I am almost as much indebted to Count Ciechanowiecki, who gave me invaluable references and introductions, and who read the typescript. I am grateful also to Dr Alvar Gonzalez Palacios, and to Professor Raffaello Causa, Soprintendente per i Beni Culturali e Artistici at Naples. Mr Reresby Sitwell did me an inestimable kindness in drawing to my attention King Ferdinand II's personal copy of *Tipi Militari* (the definitive contemporary delineation of the army of The Two Sicilies) in the collection at Renishaw; and I am indebted to Mrs Prudence Fay for her editorial criticism and suggestions.

I also wish to make acknowledgement to the following for extracts used from their editions:

David Higham and Sir Harold Acton for *The Bourbons of Naples* and *The Last Bourbons of Naples*; A. Zwemmer for Anthony Blunt's *Neapolitan Baroque and Rococo Architecture*; Sir Sacheverell Sitwell for extracts from his *Southern Baroque Art* and *Truffle Hunt*; Cambridge University Press for *The Sicilian Vespers* by Sir Steven Runciman; Collins/Harvill for *The Leopard* by Giuseppe di Lampedusa, translated by Archibald Colquhoun; George Allen & Unwin for *Memoirs of a Renaissance Pope* by Pope Pius II, translated by F.A. Gragg; Peter Gunn for *Naples: A Palimpsest*; Arnoldo Mondadori, Milan, for *Francesco II di Borbone, L'ultimo re di Napoli* by Pier Giusto Jaeger; Greenwood Press USA for *Garibaldi and the Making of Italy* by G.M. Trevelyan; Collins for *The Structures of Everyday Life* by Fernand Braudel, translated by M. Kochan; The Folio Society for *Music, Men and Manners in France and Italy in 1770* by Dr Charles Burney; Oxford University Press for *The Letters of Percy Bysshe Shelley*, edited by F.L. Jones; Weidenfeld and Nicolson for *Great Opera Houses* by S. Hughes, for *Vincenzo Bellini* by Herbert Weinstock, and for extracts by Sir Harold Acton and Giuseppe Galasso from the catalogue 'Painting in Naples 1606–1705 Caravaggio to Giordano', edited by Clovis Whitfield and Jane Martineau, which they published in conjunction with the Royal Academy of Arts.

And as usual I owe a great deal to the staffs of the British Library and the London Library – this book would never have been written without their assistance.

D.S.

1984

Introduction

The beauty of Naples is proverbial, the breathtaking bay giving it the most superb setting of any city in Europe. Goethe remarked that nobody who had seen Naples could ever be really unhappy, while the saying *Vedere Napoli e poi morire* – 'see Naples and die' – has become a cliché. Yet although wonderfully exciting, it is the least visited among the great cities of Italy. If spared the tourist hordes that mar Florence and Venice, it does not receive the respect that is its due. Many Italian cities look back with pride to the time when they were independent republics. Naples, on the contrary, prefers to remember its days as a royal capital. The surest way of rediscovering this unjustly neglected city's extraordinary fascination is to learn a little – if only a very little – Neapolitan history through the eyes of spectators of its former grandeur.

Much of the city is still elegant and prosperous. Where there is dirt, there is often colour as well – walls washed with terracotta or pale coral, silver-grey or yellow ochre. Besides medieval monasteries and castles there are Baroque churches and palaces by the hundred; the exuberance and theatricality of the Baroque appeal immediately to the Neapolitan temperament. The museums contain such local treasures as the exquisite porcelain of Capodimonte, the dramatic *chiaroscuro* paintings of the seventeenth century (exhibited in London at the Royal Academy in 1982) and the cheerful naturalistic works of the Posillipo School of the nineteenth century. The city's history is most vividly illustrated by portraits, prints and other relics of the past – including the royal state barge – up at the Certosa di San Martino on its spur overlooking the bay, from where there is the best of all views of Naples. The Museo Archeologico houses one of the world's finest collections of Classical art. The San Carlo opera house remains a glory, and there are lesser but delightful theatres, not to mention street singers; the comedy of Pulcinella and Rosetta is still alive and well. There are superlative shops in Via Roma, Via Chiaia and in Piazza dei Martiri. *La cucina*

napoletana is not to be despised, while the ordinary Neapolitan's wine
– the frothy, purple Gragnano – is cheap and delicious when drunk
chilled with *frutti di mare* or wild strawberries. There are really excellent restaurants, and cafés where cakes and ices are always superb.
Above all there is sunshine and the sea. Anyone who explores long
enough, with an open mind, must inevitably succumb to the city's siren
charm. Even Milton enjoyed himself 'by dead Parthenope's dear tomb'.

There are, of course, reasons why less adventurous tourists stay
away – the *Michelin* guide warns prospective visitors that they need 'a
very flexible outlook'. The city itself, a human anthill with over a million
and a quarter inhabitants, is the centre of a conurbation of three million
people. It suffers all the harrowing consequences of chronic unemployment; its slums and poverty are offensive even to the most hard-boiled;
its shabbiness and decay are frequently overwhelming. Newspapers
constantly report crime waves and the gang warfare of the *Camorra* –
the Neapolitan version of the Mafia. Before discussing Spacca-Napoli
(the centre of the old city), *Michelin* says sombrely, 'To avoid possible
incidents, tourists are advised to dress simply and not to draw attention
to themselves in any way. The visit should be made by day.' Mugging
and bag-snatching are endemic. The streets of the old city and the
Spanish Quarter contain some of the most glorious buildings in Europe
but have to be explored on foot because they are too narrow for coaches
or for parking cars. On wider streets the traffic has been chokingly
dense and dangerous since long before the motor age – today, according to *Michelin*, 'Tourists need courage and determination to venture
across the road.' There is bewilderment everywhere, in an ancient city
where neon lights spoil the sunset yet where a coral phallus is still
widely worn to ward off the Evil Eye, and where, in spite of a Communist
mayor, San Gennaro's blood continued to liquefy miraculously. The
shadow of Vesuvius is unnerving. So too is the inhabitants' irrepressible
mockery. Deafening noise and seemingly frenzied chaos can demoral-
ize Northerners within a few days; it has been said that Anglo-Saxons
– whether British or American – actually fear the city, and agree with

Augustus Hare that it is 'a paradise of devils'. A patronizing English aesthete once called Naples a dunghill stuffed with jewels.

But 'dunghill' is mere abuse. The blemishes enhance the beauties. If robbery is endemic, it is less vicious than in Northern Italy and tends towards sneak-thieving rather than violence. While undoubtedly fast and noisy, the traffic is safer than in New York or Paris. Hare admits that though the inhabitants may be devils, 'they are lively and amusing devils' – he also concedes: 'The spirit of fun which possesses Neapolitans is irresistible.' For peace and quiet there are the gardens of Chiaia, and there is plenty of bourgeois calm up on the Vomero.

Naples has to be recognized for what it is: a challenge – and a thrilling challenge. Nowhere else are contrasts quite so violent – of sunlight and squalor, of grandeur and decay, pleasure and misery, gaiety and despair, the best and the worst – as in 'Parthenope'. It is this that makes the city so extraordinarily exciting. A stranger who overcomes his timidity will be marvellously rewarded. For the city is still Mrs Piozzi's 'delightful and astonishing Naples', still Mme Vigée-Lebrun's '*lanterne magique ravissante*'. One can still feel with Shelley – perhaps even more so today – that it is the 'Metropolis of a ruined Paradise'. Its drawbacks are in fact assets, since they deter the casual tourist.

Nobody who drives from the seafront to the San Carlo, from Via Caracciolo past the Palazzo Reale, can fail to see that Naples was once a capital city, and a royal capital at that. 'In size and number of inhabitants she ranks as the third city of Europe, and from her situation and superb show may justly be considered as the Queen of the Mediterranean,' wrote John Chetwode Eustace in 1813. Until 1860 Naples was the political and administrative centre of the Kingdom of The Two Sicilies, the most beautiful kingdom in the world. Consisting of Southern Italy and Sicily, it had a land mass equal to that of Portugal and was the richest state in Italy. (It was often incorrectly referred to, especially when speaking of the mainland alone, as the Kingdom of Naples; the name 'Two Sicilies' commemorates a struggle, lasting from the thirteenth to the fifteenth centuries, between two rival dynasties

that both claimed Sicily, one reigning at Naples and the other at
Palermo.) Founded in 1139, for nearly 600 years the Kingdom of The
Two Sicilies was the only Italian kingdom. For five generations – from
1734 till 1860 – it was ruled by a branch of the French and Spanish royal
family of Bourbon who filled the city with monuments to their reign:
the Piazza Reale (now Piazza Plebiscito), the Piazza Dante, the Albergo
dei Poveri, the new royal palace of Capodimonte. They built, and
rebuilt, the San Carlo itself and created the Museo Borbonico – now
the Museo Archeologico.

The 'Borboni', as their subjects called them, were complete
Neapolitans, wholly assimilated, who spoke and thought in Neapolitan
dialect (indeed the entire court spoke Neapolitan). They lived in Naples
amid their people, at the vast Palazzo Reale on the seashore; or at
Capodimonte – 'on the top of the hill' – looking down the long, straight,
narrow thoroughfare of the Via Toledo; or else at Caserta, the Neapolitan
Versailles only a few miles away. Some of them, such as the 'lazzarone
king', Ferdinand I (whom Stendhal compared to Fielding's Squire
Western and who reigned longer than Queen Victoria), or that picturesque autocrat, Ferdinand II (unjustly named 'Bomba' on account of a
bombardment he never ordered), were Naples itself. Until 1860, glittering Court balls and regal gala nights at the San Carlo that staggered
foreigners by their opulence and splendour were a feature of Neapolitan
life. The last Borbone king, Francis II, died as recently as 1894, and his
widowed Wittelsbach queen, Maria Sophia (sister of the tragic Empress
Elizabeth of Austria), lived on until 1925, to be portrayed by Proust in
La Prisonnière. Sir Sacheverell Sitwell recalls seeing her, 'an old lady in
black with many pearls'. Today there is still a Borbone Pretender, the
Duke of Castro.

However, Naples is nearly 3,000 years old and saw countless marvels
long before the Borboni. Originally a colony of Greeks from Cumae in
Campania (of Athenian extraction), it takes its other name, Parthenope,
from the tomb of the siren Parthenope, a beautiful, mournful, murder-
ing sea-songstress, half virgin, half bird. (She fell in love with Odysseus,

and when he proved immune to her charms she drowned herself and her body was washed ashore in the Bay of Naples.) In the fifth century, refugees from Cumae founded a 'new city' next to Parthenope – Neapolis. Unlike the old city, Neapolis saved itself by surrendering to the Romans in 328 BC; it was besieged unsuccessfully by Hannibal but sacked by Sulla. Virgil wrote his *Georgics* here, and was buried here (his tomb now is probably under the sea). The Emperor Nero's first public theatrical performance took place at Neapolis. The ultimate Roman Emperor of the West, the boy Romulus Augustulus, was brought here after his deposition by the Ostrogoths in AD 476. Sixty years later the city was recaptured from the barbarians by the Byzantine hero Count Belisarius, only to fall to King Totila shortly afterwards, before being finally retaken for Byzantium in AD 553. During the obscure centuries that followed it existed in perilous semi-independence, though owing nominal allegiance to the Eastern Emperors. From 1139 to 1191 it was ruled by the Hauteville kings of Sicily, Norman adventurers who carved out what was to become the Kingdom of The Two Sicilies and over which they reigned brilliantly from their harems at Palermo, surrounded by French, Greek, Arab and even English, as well as Italian, courtiers. The grim Castel dell' Ovo ('Egg Castle') on its island opposite Santa Lucia was begun by the Hauteville king, William the Bad, in 1154, and was completed by a successor of the Hautevilles, Emperor Frederick II of Hohenstaufen – the 'Wonder of the World' – who also founded the university, the 'Studio'. In 1268 Naples watched with horror the execution of Frederick's sixteen-year-old grandson, King Conradin – last of the Hohenstaufen – in what was soon to be the Piazza del Mercato, by his rival, Charles of Anjou.

Naples first became a capital under this new Angevin dynasty, a branch of the French royal house. After conquering the kingdom, Charles I – Count of Anjou and brother of St Louis – established his administration at Naples rather than Palermo for strategic reasons. The loss of the other half of his realm in 1282, following the rebellion known as the Sicilian Vespers, which set up a rival dynasty at Palermo,

confirmed Naples's pre-eminence on the southern mainland and made
the city a royal capital. As though by some premonition Charles had
begun to build the Castel Nuovo – the Neapolitan Bastille – three years
before the Vespers. Boccaccio knew the court at the Castel Nuovo very
well, and met his lovely Fiammetta in the church of San Lorenzo. King
Robert the Wise (Fiammetta's putative father) entertained Petrarch in
the Castel Nuovo; and the poet has left a vivid account of his terror
during the fearful storm of 1343, when he was staying at the friary (still
occupied by friars today) next to the church of San Lorenzo. The Castel
Nuovo, together with the Castel Capuano (now the Vicaria), housed
the sinister courts of two ill-famed queens, the exquisite and perhaps
murderous Giovanna I and the depraved Giovanna II. The first had four
husbands and, some say, innumerable lovers – Boccaccio was a courtier
and may have written the *Decameron* for her – and was finally smothered in a featherbed in 1382; the second, succeeding to the throne in
1414 as a forty-five-year-old widow, gave herself up to debauchery and
to both a low-born and a high-born favourite – Pandolfello Alopo and
'Ser Gianni' Caracciolo respectively – both of whom died terrible
deaths. Eventually she brought the Angevin dynasty to an ignominious
end. Her heir, René of Anjou (father-in-law to Henry VI of England),
failed to make good his inheritance, and in 1442 that magnificent
warrior and patron of letters Alfonso of Aragon rode in through a cere-
moniously demolished breach in the walls. He was the first monarch to
call himself 'King of The Two Sicilies'. His bastard and successor,
Ferrante (who may really have been the son of a Moorish slave from
Valencia), kept a museum of mummified enemies dressed in their own
clothes at the Castel Nuovo; and he solved the problem of a turbulent
baronage simply by inviting the barons to a wedding feast that few of
them left alive – the castle banqueting-hall is still called the *Sala dei
Baroni*. There is a legend that he kept a crocodile in a dungeon and
rewarded it from time to time with a live prisoner. King Ferrante begot
an even more terrible successor in Alfonso II, a bestially cruel voluptu-
ary popularly known as *Dio della carne* (or, until he succeeded, as *Il*

feroce giovane) who was also the discerning patron of the arts who persuaded his father to build the Porta Capuana. In 1502 Federigo, the last Aragonese king, fled to France after being robbed of his throne by a Spanish cousin.

During the sixteenth and seventeenth centuries Naples was ruled from Spain, with resident viceroys and a Habsburg absentee monarch. Public life at that period was less spectacular, even provincial. Taxation was merciless and there were several despairing revolts, the most famous of these being the popular – and bloody – rebellion of 1647, led by the mad fisherman-king Masaniello. Nonetheless two hundred years under Spanish viceroys left their mark. The grave manners of the old ruling class, the use of the titles *Don* and *Donna*, and the mantillas still worn by great ladies on high occasions are relics from this period. The large number of *palazzi* is a direct consequence of the Spaniards' policy of enticing great nobles into the city so that they would be less likely to rebel; instead of lurking in a castle or villa deep in the countryside, they built in Naples enormous mansions to house themselves and their huge armies of retainers. By contrast the brief, troubled and unpopular Austrian viceroyalty of 1713–34 left little impression.

Naples became once more a truly royal capital in 1734 with the accession of Charles VII, first of the Neapolitan Bourbons, and usually known as Charles III, after his later title as King of Spain. He was the son of Philip V of Spain – Louis XIV's grandson – and of Elizabeth Farnese, and had received The Two Sicilies as part of the general rearrangement of the European map that followed the War of the Polish Succession. Just as for most historically minded people the attraction of Leningrad dates from the days before 1917 when it was St Petersburg and a capital city, so the real interest of Naples lies in the period when it too was a capital. Its cultural zenith was from 1734 to 1860 and especially the first seventy years. Among other buildings Charles created the Teatro San Carlo, the palaces of Caserta (which is larger than Versailles), of Portici and Capodimonte; Herculaneum and Pompeii were discovered; the Museo Archeologico was founded, bringing together the Farnese collections inherited by the royal family and the pick of the recent discoveries at Herculaneum and Pompeii; composers such as Porpora, Piccinni, Galuppi, Jomelli, Paisiello and Cimarosa gave lustre to the San Carlo, supported by the librettist Metastasio, by *castrati* like Caffarelli and by such female voices as those of Margherita Pozzi and la Grassini; Sir William and Lady Hamilton were in favour at Court and Nelson was welcomed as a conquering hero. In the eighteenth century all Europe, from the Holy Roman Emperor Joseph II and King Gustav III of Sweden to Prince Augustus of Great Britain (the future Duke of Sussex), from Casanova to Mozart and Goethe, from Angelica Kauffman and Joseph Wright of Derby to David and Mme Vigée-Lebrun, flocked to Parthenope.

A hundred years later Vernon Lee wrote of this heyday: 'Naples feudal and antique, at once so backward in social institutions and so happy in natural endowments, which could make Goethe feel even more of a Greek than he naturally was – Naples, which from amongst intellectual and physical filth gave Italy in the eighteenth century her philosophy and art, her Vico and her Pergolesi, her Filangieri and her Cimarosa.' Vico was the first cyclical historian, Pergolesi the inventor of *opera buffa*, Filangieri the century's most creative jurist and Cimarosa Napoleon's favourite composer. It was no accident that one of Handel's operas was *Parthenope*.

There were brief, though occasionally bloody, upheavals during the Revolutionary and Napoleonic wars. A short-lived Parthenopean Republic was brought in by the first wave of French invaders; and the second wave installed Napoleon's brother, Joseph Bonaparte, on the throne. Two years later he was given that of Spain and replaced in Naples by Napoleon's brother-in-law, Marshal Murat – half hero, half clown – who reigned as King Gioacchino Napoleone. Most Neapolitans watched with resigned amusement, but they gave a tumultuous welcome-home to the Borboni when they were restored in 1815. The San Carlo, rebuilt in 1817, saw the first triumphs of Rossini and Bellini, and some of those of Donizetti and Verdi as well, the monarch continuing to preside from his box.

Ferdinand II (1830–59) has been done a grave injustice by history and libelled as an unimaginative foreign tyrant. In reality he was both the last of the benevolent despots and the Agnelli of his age, besides being the most full-bloodedly Neapolitan of all rulers of Naples. Among his achievements were the building of the first railways and the first iron suspension-bridge in Italy, and a factory at Naples producing steam engines for locomotives and ships. He also laid down the first overland electric telegraph cable in Italy; and then an undersea telegraph cable to Naples; as well as building the Mediterranean's most advanced dockyard and its first lenticular light-house. Largely as a result of his encouragement, the merchant marine of The Two Sicilies at one time comprised the largest steamer fleet in the Mediterranean and was the first underwritten by modern insurance. In 1839 he gave his capital gas lighting in all main streets. His country's industries were among the most flourishing in Europe, encouraged by surprisingly progressive labour laws. Perhaps his most enduring monument is the clifftop road around the Sorrentine peninsula – hitherto Sorrento and Amalfi had only been accessible from the sea. And it was the same ruler who saved the San Carlo from bankruptcy time and again. Just as the last decades of Habsburg Vienna are associated with operetta and Strauss waltzes, so the last decades of Bourbon Naples are associated with *bel canto* and Romantic ballet. This paternal autocrat was deeply respected by the majority of his subjects as a royal *capo*, and tens of thousands flocked in tears to his funeral. It may even be claimed that in some ways he was to Naples what Franz-Josef was to Vienna.

Ferdinand's son, the ineffectual, unlucky, yet well-intentioned king Francis II – whom Pope Pius IX compared with Job – was fortunate enough to marry the glamorous and high-spirited Maria Sophia of Bavaria. However, despite all her courage and popularity, she was unable to save her husband from the tidal wave of the Risorgimento, which swept him off his throne in 1860. Too late, during his kingdom's last stand at Gaeta, he matured into a brave and resourceful monarch.

The Risorgimento ('resurrection'), or unification of Italy, took all save a few Italians by surprise. At the beginning of 1859 there were five other major Italian states besides The Two Sicilies – the Kingdom of Sardinia (usually known as Piedmont), the Grand Duchy of Tuscany, the Duchy of Parma, the Duchy of Modena and the Papal States under the Pope. In the north, Lombardy-Venetia formed part of the Austrian Empire. 'Italy' was a mere geographical expression, though there were a number of schemes for closer unity among Italians – including a federation presided over by the Pope or by the King of The Two Sicilies; or else a Northern, a Central and a Southern Italy. Very few people envisaged in their wildest dreams a single, unified, country. Then in the spring of 1859 the Piedmontese provoked the Austrians into declaring war on them, and the meddlesome Emperor of the French, Napoleon III – bent on acquiring military glory and on posing as the friend of nationalism everywhere – came in on their side. After a short but murderous campaign costing thousands of lives, the Austrians agreed to an armistice in June that same year, and evacuated Lombardy, which was taken over by Piedmont. The Habsburg rulers of Tuscany and Modena then lost control of their countries and Piedmontese troops marched in. They had already overrun Parma. The Papal States were next (apart from Rome, which was defended by a French garrison). It was scarcely surprising that the army of The Two Sicilies, already thoroughly demoralized, should have collapsed so quickly in the summer of 1860. Its troops redeemed their honour by their defence of the coastal stronghold of Gaeta, during which Maria Sophia showed herself a heroine, but it was in vain. In 1861 the last King and Queen sailed into exile and The Two Sicilies ceased to exist as a country. Only in 1984 will the bodies of Francis II and Maria Sophia return to Naples to be reburied at Santa Chiara with their predecessors. No doubt Italy gained a great deal from unification, but much that was worth fighting for was swept away. The Two Sicilies and Naples lost most of all.

During the last decades of Bourbon rule, Europe continued to go to Naples as a matter of course. Schiller and Humboldt, Mendelssohn and

Berlioz, Chateaubriand, Stendhal, Lamartine, Alexandre Dumas and Théophile Gautier, Shelley and Turner, Lady Morgan, Bulwer Lytton, Lady Blessington, Charles Lever, Charles Dickens, John Stuart Mill, Dr Arnold, Sir Humphrey Davy, Cardinal Newman, Gladstone, Richard Cobden and Edward Lear were among the visitors. Royal personages who came included the King and Queen of Prussia, the Comte de Chambord (Henri V, to Legitimist Frenchmen) and Don Carlos (the Carlist King of Spain) with all his brothers, together with Austrian archdukes, Russian grand dukes and countless German princes. Even the Pope took refuge there after the upheavals in Rome that followed the 1848 Revolution. The Toledo remained the most fashionable street outside Paris, and the San Carlo one of the world's two or three truly great opera houses. In 1839 that ferocious Whig Lord Macaulay was staying in the city and wrote, 'I must say that the accounts which I have heard of Naples are very incorrect. There is far less beggary than in Rome, and far more industry ... At present, my impressions are very favourable to Naples. It is the only place in Italy that has seemed to me to have the same sort of vitality which you find in all the great English ports and cities. Rome and Pisa are dead and gone; Florence is not dead, but sleepeth; while Naples overflows with life.'

The Borboni's memory has been systematically blackened by partisans of the regime that supplanted them, and by admirers of the Risorgimento. They have had a particularly bad press in the Anglo-Saxon world. Nineteenth-century English liberals loathed them for their absolutism, their clericalism and loyalty to the Papacy and their opposition to the fashionable cause of Italian unity. Politicians from Lord William Bentinck to Lord Palmerston and Gladstone, writers such as Browning and George Eliot, united in detesting the 'tyrants'; Gladstone convinced himself that their regime was 'the negation of God'. Such critics, as prejudiced as they were ill informed, ignored the dynasty's economic achievement, the kingdom's remarkable prosperity compared with other Italian states, the inhabitants' relative contentment and the fact that only a mere handful of Southern Italians were opposed to their government. Till the end, The Two Sicilies was remarkable for the majority of its subjects' respect for, and knowledge of, its laws – so deep that even today probably most Italian judges, and especially successful advocates, still come from the south. Yet even now there is a mass of blind prejudice among historians. All too many guide-books dismiss the Borboni as corrupt despots who misruled and neglected their capital. An entire curtain of slander conceals the old, pre-1860 Naples; with the passage of time calumny has been supple-mented by ignorance, and it is easy to forget that history is always written by the victors. However Sir Harold Acton in his two splendid studies of the Borboni has to some extent redressed the balance, and his interpretation of past events is winning over increasing support – espe-cially in Naples itself.

Undoubtedly the old monarchy had serious failings. Though economically and industrially creative, it was also absolutist and isola-tionist, disastrously out of touch with pan-Italian aspirations. Ferdinand II was offered the Crown of Italy and could almost certainly have imposed Neapolitan rule throughout the entire peninsula in much the same way that Bismarck's Prussia was to take over Germany; he refused, from misguided loyalty to the Papacy and exaggerated respect for his fellow-sovereigns in Piedmont, Tuscany, Parma and Modena, though he might easily have established an Italian confederation without depriving them of their thrones. (On one occasion he actually proposed the formation of a league of Italian states, but it was rejected by Piedmont; he also spoke frequently of setting up an Italian customs union.) Similarly, Sicily could have been placated by the creation of a constitutional dual monarchy to make Palermo independent of Naples – as it was until 1816. Beyond question there was political repression under the Bourbons – the dynasty was fighting for its survival – but it has been magnified out of all proportion. On the whole prison condi-tions were probably no worse than in contemporary England, which still had its hulks; what really upset Gladstone was seeing his social equals being treated in the same way as working-class convicts, since opposition to the regime was restricted to a few liberal romantics among the aristocracy and bourgeoisie. Unfortunately for Ferdinand's reputation, and for historical truth, his regime did not survive him. When he died prematurely in May 1859 he bequeathed a monolithic structure of which his timid and inexperienced young successor, only twenty-three, soon showed signs of losing control. It was undermined by a fatalist conviction in important circles that so inadequate a leader was incapable of halting the Risorgimento at his borders, and also by a widespread network of Piedmontese secret agents and bribery.

Francis II speedily confirmed even his most faithful supporters' misgivings by disbanding the Swiss regiments that were his ultimate safeguard. When, in the following year, the crisis came after Garibaldi's astonishingly successful invasion of Sicily, the vast majority of the mainland population remained loyal but all too many senior army officers and government officials doubted Francis's ability to survive, and deserted him to save their posts and pensions. Had Ferdinand II lived out a normal span of years, The Two Sicilies might still be an independent country today – or at least the senior partner in an Italian confederation. Indeed as late as April 1860, *after* Garibaldi had begun his invasion, the King of Piedmont wrote to Francis proposing that they divide the peninsula between their two monarchies. For all its faults the Bourbon realm was far more in tune with the Neapolitan character than the regime that replaced it.

The Risorgimento was a disaster for Naples and for the south in general. Before 1860 the Mezzogiorno was the richest part of Italy outside the Austrian Empire; after it quickly became the poorest. The facts speak for themselves. In 1859 money circulating in The Two Sicilies amounted to more than that circulating in all other independent Italian states, while the Bank of Naples's gold reserve was 443 million gold lire, twice the combined reserves of the rest of Italy. This gold was immediately confiscated by Piedmont – whose own reserve had been a mere 27 million – and transferred to Turin. Neapolitan excise duties, levied to keep out the north's inferior goods and providing four-fifths of the city's revenue, were abolished. And then the northerners imposed crushing new taxes. Far from being liberators, the Piedmontese administrators who came in the wake of the Risorgimento behaved like Yankees in the post-bellum Southern States; they ruled The Two Sicilies as an occupied country, systematically demolishing its institutions and industries. Ferdinand's new dockyard was dismantled to stop Naples competing with Genoa (it is now being restored by industrial archaeologists). Vilification of the Borboni became part of the school curriculum. Shortly after the Two Sicilies' enforced incorporation into the new Kingdom of Italy, the Duke of Maddaloni protested in the 'national' Parliament: 'This is invasion, not annexation, not union. We are being plundered like an occupied territory.' For years after the 'liberation', Neapolitans were governed by northern *padroni* and carpet-baggers. And today the Italians of the north can be as stupidly prejudiced about Naples as any Anglo-Saxon, affecting a superiority that verges on racism – 'Africa begins South of Rome' – and lamenting the presence in the north of so many workers from the Mezzogiorno. (The ill-feeling is reciprocated, the Neapolitan translation of SPQR being *Sono porci, questi Romani*.) Throughout the 1860s 150,000 troops were needed to hold down the south.

Neapolitan regret at the change of regime is undeniable. Farini, the Piedmontese 'Lieutenant-General for the Neapolitan Provinces', estimated that there were 'less than a hundred believers in national unity among seven million inhabitants', despite a supposedly unanimous Neapolitan plebiscite in favour of it. Soon many southerners who had fought for Garibaldi openly regretted their victory. In 1861 a cheering mob ran up the Borbone flag in the centre of Naples; and guerrillas loyal to the King waged a grim war in the mountains until 1865, led by officers from the old army and aided by committees at Rome, Marseilles and Trieste. (In 1866 Sicily too rose against the 'liberators'.)

A government and a court in exile, recruited from countless faithful Neapolitans, existed for many years. When Francis II died in 1894, Austro-Hungary and the Holy See recognized his brother, the Count of

Caserta, as King Alfonso of The Two Sicilies. The Holy See only ceased to receive an ambassador from The Two Sicilies in 1902. Even today the Vatican accords recognition to the exiled dynasty's orders of chivalry – those of San Gennaro and Constantinian St George. (Indeed the Italian Republic has recently given official permission for Italian citizens to wear the latter, alone of all Italian dynastic orders.) Mezzogiorno Jacobitism is far from extinct as a sentiment, and is surprisingly widespread: the Pretender's photograph has an honoured place in an unsuspectedly large number of Neapolitan drawing-rooms, while only recently the Naples football club adopted the Bourbon lily as its emblem. The San Carlo has renewed its homage to its creators: during restoration work some years ago the old royal arms over the royal box were discovered intact beneath the Cross of Savoy that had been painted over them – now the full armorial achievement of the House of Borbone delle Due Sicilie dominates the beautiful opera house, once more.

However, there is of course no question of separation, of renewed independence; no political dimension. The Kingdom of The Two Sicilies has vanished as irrevocably as the Republic of Venice. All that has been bequeathed to its people's heirs is a sense of history. Just as some men of distinguished ancestry who suffer reverses and poverty look back to their great forebears for reassurance, so many Neapolitans cherish the noble past of *Napoli Gentilissima*.

The seismic shock experienced by Naples at ceasing to be not only a capital, but the principal, Italian city may still be felt. Its consequences cannot be exaggerated – political, economic, social and cultural. The blow to Neapolitan self-esteem was incalculable. In 1859 Rome had been a city of the past, the preserve of priests and antiquaries; Florence was scarcely more than a museum, even though it was the seat of the Grand Duke of Tuscany; Milan and Venice were occupied by Austrians; and Turin was a rustic backwater, for all its rulers' pretensions. After what was in only too many ways a northern conquest, Naples had to learn to be governed by strangers from afar, to become a provincial city.

It was no longer visited by royalty and international society and was abandoned by the diplomatic corps – intellectuals continued to come, but fewer and fewer of them. Compared with that of its rivals, the history of the city's image since the Borboni's departure is one of steady decline. Apart from the dreary Corso Umberto and that neo-Renaissance monstrosity of 1890, the Galleria Umberto, nothing of any real architectural significance has been added. The splendour and the elegance have vanished.

The last lines of Wordsworth's sonnet *On the Extinction of the Venetian Republic* can just as well be applied to the end of Parthenope as the royal capital of The Two Sicilies:

> And what if she had seen those glories fade,
> Those titles vanish, and that strength decay?
> Yet shall some tribute of regret be paid
> When her long life hath reached its final day:
> Men are we, and must grieve when even the shade
> Of that which once was great is passed away.

Nevertheless, enough of past glories survives to enable the nostalgically inclined to recapture something of the old Naples. Moreover one is helped by the fact that, unlike the Venetians, the Neapolitans themselves remain largely unchanged. It is almost impossible to walk twenty yards through Spacca-Napoli without seeing not merely a wonderful building, but a memorable human being as well – whether a gargoyle in tatters or a beautiful woman. Nor can one fail to be impressed by the courage with which the all but destitute in this sorely afflicted city cope with conditions that would drive many others to hopeless despair. The hackneyed phrase 'working-class culture' has some meaning in Naples, especially during the music festival of Piedigrotta in the autumn when whole streets are turned into concert halls. The *borghesi* may be indistinguishable from any other Italian *popolo grasso* throughout the peninsula; yet the ordinary people continue to be oddly Greek in face and manner, small dark men with grave features that suddenly erupt into vivacity. They are best observed in the ancient narrow streets of the old town, whose gridiron pattern dates from Graeco-Roman times, and where thousands still live in one-room *bassi* filled by a single family bed (nowadays supplemented by television sets, and even by video-cassettes as well). The rarely glimpsed, though still very strongly established, aristocracy displays an equal debt to history in its appearance, being often surprisingly tall, grave and Spanish-looking. Both proletariat and nobility share the same attractive if peculiar temperament, and the latter break into Neapolitan dialect in moments of stress. In the seventeenth century John Evelyn called the Neapolitans 'merry, witty and genial', and in the nineteenth the humourless Gladstone commented: 'While they seem to be most amiable for their gentleness of tone, and for their freedom from sullenness and pride, they are, I must say, admirable in their powers of patient endurance, and for all their elasticity and buoyance.' They are just the same today. But though exuberantly gay, kindly and courteous, if always subtly mocking, they may seem melancholy and, ultimately, extraordinarily reserved. Their character heightens the mystery of this most secret of cities.

'Pot che Napoli tua non è più Napoli' – 'Your Naples is Naples no more' – was probably a cliché when Jacopo Sannazzaro first wrote it down in the fifteenth century. History is the sole means of appreciating this amazing, battered, yet siren-like metropolis, of allowing the *genius loci*, Parthenope, to continue casting her potent spell. Revealingly, the most down-to-earth Neapolitan will occasionally remind a visitor, 'This used to be a capital, you know.' In Venice it is not too difficult for a tourist to imagine what it was like to be a Venetian under the *Serenissima*; it is much harder in Naples to recapture what it must have been like to be a Neapolitan during the *Regno*. One should see the old Naples while one can, for the Neapolitan heritage is crumbling at an inexorably increasing pace. The threat may be different from that facing Venice but, if not so dramatic, it is even more menacing. Magnificent *palazzi* in what was once the aristocratic quarter are now dingy and decaying tenements, however colourful and amiable their swarming modern inhabitants. A considerable number of medieval buildings were destroyed during the construction of the Corso Umberto in the 1880s. There was heavy Allied bombing – and German reprisals – during the Second World War. More recently there have been waves of demolition and speculative building. The horrific earthquake of 1980 damaged the Spanish Quarter so badly that there have even been suggestions that it should be pulled down in its entirety – as it is, parts are still roped off. One asks (without too much hope) why, if Paris has been able to regenerate the Marais so brilliantly, cannot the Neapolitans do the same with their city's historic centre? A partial reclamation, on the most limited scale, might well contribute towards a tourist revival and at least do something to ameliorate the present heart-rending unemployment and poverty. But one must not despair. In 1688 Maximilien Misson wrote of Parthenope: 'Tho' it hath often endured terrible assaults, 'tis still one of the most noble and perhaps finest cities in the world.' In many ways a Naples in Peril fund would be quite as justified as the Venice in Peril fund – and it is not beyond the bounds of possibility.

Encouragingly, there are signs that, after the heavy curtain of obscurity that followed the Risorgimento, Naples is at least ready to take a more positive attitude towards her royal past. In 1980 all Neapolitan museums combined to stage a truly magnificent exhibition of their city's art in the eighteenth century. Significantly it was named 'The Golden Age of Naples'; there was a special ceremony in honour of the formal visit by the royal family, who were led by the Pretender, the Duke of Castro. This reminder of former glories did much to help the Neapolitan people rediscover their pride in their city and raised their morale despite the horrors of the earthquake. In 1984 the bodies of the last King and Queen of The Two Sicilies are to be re-interred with fitting ceremony at Santa Ghiara, the traditional burial place of the Borboni, in the presence of the royal family; and during the ceremony the old royal anthem, by Paisiello, will be played once more. A fundamental re-evaluation of Neapolitan culture is taking place, both in Italy and abroad. In time to come perhaps even Anglo-Saxons may regain their forebears' passion for Naples.

Too much, far too much, has been written in recent years about the seamier aspects of Parthenope. I have therefore concentrated in this book on her neglected grandeurs and veiled beauties. The city is undeniably an acquired taste, yet also a taste infinitely worth acquiring, and this anthology is intended to help visitors do so. It is a guide to the Naples that was once a capital, and to its inhabitants down those centuries. Since the book is inspired by the firm conviction that Naples can truly be understood only by seeing it as a royal capital, it ends with the fall of the Kingdom of The Two Sicilies in 1860. It cannot be concerned with Naples after that date – not even with such events as the Black Death of 1884 (cholera) and the vast slum-clearance and rebuilding that ensued; with the building of the funicular railway up Vesuvius; with the *camorra* epics of the early 1900s; the rising against Germans in the Second World War; or the recent earthquake. Those are the experiences of Naples as a provincial city.

Most of the translations are my own, and I have sometimes modernized the spelling and punctuation of older English writers. Occasionally I have chosen English writers in preference to more authoritative Neapolitans – for example, Augustus Hare or Lacey Collison-Morley instead of Benedetto Croce or Gino Doria – simply because they provide more compact extracts. I have been limited by space and by the sheer mass of material available, and also by the realization that few visitors to Naples are likely to be acquainted with its history. As Doria says, in his *Storia di una Capitale*, the real difficulty in telling the city's story lies in the fact that it is also the story of a country.

The introduction, together with the chronology and list of sovereigns at the end of the book, is consequently designed to give the briefest possible outline of Neapolitan history. Extracts in this anthology begin in the thirteenth century, when the city first became a great capital under Charles of Anjou, and end in the nineteenth with the Risorgimento and the departure of Francis II. It is arranged in sections around the most important and most beautiful buildings in and about Naples. Sadly, there is not sufficient room to include such landmarks as the Museo Archeologico, 'Virgil's Tomb' or nearby Herculaneum, though there is a section on Vesuvius and Pompeii. Some readers may be a little daunted by the number of churches, but the city would not be Naples without them; those listed here are only a small selection of the most interesting out of more than 200 (once there were 400), and there are perforce all too many omissions.

My intention has been to stimulate the imagination of historically minded travellers, so that they may catch a glimpse of the old royal Naples. Before visiting a palace, a castle, a church or any other outstanding monument, they should first read what this book has to say about it. I hope that at the same time they may begin to appreciate the Neapolitans, who have remained so astonishingly unaltered through all the vicissitudes of their history.

Map of city
locating the places described

Vomero

Via Piedigrotta

Mergellina

▲ to Posillipo

Naples

Naples

(Fynes Moryson (1566–1630) was probably the most authoratative of
all Elizabethan travel writers.)

Naples was of old called Parthenope of one of the Sirens there buried,
whom they write to have cast herself into the sea for grief that by no
flattery she could detain Ulysses with her. The citizens of old Cumae
built Naples and, lest it should grow great to the prejudice of Cumae,
they pulled it down again till at last oppressed with a great plague, upon
the warning of an oracle they built it again, and changing the old name
Parthenope, called it Naples which in Greek signifies a new city.

The Castel Nuovo, the Capuan Gate, the Vicaria, and the Piazza del Mercato

[2] THE FIRST ANGEVIN KING, CHARLES I (1266–85), WHO MADE NAPLES A CAPITAL AND BUILT THE CASTEL NUOVO, 'THE NEAPOLITAN BASTILLE'; FROM THE *CRONICHE FIORENTINE* OF GIOVANNI VILLANI.

(A Florentine, born in 1280 and killed by the Black Death in 1348, Giovanni Villani had met many people who had actually seen the King.)

Harsh and much feared ... speaking little and acting much, rarely smiling, chaste as a monk, Catholic, harsh in judgement, and of a fierce countenance, tall and stalwart in person, olive coloured and large nosed.

[3] CHARLES I RECEIVES NEWS IN 1282 OF THE SICILIAN VESPERS AND OF THE LOSS OF HALF HIS KINGDOM; FROM SIR STEVEN RUNCIMAN'S *THE SICILIAN VESPERS*.

Charles was at Naples when in the first days of April a messenger sent by the Archbishop of Monreale told him of the massacre at Palermo. He was angry; for it meant the postponement of his eastern expedition for a while. But he did not at first take the revolt seriously. It was a local affair, he thought, with which his Vicar, Herbert of Orléans, could deal. He merely ordered the vice-admiral Matthew of Salerno to take four galleys to attack Palermo. The order was given on 8 April; but when Matthew arrived off Palermo he found the Messinese squadron already cruising ineffectually outside the harbour and did not venture to press any attack. When Messina joined in the revolt, the Messinese ships attacked him and captured two of his galleys. He retired with the others to Naples.

It was the rising in Messina and the destruction of his fleet there that brought Charles to realize the seriousness of the rebellion. 'Lord

God', he cried, 'since it has pleased You to ruin my fortune, let me only go down by small steps.'

[4] The abdication of the hermit pope, St Celestine V, at the Castel Nuovo in 1294; from H.K. Mann's *Lives of the Popes in the Middle Ages*.

When Celestine arrived in Naples, he was lodged in the Castel Nuovo, which, begun by Charles I (1283), overlooks with its five great round towers the so-called military harbour (porto militare). In one of its great halls, when one of the saint's 'Lents' drew nigh – that of St Martin, Nov. 11 – Celestine ordered a wooden hut to be constructed, and decided to remain in it all alone, as he had been accustomed to spend his 'Lents' in the past. To ensure that he would be left undisturbed, he caused a document to be drawn up by means of which all the pontifical powers were to be handed over to three cardinals. However, before it was sealed, Cardinal Matteo Rosso induced him to withdraw it, 'lest the Spouse should come to be thought to have married three husbands' [meaning that he would simply have created three more Popes] . . .

The cardinals were ordered to meet the Pope on the feast of St Lucy (Dec. 13), in the great lofty central hall of the Castle, now known as the Sala S. Luigi or the Sala dei Baroni. Swinging open the very door which still gives entrance into this magnificent apartment, they found the Pope seated on his throne in full pontificals.

When he had signified that he did not wish any interruption, Celestine suddenly produced the deed of renunciation which, with pale face but determined mien, he read out clearly to the assembled fathers. He told them that of his own accord (*sponte*) and free will (*libens*), he resigned the papacy, as his age and other defects rendered him incapable of fulfilling its duties, and he wished to put an end to further disasters, and to attend to his soul's salvation. He then exhorted the cardinals to show their care for the world by electing a worthy pastor who would lead the flock to pastures abundant and fresh, and who would correct the many mistakes he had made. Then, to the profound astonishment of the cardinals in front of him, straightway descending from the throne, he took off, one after another, the insignia of the papacy – his mitre with its one crown, the red mantle, the ring, and the other *pontificalia* even to the alb. All this he did, so we are assured by Petrarch, who had his information from eye witnesses, 'with every sign of joy. If he took the chair of Peter with sorrow, he left it with gladness: *Ascensus moestus, descensus laetus.*'

He then withdrew for a moment, and returning, clad in the simple garb of his Order, he took his seat on the lowest step of the throne, and said: 'Behold, my brethren, I have resigned the honour of the Papacy; and now I implore you by the Blood of Jesus and by His Holy Mother, quickly to provide for the Church a man who will be useful for it, for the whole human race, and for the Holy Land.' When he had said this, he rose to go, but the cardinals who had not been able with dry eyes to look at this scene so touching in its simple humility, entreated him not to leave them until he had duly provided for the future.

[5] PETRARCH IS RECEIVED BY KING ROBERT AT THE CASTEL NUOVO IN 1340; FROM HIS *EPISTLE TO POSTERITY.*

(Francesco Petrarch (1304–74), a Florentine, is the most famous Italian scholar, poet and man of letters of his day.)

I decided to visit Naples first and present myself to that distinguished philosopher, King Robert – illustrious in letters as well as in rank, the only monarch of our time who loved learning and virtue – to see how he would judge me. I still wonder at his most flattering estimate and his kindest of welcomes and if you who read this had experienced them yourself, you would be no less amazed. Hearing why I had come, he was surprised and also delighted, considering that my youthful trust in him – perhaps too the honour which I was seeking – would contribute to his own glory, since I had sought him out as being alone competent to judge. Need I say more? After countless discussions I showed him my *Africa* and he was so pleased with it that he asked me to dedicate it to him as a particular favour, a request I could scarcely refuse – not that I wished to. Eventually he fixed a day for my examination. He kept me from noon to night, doing the same on the two following days, until he had discovered how very little I really knew. However after three days he decided that I really was worthy of the poet's laurel crown. He wanted to place it on my head at Naples, and actually begged me to let him do so, but my love of Rome took precedence over even the august request of a king. When he saw that I was immovable, he gave me messages and letters to the Roman Senate, in which he declared his approval of me in the most flattering terms.

[6] KING ROBERT THE WISE AT THE CASTEL NUOVO; FROM EDWARD TATHAM'S *FRANCESCO PETRARCA*.

Robert's reputation as a sage did not rest entirely on his theological bent. He was content to learn as well as to teach. He was a great supporter of the University of Naples, forbidding the civil law to be taught at any other place in his realm. He often himself attended the lectures, standing throughout their delivery. He was a diligent collector of books, and appointed a man of real learning, Paolo di Perugia, to the charge of his library at the salary – princely for those days – of 225 gold florins a year. Robert employed copyists of Arabic and Greek manuscripts, and caused works of Aristotle and Galen to be translated into Latin. Moreover, though accused by his enemies of avarice, he strove to promote learning by inviting scholars to his court and acting as their patron. So far as possible, he chose his officers and advisers from men of this stamp; and his chief minister, Bartolomeo da Capua, was an eminent jurist . . .

The King was accustomed to relieve his mind from the heavy cares of state not merely by literature and study, but by regular bodily exercises. He was specially devoted to archery – i.e. to competitions with a crossbow, either at a fixed target or perhaps at pigeons let loose for the purpose; and every day at a fixed hour he resorted to an open space in the castle grounds, sloping down to the harbour but elsewhere surrounded by a wall, and took part in contests, in which, according to Petrarch, he excelled the greatest masters of the craft. The poet was often present on these occasions, either among the general crowd of courtiers or as one of a privileged few; but he does not say whether he figured as a competitor. From a chance expression in a later letter we may infer that he was shocked at the contrast between the simple, religious life led by Robert and his devout Queen Sancia, and the dissolute habits of some of the courtiers.

From scattered notices in his works we may conclude that [during Petrarch's visit in 1340], after the three days' public display, he was honoured with frequent private interviews on literary topics. We may fancy that these conferences took place in an embrasure of the royal study, from which Robert loved to contemplate the beauties of the Bay of Naples. We know that not only poetry, but history and geography were discussed. It was at the King's instance that Petrarch used every effort to discover the second decade of Livy, but without success. In the following century a map of Italy was in existence which was said to have been prepared by the poet in collaboration with Robert.

[7] QUEEN GIOVANNA I; FROM L. COLLISON-MORLEY'S *NAPLES THROUGH THE CENTURIES*.

(Lacey Collison-Morley was a travel writer whose *Naples through the Centuries* appeared in 1925. He was a close friend of Benedetto Croce and of the Neapolitan dialect poet Salvatore di Giacomo, and his book also won the approval of Gino Doria – in his day one of the most popular of all historians of Naples.)

The beautiful, pleasure-loving, weak, sensuous Giovanna I (1343–82), who has become legendary as a modern Semiramis the living embodiment of every sensual vice, was from the first repelled by her gloomy, clumsy husband [Andreas of Hungary], and her repulsion was fomented by Filippa de Cabannis, who ruled her. She is said to have made open fun of him before the Queen, who did not reprove her. Giovanna threw herself into every amusement. The Castel Nuovo became the centre of riotous gaiety, and the crowds in the Corregge increased daily. Robert's devout widow, Sancia, retired to the convent of S. Croce, and took the veil in despair. The Queen was utterly unfit to govern. The State was ruled by Fra Roberto and the Hungarians, and the King of Hungary was soon insisting that Andreas should be crowned King, in spite of Robert's expressed wish.

The Neapolitan barons were highly indignant. The result was the murder of Andreas at Aversa, where he was called from his room at dead of night on the plea of the arrival of a messenger on urgent business, seized and strangled with a silken cord, his body being thrown out of the window, on September 18, 1345, while his Hungarians, who had drunk heavily, were sunk in sleep. Whether she was an accomplice or not, the murder was a great shock to Giovanna, who shut herself in the Castel Nuovo, where the boy was born. The fact that the Pope stood godfather did not guarantee the child's parentage in the eyes of the world. An angry crowd invaded the castle gardens, demanding the punishment of the murderers, chief among them Filippa de Cabannis and her daughter. They were seized and tortured. Filippa died in the Vicaria, but the others were executed with the utmost rigour of the law.

The Queen now had to choose a new husband, and her choice fell upon her cousin, Luigi di Taranto. But the King of Hungary was bent on vengeance and advanced upon the Regno. After punishing the guilty nobles who came to meet him at Aversa he led his army towards Naples, preceded by a banner with a strangled king upon it, inscribed 'Vendetta'. Here he sacked the houses of the conspirators and the inhabitants were roughly treated by the Hungarian soldiery. Giovanna meanwhile fled to Avignon, on the plea that she wished to justify herself before the Pope. The Pope pronounced her innocent and recognized her marriage, declaring that, if there was evidence of a not altogether perfect conjugal love, this was not due to any evil disposition on her part, but to magic and witchcraft, which, being but a weak woman, she was not strong enough to resist. She provided herself with funds by selling him Avignon for 80,000 gold florins, with which she returned to Naples, landing at the bridge over the Sebeto, as the Castel Nuovo was held by the Hungarians. In 1351 the Pope induced the King of Hungary to renounce his claim and in the following year Joan [Giovanna] was crowned with great splendour . . .

In 1372 St Bridget of Sweden came to Naples and vented her holy wrath upon what she found there. When asked to intercede on behalf of the people, who were threatened by a plague, she announced that it was due to pride, avarice and bestial sensuality. Two vices especially she denounced among the women, the painting of their faces and the luxury of their dress. The Queen ordered her denunciation to be read in the churches, but it had no effect in staying the plague, which grew steadily worse; and we may doubt whether it had much effect upon the ladies, or at least upon the more attractive among them. In the Castel Nuovo St Bridget was visited by ecstatic visions of Giovanna's wickedness, and there is even a wholly unfounded legend that a son of the saint was among her lovers . . .

On the death of Luigi of Taranto, Giovanna married the Infante of Majorca, who was soon killed in battle. She then adopted Charles of Durazzo, who had married her niece, who was also his own first cousin, as her heir. But in 1376 she married her fourth husband, Otto of Brunswick. The indignant Charles of Durazzo rose in revolt and was supported by Urban VI. Giovanna was true to the Anti-Pope, Clement VII, whom she welcomed in the Castel dell' Ovo; but the people of Naples rose against him and he fled to Avignon. She now made Louis d'Anjou, the King of France's brother, her heir. But she obtained little support, though Clement VII did all he could for her. Charles easily occupied Naples and she shut herself up in the Castel Nuovo. Her husband made a plucky and desperate attempt to rescue her, but without success, and she was obliged to surrender.

Charles imprisoned her in the castle of Muro in the Basilicata, where at last, under pressure, it is said, of the King of Hungary, he had her smothered ... Her violent death has helped to consecrate the Regina Giovanna legend, and most of the classical stories of queenly lust have been fastened upon her, even to making away with each lover, as soon as she had tired of him. Her name has been given to more than one ruined castle or bath, such as the picturesque unfinished castle of Donn'anna on the coast at Mergellina, begun by Fanzago for Anna Carafa, wife of the Viceroy Medina, or the Bagni di Regina Giovanna beyond Sorrento, a delicious place for a picnic and a bathe, which is obviously of Roman origin. The boatmen will speak with awe, not unmixed with envy, of the Queen's luxurious life. Her reputation has undoubtedly suffered from confusion with her great-niece, Giovanna II, who far exceeded her in viciousness, though she died in her bed. One benefit she conferred upon her sex. It is due to Giovanna I that in Naples women can inherit titles on an equality with men.

[8] PETRARCH'S DESCRIPTION OF FRA ROBERTO DA MILETO, A 'SPIRITUAL' (I.E. HERETICAL) FRANCISCAN FRIAR WHO WAS CONFESSOR TO ANDREAS OF HUNGARY AND WHO DOMINATED THE YOUNG QUEEN GIOVANNA I AND HER MOTHER AT THE BEGINNING OF HER REIGN; FROM PETRARCH'S LETTER TO CARDINAL COLONNA, 29 NOVEMBER 1343.

I saw a horrible thing walking on three legs, hooded and barefoot, preaching poverty but dissipated by vice – a bald, red-faced dwarf, whose bloated limbs were barely covered by a tattered cloak which deliberately reveals a good deal of his unpleasant body – an apparition who in his insolence rejects not just your plea but the Pope's as well, from the high peaks of his 'saintliness'. One shouldn't be surprised. His pride is solidly founded, however – on gold. The general rumour is that his rags are in complete contradiction to his private treasure. This. venerable figure is named Roberto. The late most majestic King Robert, the greatest glory of our age, has, to its everlasting shame, made way for another Robert. From now on I shall find it much easier to credit a snake's being born from the marrow of a corpse's bones, after such a viper has crawled forth from the royal sepulchre. Is it fit that such a creature should succeed a truly great king? He is a man who practises a new sort of tyranny, sporting neither diadem, purple or sword but only a dirty cloak – and not even a whole cloak but hitched up all round – crooked from hypocrisy rather than age, relying on sullen silence instead of eloquence. The animal swaggers through the Queen's palace with an arrogant expression, at the same time supporting himself ostentatiously with a staff . . . the ship of state veers from side to side and, in my opinion, there is about to be the most dreadful shipwreck.

[9] QUEEN GIOVANNA I IS DEPOSED IN 1381 BY HER
NEPHEW AND FORMER ADOPTED HEIR, CHARLES
OF DURAZZO (KING CHARLES III); FROM PIETRO
GIANNONE'S *ISTORIA CIVILE DEL REGNO DI NAPOLI*.

(Pietro Giannone (1676–1748) is the most famous of all Neapolitan historians. A lawyer from the Gapitanata who came to Naples at the age of eighteen, he was violently anti-clerical. When the *Istoria* – his *magnum opus* – was published in 1723, its attacks on the Church caused uproar and he was banished. Later he attacked the Papacy directly in *Il Triregno*, and he ended his days in a Piedmontese dungeon.)

Charles invested the Castel Nuovo. Most Neapolitan ladies of rank had taken refuge there, since they were frightened of being ill treated on account of their loyalty to the Queen; there were also a very large number of noblemen with their families. This quickly led to disaster as the Queen, partly from her natural kindness and partly because she expected that galleys with fresh provisions would soon arrive from Provence, fed them all, with the consequence that the castle's entire stock of victuals was eaten in a single month when in normal circumstances it would probably have sufficed the garrison for six months. The Prince (Giovanna's fourth husband, Otto of Brunswick) tried everything possible during the siege to relieve the Queen. He advanced on Naples and took up a position in the marshes, hoping that Charles would come out and give battle; The latter's commanders told him to stay put; it was better to use his troops to hold down the city and invest the castle, since they knew how many people were inside and that very soon hunger must force the garrison to surrender.

Meanwhile the Queen was beginning to run short of provisions. Her one hope was that the galleys would arrive; she not only intended to escape in them, but to go in person to the King of France and Pope Clement to ask them for armed assistance so that she could return with her new adopted heir [Louis, Duke of Anjou] and expel the invader. But the galleys did not come – the castle was in serious difficulty from lack of provisions. On 20 August the Queen sent Ugo Sanseverino, the Great Protonotary of the Kingdom, to King Charles to arrange for a surrender and negotiate terms.

The King knew that any chance of success depended on the straits in which the Queen found herself. He received Sanseverino honourably enough, since he was his cousin, but would not agree to any delay longer than five days; if by that time Prince Otto had not relieved the castle and raised the siege, then the Queen must surrender to him in person. Sanseverino went back to the Queen with the conditions, and Charles sent men of his own household after him with a present for her of chicken, fruit and other food, ordering that she be supplied every day with whatever dishes she desired . . . More important, he sent envoys to her to make excuses for the way in which he had behaved, and to say that he genuinely respected her position as Queen and would continue to do so . . . [On 24 August] the Queen sent Ugo de Sanseverino to surrender and to beseech Charles to spare those under her protection in the castle. That very same day the King, accompanied by his guards and Sanseverino, entered the castle and paid his respects to the Queen,

assuring her that he would keep his promises, that he wanted her to
stay in the castle as Queen, not as a prisoner, and that she would be
waited on by her own household.

On 1 September ten Provençal galleys commanded by the Count of
Caserta sailed in to Naples to take the Queen to France. King Charles at
once went to see her, imploring her to be good enough to make him
heir to her entire inheritance so that after her death he would have her
lands in France, and to invite the Provençals in the galleys to come
ashore as friends . . . He sent a safe conduct and allowed them to go to
her apartments and to talk to her alone.

As soon as they entered, the Queen addressed them. 'Gratitude to
my forebears and the allegiance which the County of Provence owes to
me should have made you come much faster than you have done to my
rescue. After being exposed to hardships which would be a great trial
for the strongest soldiers, let alone women, including having to eat
disgusting meat from filthy animals, I have been forced to surrender
myself into the hands of an extremely cruel enemy . . . Never accept as
your sovereign this ungrateful robber who has turned me from a Queen
into a slave. If any document is ever cited or produced stating that I
have made him my heir, do not believe it but reject it as either a forgery
or else extorted from me by force. I wish you to acknowledge the Duke
of Anjou as your lord, not only in the County of Provence and in my
other lands across the Alps, but in this realm as well, to all of which I
have already made him my heir and now make him my avenger . . .'

When King Charles went to the Queen to find out what had been
discussed with the Provençals, he realized that it was the reverse of
what he wanted. He at once changed his behaviour, placing a guard on
the Queen and treating her as a prisoner. A few days later he sent her to
the castle of Muro on his estates in the province of Basilicata . . .

Charles of Durazzo then wrote to the King of Hungary, explaining
what had happened and asking how he should dispose of Giovanna.
The answer was that she should be treated in just the same way as the
late King Andrew [her Hungarian first husband, who had been

murdered]. This was done accordingly in the next year, 1382, in circumstances of the greatest cruelty; he had her smothered with a bolster at
the castle of Muro. Her body was taken back to Naples to lie for seven
days unburied in the church of Santa Chiara, so that everybody could
see it and her supporters finally lose hope. At last she was buried,
between the monument of her father the Duke and the door of the
vestry, without ceremony, though under a fine tomb which may still be
seen today. Such was the end of Queen Giovanna I, a truly excellent
lady who had been brought up under the tuition of King Robert and of
his wise and virtuous Queen Sancia. . . At the time, and later by historians, she has been accused of having had a hand in the death of her
first husband, King Andrew. However, she provided so much evidence
in favour of her innocence that even in those days the best informed
and most intelligent observers considered her guiltless.

[10] THE LAST ANGEVIN KING, RENÉ OF ANJOU (FUTURE
FATHER-IN-LAW OF HENRY VI OF ENGLAND), LOSES NAPLES TO
ALFONSO OF ARAGON IN 1442 AND DEPARTS FROM THE CASTLE
NUOVO; FROM LE ROI RENÉ BY A. LECOY DE LA MARCHE.

Alfonso was browsing in a book which the poet Leonardo Aretino –
Secretary of the Florentine Republic – had just sent him after translating it from Greek into Latin. A keen admirer of classical literature, he
was enjoying himself when, during a page dealing with Belisarius's war
against the Goths, he suddenly stopped; he had been reading how the
Roman general had entered Naples through an aqueduct which brought
water from three miles away to a point inside the city. Alfonso was
determined to repeat the exploit. In that countryside littered with ruins
of antiquity, much better preserved than in our own time, it would
surely be possible to rediscover the aqueduct. His men searched for it,
found it, and saw that it was big enough to squeeze through. . .situated
on the northern side of the city, it led to several wells dug behind the
walls, of which one was in the house of a tailor called Citello near the

Santa Sophia gate – only a short distance from the Castel Capuano where King René was in residence . . .

The besiegers prepared to attack. The King of Aragon summoned his bastard son Ferrante, the Prince of Salerno, Urso dei Ursini, Ramon Buil, Pedro and Alfonso de Cardona, Alvar de Castro, and many other lords. He explained his wonderful plan to them and said he hoped that they would fight at his side if it succeeded. Told by Sacchettiello that the right moment had come, he chose a hundred tough men from young Ferrante's troops. Led by Pedro de Corella, by Miguel Juan (a knight from Valencia), by Pedro Sanchez and by Matteo de Guinnaro (a Sicilian nobleman), these entered the aqueduct at night. The passage was so narrow that the only weapons they could carry were crossbows and half-pikes. Nonetheless, the exit was unguarded and eventually they broke through the last barrier. At first light on the morning of 2 June, forty-six of them burst out into the house of the tailor Citello.

The tailor's wife and daughter were alone. They were speedily bound and gagged. Not daring to go outside yet, the attackers waited. Soon Citello's young son knocked at the door and came in. They tried to seize him too. He escaped and ran out yelling, 'The enemy! The enemy are coming up from under the ground!' At his shouts everyone barricaded themselves in their houses – the alarm spread and the entire town gave way to panic. The forty-six were no less terrified at being discovered. They rushed desperately into the street, hoping to climb the walls and reach safety. But in the meantime King Alfonso had advanced right up to the walls from the other side with his men and had been seen by sentries; thinking themselves surrounded, the latter abandoned their posts and let the attackers capture the Santa Sophia gate – soon the banner of Aragon was flying from it . . .

René could not be everywhere. While he was fighting like a lion at the Santa Sophia gate, the San Gennaro gate not far off was opened to enemy troops by one of the besieged at the end of his tether, who told them that he did not want to die of hunger. Thereupon 300 Genoese responsible for guarding this gate fell back to the Castel Nuovo. The flood of attackers, some disguised in Angevin livery, increased each moment. The abbess of the convent next to Santa Maria Donna Regina – a member of the Caracciolo family – let them in through her nunnery, which was how Pedro de Cardona got in. Pedro advanced as far as Via Maestra, one of the principal streets, capturing Sarro Brancazzo en route; he pulled him off his horse, mounted it and galloped towards the Santa Sophia gate to take King René in flank. Seeing an Aragonese on horseback, René thought that the town had been stormed from the other side. Despair merely infuriated him. He ran to the Capuan gate. 'We must retreat', a French knight Louis d'Epinay shouted at him, 'we must retreat, the Aragonese are everywhere.' René answered, in one of history's better asides, 'You're telling a king to retreat!' and split his head in a rage. Then a Catalan accosted René, saying he was his prisoner – with a single blow of his sword the King cut down his would-be captor.

However prodigies of valour were to no avail. The attackers were surging in everywhere. If René waited any longer, he would suffer the same fate he had met with at Bulgnéville [several years in captivity]. A last refuge remained. Abandoning the Castel Capuano, whose outworks had already fallen, he retreated step by step towards the shore and shut himself up in the Castel Nuovo with all that was left of his army. Then began the sack of the unhappy city of Naples . . .

René obtained a ten-day truce. The Castel Capuano was still holding out, stubbornly defended by Giovanni Cossa. That faithful officer received orders to surrender it, to save his life and those of his men; he obeyed and was allowed to rejoin his master. Inside, the Aragonese found only a few bombards and a little ammunition. Fort Sant'Elmo surrendered shortly after, in much the same way. But the Castel Nuovo could only be taken on terms. From this final refuge the King entrusted negotiations to, the Genoese Antonio Calvi, whose city he owed a considerable sum of money, authorizing him to open the gates to the enemy on condition they guaranteed his safety and pardoned all Angevin supporters (as head of whom he named Ottone Caracciolo).

Alfonso accepted the terms, occupying the castle later that month after paying off Calvi, who went home to Genoa.

Two Genoese galleys, which only a short time before had sailed out to buy provisions for the garrison, returned to port at Naples on 3 June. René took this last opportunity and embarked with the few French knights he had left, together with a few Neapolitans who wanted to stay with him – Cossa, Caracciolo, Arteluche d'Alagonia, and others less well known. Later he would richly reward these comrades in misfortune and indeed all who had come to Italy with him. But in the meantime it seemed that he had nothing to offer them save banishment and poverty. He set sail.

[11] ALFONSO I – THE FIRST RULER TO CALL HIMSELF KING OF THE TWO SICILIES – AT THE CASTEL NUOVO; FROM JACOB BURCKHARDT'S *CIVILISATION OF THE RENAISSANCE IN ITALY*.

(Jacob Burckhardt (1818–97) was a Swiss historian and art critic, and Professor of History at Basel University for nearly fifty years. This immensely influential book, his masterpiece, was first published in 1860.)

The great Alfonso, who reigned in Naples from 1442 to 1458, was a man of another kind than his real or alleged descendants. Brilliant in his whole existence, fearless in mixing with his people, dignified and affable in intercourse, admired rather than blamed even for his old man's passion for Lucrezia d'Alagno, he had the one bad quality of extravagance, from which, however, the natural consequence followed. Unscrupulous financiers were long omnipotent at Court till the bankrupt king robbed them of their spoils; a crusade was preached as a pretext for taxing the clergy; when a great earthquake happened in the Abruzzi, the survivors were compelled to make good the contributions of the dead. By such means Alfonso was able to entertain distinguished guests with unrivalled splendour; he found pleasure in ceaseless expense, even for the benefit of his enemies, and in rewarding literary work knew absolutely no measure. Poggio received 500 pieces of gold for translating Xenophon's *Cyropaedeia* into Latin . . . .

It appears that his zeal was thoroughly unaffected, and that the monuments and writings of the ancient world made upon him, from the time of his arrival in Italy, an impression deep and powerful enough to reshape his life. With strange readiness he surrendered the stubborn Aragon to his brother, and devoted himself wholly to his new possessions. He had in his service, either successively or together, George of Trebizond, the younger Chrysoloras, Lorenzo Valla, Bartolommeo Fazio and Antonio Panormita, of whom the two latter were his historians; Panormita daily instructed the King and his court in Livy, even during military expeditions. These men cost him yearly 20,000 gold florins. He gave Panormita 1,000 for his work; Fazio received for the *Historia Alfonsi*, besides a yearly income of 500 ducats, a present of 1,500 more when it was finished, with the words, 'It is not given to pay you, for your work would not be paid for if I gave you the fairest of my cities; but in time I hope to satisfy you.' When he took Giannozzo Manetti as his secretary on the most brilliant conditions, he said to him, 'My last crust I will share with you.' When Giannozzo first came to bring the congratulations of the Florentine government on the marriage of Prince Ferrante, the impression he made was so great that the King sat motionless on the throne, 'like a brazen statue, and did not even brush away a fly, which had settled on his nose at the beginning of the oration'. His favourite haunt seems to have been the library of the castle at Naples, where he would sit at a window overlooking the bay, and listen to learned debates on the Trinity. For he was profoundly religious, and had the Bible, as well as Livy and Seneca, read to him, till after fourteen perusals he knew it almost by heart. Who can fully understand the feeling with which he regarded the suppositious remains of Livy at Padua? When, by dint of great entreaties, he obtained an arm-bone of the skeleton from the Venetians, and received it with solemn pomp at Naples, how strangely Christian and pagan sentiment must have been blended in his heart! During a campaign in the Abruzzi, when the distant Sulmona, the birthplace of Ovid, was pointed out to him, he saluted the spot and returned thanks to its tutelary genius. It gladdened him to make good the prophecy of the great poet as to his future fame. Once indeed, at his famous entry into the conquered city of Naples (1443) he himself chose to appear before the world in ancient style. Not far from the market a breach forty ells wide was made in the wall, and through this he drove in a gilded chariot like a Roman Triumphator. The memory of the scene is preserved by a noble triumphal arch of marble in the Castello Nuovo.

[12] ALFONSO I'S MISTRESS; FROM *MEMOIRS OF A RENAISSANCE POPE* BY POPE PIUS II.

(Pius II – Enea Silvio Piccolomini (1405–64) – was Pope for the last six years of his life. A humanist and a great patron of the arts, he was a little too cynical and a little too outspoken in these memoirs for the good of his own posthumous reputation. He must often have met both Alfonso and Lucrezia.)

She was a beautiful woman or girl, the daughter of poor but noble Neapolitan parents (if there is any nobility in poverty), with whom the King was so desperately in love that in her presence he was beside himself and could neither hear nor see anything but LuCrezia. He could not take his eyes off her, praised everything she said, marvelled at her wisdom, admired every gesture, thought her beauty divine. He had made her many presents, had given orders that she was to receive the honours of a queen, and at last was so completely dominated by her that no-one could get a hearing without her consent. Marvellous is the power of love! A great king, lord of the noblest part of Spain, obeyed by the Balearic Islands, Corsica, Sardinia, and Sicily itself, who had subdued many provinces of Italy and defeated the most powerful generals, was finally conquered by love and like any captive of war was a slave to a weak woman! He had no intercourse with her (if report is true) and they say she used to declare, 'Never with my consent shall the King ravish my maidenhood! But if he should attempt force, I shall not imitate Lucretia, the wife of Collantinus, who endured the outrage and then took her own life. I will anticipate the outrage by my death.' But noble acts are not so easy as noble words nor did her after-life bear out her protestations. For after Alfonso's death she went into Piccinino's camp, where she had no reputation for virtue; indeed it was common talk that she was his secretary's mistress and had a child by him. But Alfonso thought there was nothing in the world more divine. Though wise in everything else, in regard to this and hunting he was stark mad.

[13] KING FERRANTE'S WELCOME AT THE CASTEL NUOVO IN 1465 FOR THE *CONDOTTIERE* JACOPO PICCININO, A FORMER LEADER OF THE ANGEVIN PARTY WHO HAD FOUGHT AGAINST HIM; FROM *HISTOIRE DES RÉPUBLIQUES ITALIENNES DU MOYEN AGE* BY J.C.L. SISMONDI.

(Claude Simonde de Sismondi (1773–1843) was a Swiss historian, whose conviction that Italy prospered best under republican governments made him instinctively hostile to the monarchy at Naples.)

Ferrante invited Piccinino to return to his court and Broccardo Persico, Piccinino's lieutenant, delighted by the welcome he had received at Naples, assured his master in every despatch that far from there being anything to fear he would be laden with honours if he went back . . .

On the way Piccinino visited Borso d'Este at Ferrara and Domenico Malatesta at Cesena. They both disapproved of his going and tried in vain to stop him – they had been given good reason not to trust Ferrante. Piccininio himself felt very uneasy from time to time, yet a sort of fatalism drew him back to Naples. Broccardo Persico, who rejoined him, could speak of nothing but the honour which had been done him. So Piccinino went on, and as soon as he had crossed the frontier the compliments paid to him made him forget his fears. All the leading nobles of the realm had been waiting at Naples for three days to welcome him, there were celebrations at every little town through which he passed and the King himself stood in front of his capital's gates with his court to greet him. He embraced him affectionately, treating him like a brother. For twenty-seven days there was one party after another in his honour and Ferrante never flagged for a moment in flattering attentions. Finally Piccinino asked for a farewell audience before departing for Sulmona and was granted one; on St John's Day, 24 June, he was taken in to the King at the Castel Nuovo, who showed all the same signs of affection and said good-bye with still more embraces. Ferrante had scarcely left the room when royal archers hurled them-selves on Piccinino and dragged him off to a dungeon. His son Francesco, his lieutenant Broccardo, and several officers were seized at the same time. In fact during the celebrations in his honour orders had been in force on all the main roads, sent to every provincial governor, to arrest him if he tried to escape, sieze his goods and attack his troops without warning. In the event, the latter were robbed of everything they possessed. Bereft of officers, their arms and equipment stolen, his men only reached Domenico Malatesta at Cesena with the greatest difficulty . . .

The King said later that Piccinino, excited by the people's cheers at the royal fleet's returning to port, had hung out of a high window to see what was happening, and had fallen down and broken his thigh. After twelve days he had died.

[14] KING FERRANTE'S BANQUET FOR HIS REBELLIOUS
BARONS AT THE CASTEL NUOVO IN 1486; FROM PIETRO
GIANNONE'S *ISTORIA CIVILE DEL REGNO DI NAPOLI*.

The King and the Duke of Calabria were determined to destroy the Count of Sarno and the Secretary [Petrucci] together with their sons – the other barons had made them the scapegoats for the recent civil war and were more or less forgiven – and laid a plot to seize them.

They had to persuade them to meet in the same place at the same time. They therefore hastened a marriage already arranged between Marco Coppola (the Count of Sarno's son) and the Duke of Melfi's daughter (the King's grandchild) and persuaded the Duke to agree that the wedding should take place in the great hall of the Castel Nuovo. When the guests had assembled and were busy dancing and feasting, their merry-making turned in a moment into grief and bitter lamentations. For regardless of hospitality and the wedding, of the Pope's wishes, and of the fact that the Spanish King had guaranteed the peace treaty, Ferrante suddenly ordered the arrest of the Count of Sarno and his sons (the bridegroom Marco, and Filippo), of the Secretary Petrucci and his sons (the Counts of Carniola and Policastro), with his brother-in-law and a Catalan called Joan Impore. He also gave orders for their palaces at Naples and Sarno to be sacked. As his action was universally decried, everyone speaking of it with horror, he did not have them put to death at once, but appointed a court of four judges to try them and find them guilty of felony and high treason according to the letter of the law . . . However he did not want them to die all on the same day; first he had the Secretary's sons beheaded in the Piazza del Mercato; a few months later, on 11 May 1487, the Secretary and the Count were beheaded on a scaffold behind the Castel Nuovo's gatehouse, which had been built at such a vast height that the executions could be seen from the city.

Some time after these sentences had been carried out, on I October following, King Ferrante arrested the Princes of Altamura and Bisignano, the Dukes of Melfi and Nardo, the Counts of Morcone, Lauria, Melita, and Noja, with many other noblemen. Urged on by the Duke of Calabria he had them all put to death, secretly, at different times and in different ways; to complete the tragedy Marino Marzano, who had spent twenty-five years in prison, was also murdered. To make people think that they were all still alive, the King continued to have food sent into them at their prisons. However, shortly afterwards the public executioner was seen wearing a gold chain which had once adorned the neck of the Prince of Bisignano. It was generally believed that they had been strangled, put in sacks, and thrown into the sea. In addition their wives and children were arrested and their estates confiscated, on the pretext that they were planning to flee the kingdom and stir up another civil war. Only Bandella Gaetani, Princess of Bisignano, and her children escaped, in a small boat.

[15] Alfonso II's reasons for fleeing from the Castel Nuovo in 1495; from *Istoria di Italia* by Francesco Guicciardini.

(Francesco Guicciardini (1483–1540) was a Florentine statesman and historian whom Edward Gibbon compared with Thucydides. His *Istoria*, which deals with events in Italy from the French invasion of 1494 until the death of Pope Clement VII in 1534, is one of the world's great historical works.)

When Alfonso heard that his son had fled from Rome [before the French] he became so terrified that, forgetting all the fame and glory he had won during numerous campaigns in many Italian wars, and abandoning all hope of surviving this dreadful menace, he made up his mind to leave the kingdom of Naples for ever, giving up his royal title and kingly authority to [his son] Ferrantino.

It was rumoured (if one may be allowed not to despise such matters entirely) that on a number of nights the ghost of old Ferrante had appeared to the Court's chief surgeon, Iacopo, and, beginning gently but ending with the most terrible threats, had ordered him to tell Alfonso in his name that he had no hope of resisting the French King, since it was predestined that his descendants, after suffering countless hardships and being at last deprived of their illustrious kingdom, would cease to exist. For the Aragonese dynasty was to pay the price for its crimes ... in particular because Ferrante, persuaded by his son [Alfonso], had in secret ordered the murder of many of the barons of the realm ...

Whether this is true or not, Alfonso certainly decided to flee – in agony from his conscience, without peace of mind by day or by night, the dead lords' ghosts appearing to him in his dreams, and his people rising in rebellion because of his cruelties. However he only told his mother-in-law, the Queen, what he meant to do, and despite her prayers would not tell his brother or his son. For he had no wish to stay for the two or three days which would have completed the first year of his reign.

Alfonso left Naples, accompanied by four light galleys which were laden with treasure. While he was leaving he shook all over, as though the French were already upon him, trembling with fear at the slightest noise like a man who was frightened that heaven and earth were plotting against him. He fled to Mazari, a Sicilian town with which he had recently been presented by King Ferdinand of Spain.

[16] THE EMPEROR CHARLES V VISITS NAPLES AND THE CASTEL
NUOVO IN HIS CAPACITY AS KING OF THE TWO SICILIES; FROM
L. COLLISON-MORLEY'S NAPLES THROUGH THE CENTURIES.

Nothing made Spanish rule more popular than its success against the corsairs, and every assistance was given in the wars. So when Charles V spent the winter of 1535–6 in Naples after the capture of Tunis, making his entry by the Porta Capuana and along the Tribunali, he was welcomed with more than the usual enthusiasm. Naples lies under the Ram, a fickle and changeable planet, says a traveller of the day. The leading princes of Italy thronged the Castel Nuovo, which, for the last time, witnessed a revival of its former splendour. It was becoming old-fashioned as a royal residence . . . To Naples now came the Dukes of Urbino and Florence, and Pier Luigi Farnese, and some of the loveliest women in Italy. Court life was one long round of gaiety, marred only by the jealousies between Spaniard and Italian. The Neapolitans maintained that titles gave rank, whereas the Spaniards held that the Grandee of Spain, who remained covered in the presence of the King, should take precedence of all others. At last Charles was obliged to order all chairs to be removed from the Chapel of S. Barbara [in the Castel Nuovo], when he attended Mass there with his Court.

[17] THE CASTEL NUOVO IN 1594; FROM FYNES MORYSON'S *AN ITINERARY* . . .

On the outside of the said *Molo*, or fortification upon the haven, towards the west and near to the shore lies the most strong fort called Castello Nuovo, seated in a plain, and built by Charles I of Anjou and so fortified by Alfonso I, King of Aragon, as it is numbered among the chief forts of Europe. The inward gate is most fair, all of marble, and it hath a little four-square hall in which the Parliaments are yearly held and the Viceroys weekly sit in judgement. Near this hall is a fair tower in which the kingly ornaments are laid up; namely a sceptre of gold with great diamonds on the top, the sword with the haft and scabbard of gold adorned with precious stones, the King's crown shining with precious stones, a golden cross, an huge pot of gold set with precious stones, great unicorns' horns, and the chief kinds of precious stones.

Further towards the west (yet so near as the garden of the palace lies upon the ditch of this castle) is the Viceroy's palace, which hath a large and most sweet garden and delicate walk paved with divers coloured and engraven marbles. And in this garden are two banqueting houses, whereof one is very stately built and hath a sweet fountain close to the table continually pouring out water. Also there is a delicate cage of birds wrought about with thick wire, and it is as big as an ordinary still-house, delicately shadowed round about, wherein are many kinds of singing birds as well of Italy as foreign countries.

[18] THE MURDER OF 'SER GIANNI' CARACCIOLO, THE
GRAND SENESCHAL AND LOVER OF QUEEN GIOVANNA II, AT
THE CASTEL CAPUANO IN 1432; FROM J.C.L. SISMONDI'S
HISTOIRE DES RÉPUBLIQUES ITALIENNES DU MOYEN AGE.

Queen Giovanna II had more or less exiled her adopted son Louis III of
Anjou, and kept him far away administering Calabria, so that she could
give herself and her kingdom unconditionally to Giovanni Caracciolo,
her Grand Seneschal. Born in 1371, Giovanna had now passed her sixti-
eth year and her irregular life had aged her prematurely. Caracciolo was
sixty too, and the passion to which he owed his success was no longer
felt by himself or by the Queen. However habit had replaced love; the
ambitious Caracciolo remained the ruler of the sovereign who had
taken him for her lover long ago. Even now he had not yet had his fill of
honours, wealth, and power; every day he demanded some new favour
from Giovanna. He was Duke of Venosa, Count of Avellino and Lord,
but not Prince, of Capua, since he did not quite dare to take a title
borne only by heirs to the throne; in addition he wanted the Duchy of
Amalfi and the Principality of Salerno, which Giovanna had confiscated
from Antonio Colonna on the death of his uncle, Pope Martin V. Such
excessive demands aroused the jealousy of other members of the Court,
who would have liked some of these favours for themselves. To find
refuge from the misery which Caracciolo's domineering temper was
causing her, the Queen began to confide in her cousin Cobella Ruffo,
Duchess of Sessa. That lady, no less haughty and violent than the Grand
Seneschal himself, sought to destroy this insolent minister whom she
regarded as an upstart, and took every opportunity to aggravate her
mistress's resentment.

One day the Duchess of Sessa was in an ante-chamber when she
heard Caracciolo loudly repeating his demands for Amalfi and Salerno.
Infuriated at the Queen's refusal, and believing that he was alone with
her, he began to upbraid her in such a brutal and abusive way, and was
so angry and insulting, that Giovanna II burst into tears. When the

Seneschal had gone, the Duchess did her best to see that tears gave way to fury and also to frighten Giovanna about Caracciolo's future plans. He was marrying his son to the daughter of Jacopo Caldera, the realm's one genuinely capable general: the Duchess claimed that the marriage showed that he was conspiring, and that the Seneschal wanted to make sure of all the troops in the country, since he intended to seize the throne. There was barely time, so she said, in which to stop him. With the Queen's permission, she, the Duchess, would assemble Caracciolo's opponents and tell them that he was going to be deprived of the power he had usurped. She was sure they would help.

The marriage between Caracciolo's son and Caldera's daughter was celebrated with great magnificence on 17 August 1432. The festivities were to last for an entire week at the Queen's own castle. On the night before the last of these days of games and tournaments, when the feasting and dancing were over and when the Court had gone to bed, Caracciolo, instead of going home with the happy couple, went to spend the night in a chamber which he had at the castle. Then one of the Queen's pages knocked on his door and shouted that Giovanna had had a stroke and wanted to see him before she died. Caracciolo at once ordered the door to be opened, while his servants dressed him. The conspirators, who had tricked him with a false message, rushed in and killed him on his bed with swords and axes. Next morning, when the news spread through the city, both nobles and commons who had trembled in the Grand Seneschal's presence and had seen him govern with unlimited authority, whom neither the Queen's husband nor her two adopted sons had ever been able to control, crowded into the room to gaze on his dead body. He was lying on the floor, half dressed and wearing only one stocking; nobody had bothered to finish dressing him or place him on the bed. The Queen, who had simply agreed to sign an order for his arrest, had never dreamt that people wanted to kill him. She seemed to display the deepest grief when told that Caracciolo's resistance to her commands had made it necessary to use force, and that he had died in consequence. Nonetheless she pardoned the conspirators who had murdered him, ordered the confiscation of all his estates on the grounds of rebellion, arrested his son and entire family, and allowed the mob to plunder their palaces.*

[19] THE BUILDER OF THE PORTA CAPUANA AND REBUILDER OF THE CASTEL CAPUANO (NOW THE VICARIA), KING FERRANTE; FROM JACOB BURCKHARDT'S *CIVILISATION OF THE RENAISSANCE IN ITALY*.

Ferrante, who succeeded Alfonso I in 1458, passed as his illegitimate son by a Spanish lady, but was not improbably the son of a half-caste Moor of Valencia. Whether it was his blood, or the plots made against his life by the barons, which embittered and darkened his nature, it is certain that he was equalled in ferocity by none among the princes of his time. Restlessly active, recognized as one of the most powerful political minds of the day, and free from the vices of the profligate, he concentrated all his powers, among which must be reckoned profound dissimulation and an irreconcilable spirit of vengeance, on the destruction of his opponents. He had been wounded at every point on which a ruler is open to offence; for the leaders of the barons, though related to him by marriage, were yet the allies of his foreign enemies. Extreme measures became part of his daily policy. The means for this struggle with his barons, and for his external wars, were exacted in the same Mohammedan fashion that Frederick II had introduced: the Government alone dealt in oil and corn; the whole commerce of the country was put by Ferrante into the hands of a wealthy merchant, Francesco Coppola, who had entire control of the anchorage on the coast and shared the profits with the King. Deficits were made up by forced loans, by executions and confiscations, by open simony, and by contributions levied on the ecclesiastical corporations. Besides hunting, which he practised regardless of all rights of property, his pleasures were of two kinds: he liked to have his opponents near him, either alive

---

* See page 83 for Caracciolo's tomb.

in well-guarded prisons, or dead and embalmed, dressed in the costumes which they wore in their lifetime. He would chuckle in talking of the captives with his friends, and make no secret whatever of the museum of mummies. His victims were mostly men whom he had lured into his power by treachery; some were seized while they were guests at the royal table. His conduct to his prime minister, Antonello Petrucci, who had grown sick and grey in his service, and from whose increasing fear of death he extorted 'present after present', was literally devilish. At length a suspicion of complicity with the last conspiracy of the barons gave the pretext for his [Petrucci's] arrest and execution. With him died Coppola. The way in which all this is narrated in Caracciolo and Porzio makes one's hair stand on end.

[20] THE VICEROY DON PEDRO DE TOLEDO (1532–53)
REFORMS THE LEGAL SYSTEM AND CONVERTS THE OLD
ROYAL PALACE OF THE CASTEL CAPUANO INTO THE
VICARIA; FROM ALFRED VON REUMONT'S *DIE CARAFA VON*
MADDALONI. NEAPEL UNTER SPANISCHER HERRSCHAFT.

(Alfred von Reumont was a nineteenth-century German historian.)

There were three High Courts of Justice in Naples – the Sacro Consiglio of Santa Chiara, which took its name from being held in the monastery of Santa Chiara; the Court of the Vicaria; and the Royal Chamber. To the first were assigned civil causes, which it decided even up to a third hearing; it consisted of fifteen counsellors – ten Italian and five Spanish, one of them bearing the title President – and was divided into three chambers. The Court of the Vicaria consisted of the higher criminal tribunal with four judges; and the Court of Appeal with three judges for civil cases. The Supreme Court of Judicature of the Sommaria judged all fiscal cases, whether criminal or civil. The very important office of Lieutenant of the Exchequer was for life. Toledo housed the three high courts together in the rebuilt Castel Capuano, where from henceforward sat the President of Santa Chiara, the Governor of the Vicaria, and the Lieutenant of the Exchequer. The old palace's arched halls were transformed into courtrooms and its basement into cells.

[21] NEAPOLITAN JUSTICE AND ITS PENALTIES AT THE VICARIA
IN THE LATE EIGHTEENTH CENTURY; FROM *VOYAGE D'UN*
FRANÇOIS EN ITALIE BY THE CHEVALIER DE LALANDE.

(Joseph-Jérome Lefrançais de Lalande (1732–1807), although best known as an astronomer, produced perhaps the most internationally successful of all eighteenth-century guides to Naples.)

The Vicaria (or *Palais de Justice*) contains all those tribunals which deal with legal matters. The Lord Chief Justice is called the *Regente della Vicaria*; he does not give judgements but assigns all cases to the judges . . . The *Camera Reale di Santa Chiara* is a supreme tribunal, analogous to the Parlement of Paris, which the King occasionally consults though only when it pleases him and to which he gives his commands, where the laws which he ordains are enacted without any form of debate; it consists of a President and the heads of the four rotas of the Sacro Consiglio, together with a procurator fiscal and a secretary. Petitions presented to this tribunal must open with the words 'Sacred Royal Majesty'. Criminal cases are first examined at the Vicaria by the *Regente della Vicaria* . . .

The ordinary torture is that called the cord or *strappado*, as in every Italian city. The more severe torture – *Tortura Acre* – consists of the accused hanging by his arms from cords for an hour. It is very rarely used. However another type of torture is also in use in Naples. The criminal is confined naked in a damp cell whose walls are running with water; he has neither stool nor bed, nothing on which to sit; he is fed at certain specified hours and if he refuses to eat he is fed by force. People are always ready to face it, but very few can stand it for longer than four days at most.

According to the letter of the law any thief is liable to the death penalty, even for stealing a mere ten ducats [about 5s. in English money of the period]. Carrying weapons such as pistols, knives or stilettos is punishable by fifteen years in the galleys, a penalty which is only too necessary in a country where there are so many beggars. Formerly criminals were hanged here for very slight offences, and frequently a little too arbitrarily, but it is not so nowadays. On the contrary the death penalty is rarely carried out, either because fewer crimes are committed or because criminals find it only too easy to get off. People say that money can stop the investigation of even the most atrocious crimes. What is certain is that capital punishment is very rarely seen at Naples.

[22] THE EXECUTION OF THE SIXTEEN-YEAR-OLD KING CONRADIN BY HIS RIVAL, CHARLES OF ANJOU, IN THE PIAZZA DEL MERCATO IN 1268; FROM GIOVANNI VILLANI'S *CRONICHE FIORENTINE*.

When the King had Conradin and Conradin's lords in his power he took counsel as to what he should do. Finally he decided to put them to death and, to give an air of legality to the proceedings, he had them indicted as traitors to the Crown and as enemies of Holy Church, which was done accordingly ... Conradin, the Duke of Austria, Count Calvagno, Count Bartolommeo and two of his sons, and Count Gherardo (of the Counts of Doneratico of Pisa) were beheaded in the market place at Naples, beside that stream of water which flows past the church of the Carmelite friars. The King would not allow them to be buried in consecrated ground, but only under the sand in the market place, since they were excommunicated ... When the judge who condemned Conradin had finished reading the sentence, Robert, son of the Count of Flanders and the King's son-in-law, gave him a sword-thrust, saying that it was not lawful for such as he to sentence to death so great a gentleman, from which thrust the judge died; this was done in the presence of the King, but not a word was said about it.

[23] GIOVANNA II's LOW-BORN LOVER, AND HIS
DEATH IN THE PIAZZA DEL MERCATO; FROM PIETRO
GIANNONE's *ISTORIA CIVILE DEL REGNO DI NAPOLI*.

When she was Duchess of Austria, Giovanna had fallen in love with her cup-bearer, or as others say her carver, Pandolfello Alopo, to whom she secretly prostituted her person. When she became Queen she shook off any lingering shame and restraint and prostituted her kingdom's government in just the same way; she made him Lord High Chamberlain, an office which entrusted him with the management of all Crown lands and revenues and allowed him to administer everything as he saw fit – in theory the entire realm was at his disposal . . .
[*However the Queen then married a French prince, Jacques de La Marche, who became King Consort.*]

The day after his entry the King had Count Pandolfello arrested and imprisoned in the Castel dell' Ovo, where he was horribly tortured and, after confessing everything that the King wanted to know, was condemned to death. On 1 October he was led out to the Piazza del Mercato where he was beheaded, after which his body was treated with the utmost dishonour, being dragged through the city and then hung up by the feet – to the great grief of the Queen and to the no less great joy of those who had once served King Ladislao.

[24] THE PIAZZA DEL MERCATO IN THE SECOND
HALF OF THE NINETEENTH CENTURY; FROM AUGUSTUS
HARE's *CITIES OF SOUTHERN ITALY AND SICILY*.

(Augustus Hare (1834–1903) was one of the greatest and most knowledgeable of English travel writers – even today he is still readable and informative.)

The adjoining Piazza del Mercato, where a great market is held on Mondays and Fridays, is a spot where strangers may well study

Neapolitan life amongst the lower orders, and where artists may find plenty of subjects amongst the booths, the pretty stalls of the lemonade-vendors, hung with bright festoons of lemons like pictures of Girolamo dai Libri, and the groups of women round the three fountains. Of these, the largest is called Fontana di Masaniello, for it is here that, in 1647, the young fisherman Tommaso Aniello – Masaniello – of Amalfi, roused to fury by the fact of his young wife having been fined a hundred ducats for trying to smuggle three pounds of flour into Naples in a stocking to evade the octroi, first roused the people to the revolution, which led to his sovereignty of eight days, and ended in his early death. In the famous executions which have taken place here, the Mercato answers to Tower Hill in London, and the Place de Grève at Paris. The scaffold called La Madaja was appropriately erected in front of the Vico del Sospiro. It was here that Conradin was beheaded, October 29, 1268.

On the north of the piazza stands the gay and thoroughly Neapolitan Cappella della Croce, where in the second sacristy (entered at the end of the right wall) are preserved the carved block of stone on which Conradin suffered, and the porphyry pillar, supporting an ancient crucifix, which formerly stood on the site of the scaffold, commemorating the treachery of Giovanni Frangipani, Lord of Astura, by whom the young prince was betrayed, in the inscription.

> Asturis ungue leo pullum rapiens aquillinum
> Hic deplumavit, acephalumque dedit

a horrible play upon the word *Astur* (vulture) and the castle of Astura. The block and cross, however, are the most interesting memorials of Conradin; the church, with its statue and inscription, are all of recent date.

On the south-west of the piazza, near an old stone cross, is the church of S. Eligio (S. Loo – the patron of workers in metal), with a beautiful Gothic porch of the fourteenth century and a statue of the saint. A gate crosses the narrow street below the church, and, upon it, two heads below the clock record the romantic administration of justice upon this spot by the Regent Isabella of Aragon, daughter of Alfonso I, who, in 1501, insisted upon the marriage of a Baron Caracciolo with a young girl whom he had deflowered, upon the scaffold in the market-place, and had him beheaded immediately afterwards in the presence of his bride.

[25] MASANIELLO'S REBELLION; FROM LADY MORGAN'S *THE LIFE AND TIMES OF SALVATOR ROSA*.

(Sydney Owenson, Lady Morgan, (1783–1859) was an Irish novelist and travel writer very popular in her day. Her best-known book was *The Wild Irish Girl*.)

In the summer of 1647, when the public fermentation was beginning unequivocally to declare itself, the approaching celebration of the great national and religious festival of *Our Lady of Carmel* appeared, for the moment, to obliterate all less joyous impressions. The principal spectacle of this '*gran festa*' was a sort of war-game, played by the youths of the city. A Turkish fortress was erected in the centre of the *Mercato del Carmine* [Piazza del Mercato]. The crescent glittered on its ramparts, and it was defended by three or four hundred youths, who, with the name of Alarbes, were supposed to represent a species of Turkish militia. The besiegers of this stronghold of infidelity, the representatives of the Neapolitan nation, never failed to conquer the Alarbes; as the people never failed to rejoice in a victory which imaged the triumph of the cross over the crescent – of the Neapolitans over their hated neighbours, the Turks!

The chiefs elected to command these opposed forces were Scipione Gannatajo Pione, a bold brave youth of eighteen, who led on the Turks, and Tommaso Angelo Maya, the captain of the Neapolitans, whose familiar and abbreviated appellation of Masaniello now belongs to history. On the morning of the seventh of July, the two commanders came to review their forces in the market, previously to the celebration of the *festa*. They were all habited alike in the customary Neapolitan suit of coarse linen trowsers and tunic, fastened with as coarse a girdle, and without stockings; their arms were long canes or reeds, to which a pitched faggot was attached for burning the citadel at the hour of attack. Every eye was turned on Masaniello as he marched into the Mercato; for his elevation was a preconcerted event, and he had long been looked on as one who represented in his story and condition, the sufferings and the grievances of the people at large. Masaniello was a handsome youth, of a lofty stature and prepossessing air, acute, vivacious, endowed with an instinctive love of justice and hatred of oppression, and with a simple but powerful eloquence, the language of strong feelings and clear intellect. Though his profession was no higher than that of a fisherman, carrying on a little commerce between Amalfi (his native village in the gulf of Salerno) and the market of Naples, yet he is said to have taken a pride in an employment which the founder of his church, and the favourite apostle of his Redeemer, had rendered sacred; and at an early age he obtained an extraordinary influence over his companions.

Masaniello, though he had married in boyhood, and was already a father, had by prudence and industry contrived to save a small sum of money, and to support his little family with respectability for one so humble, when his young wife, who attended the markets with grain and fruits, endeavouring to pass the barriers without paying the toll, was seized and thrown into prison, and a fine levied on her husband of an hundred ducats. Plunged into the deepest indigence by an exaction which exhausted the savings of his laborious life, the hatred of the beggared fisherman of Amalfi against the tyranny of the underlings in office, became deep as the wretchedness into which they had plunged him. From effects so personal, his sullen and discontented spirit extended its broodings to the causes in which they originated; and in this mood he was found in the hut, which now (in the place of the vine-covered cottage he had been forced to abandon) afforded him a temporary shelter; and he was elected captain of the Neapolitan Lazzaroni, to fight for the honour of Christ and Our Lady of Carmel.

Masaniello and Pione had severally taken the field at an early hour of the morning, and begun their ordinary evolutions in the Mercato, when a dispute arose between the gardeners of Pozzuoli, their customers, and the officers of the new *gabelle* on fruits. The peasantry and the citizens alike refused to pay a tax which the Viceroy had solemnly promised to abolish from the 30th of the preceding month. The officers insisted, and the conflict became general and fearful. The gardeners flung their fruits on the earth, declaring they would rather give them to the people, than permit them to be seized by their common bloodsuckers. The General of the police attempted to interfere, by order of the Viceroy, and the tumult became still more violent, when Masaniello, springing on the steps of the church, commanded silence; and with the air and voice of one inspired, exclaimed, 'My people, from this moment there is no *gabelle* in Naples!' He was answered by the approving acclamations of thousands. His own little troop, and that of Pione, rallied round their leaders, and were joined by some others. This force he divided into two corps, and placing himself at their head, he marched forth amidst the *vivats* of all Naples, to the Viceroy's palace, to demand a religious performance of the promise so often reiterated and so often broken. The shrewd and clever Duc D'Arcos, the profound diplomatist and master of that '*fourberie que l'on appelle politique*', thus taken on the hip, was confounded and intimidated. He sent away his family to the citadel of the Castello-Nuovo; he doubled his German guards, surrounded himself with his court, and trembled as he presented himself at the open balcony, beneath which the young fisherman of Amalfi, at the head of his boy-bands, armed only with reeds, called for a parley with the representative of majesty.

The Viceroy again promised the abolition of the *gabelle* upon fruit; but when the multitude cried out 'upon flour also' he replied, with a show of returning firmness, 'that he might *moderate*, but could not abolish, any *gabelle* save that on fruit'. It was then that, after a moment's pause, Masaniello ordered his troop to follow him; and rushing through the gates of the palace, forced the foreign troops to fly before him. Traversing the sumptuous apartments, he commanded that all the splendid trappings of luxury, which were there accumulated at the expense of the people's blood, should be destroyed, without reserving a single object save the king's picture . . .

The Viceroy shut himself up in St Elmo, and thus formally abandoned the city to a low-born youth of three-and-twenty, who in the space of a few hours beheld himself its absolute master, without having incurred the reproach of shedding one drop of blood.

The first acts of his authority were to disarm the foreign guards, to open the state prison of St Giacomo, where hundreds of persons were incarcerated for the non-payment of taxes, which they had not the means to discharge, and to proclaim by sound of trumpet the abolition of the *gabelles* on all articles of subsistence . . .

He scarcely took any food, slept but little, was in perpetual activity. At once mild and resolute, severe and just, he remodelled the police, and directed its operations with absolute authority and with admirable intelligence. He erected batteries on the most exposed points, threw artillery into suspicious situations, invested the Convent of San Lorenzo, the repository of the arms and archives of the city, and took it almost without resistance, although the government had stationed a party of Calabrian banditti in the belfry to defend it. He restrained the people from all acts of violence, protected the nobility, and administered justice with inflexible impartiality. As unambitious as disinterested, he was solely occupied with the great object of restoring the people to their ancient franchises, and forcing the Viceroy to a formal renunciation of the *gabelles*. While the high-born Duc d'Arcos shut himself up in the Castello-Nuovo, to which he had fled from St Elmo, as being nearer the sea – while he affected to negotiate, in order to gain time, and *betray* the man he could not *conquer* – Masaniello, in his fisherman's habit, stood unarmed at the open casement of his own humble dwelling, giving orders with an authority none disputed . . .

Masaniello was proceeding carelessly towards the church [of the Carmine] when a single shot from an arquebus whistled by him in the cloisters, and he had scarcely pronounced the word '*traditori*', when a discharge of fire-arms, mingled with the shrieks of thousands, echoed through the vast edifice. The cry of 'Masaniello is assassinated – down with the banditti', repeated through the church, was heard in the market-place. The multitude rushed in to the assistance of their chief; the assassins were driven out and forced to fly; some few were poniarded on the steps of the altar; others were stuck down in the cloisters, and all was confusion and sanguinary contest, when Masaniello arrested the carnage . . .

On a special invitation from the Viceroy, Masaniello gave a reluctant consent to visit him in the Castello-Nuovo. It was not till the Cardinal had suggested the necessity for a frank and open reconciliation, and of setting the example of confidence, that the unambitious Captain-General agreed to the meeting. When the Cardinal and officers of state came to conduct Masaniello to the Castle, he was still in his white linen jacket and fisherman's cap; and to all remonstrances on the unfitness of his garb for the occasion, he replied that 'It was the dress of his class and profession, the dress in which he had fought for the rights and privileges of the people, and the only dress he should ever wear with pride, or look upon with triumph'. At length, however, a threat from the Cardinal, of excommunication, forced him to yield; and when he again appeared before the people, he was mounted on a superb charger, dressed in a rich habit of white and silver, his velvet hat shaded with a profusion of feathers, and his air that of a graceful and handsome cavalier. The people could not satiate themselves with gazing on him; and when the procession began to move to the Castello-Nuovo, he was followed by sixteen companies of cavalry and infantry, well armed and accoutred, and by 50,000 of the Neapolitan population. The Cardinal rode beside him in grand pontificals; and the officers of state went before in the Viceroy's carriages. At the gates of the Castle the captain of the guards welcomed him with military honours; and in the Viceroy's name invited him to alight and enter . . .

A conference followed; Masaniello was confirmed in his post of Captain-General of the People by the government, and was reconducted in state to his hovel in the Mercato, by the equipages and principal officers of the Viceroy's court.

But his mission was nevertheless now hastening to its close. On the 13th of July, he accepted an invitation to a fête, at which some of the court were to be present, at Pausilippo. The party proceeded by water; and in the course of this splendid little voyage, Masaniello, exhausted by the fatigues of the day, called for iced water, which was presented to him by Onofrio Caffriero, one of the Viceroy's officials and familiars. Whether he really was poisoned in this draught, as was generally asserted, is uncertain. Extraordinary exertions, long want of sleep, and an over-worked brain, are causes of mental derangement, which have affected wiser men than the fisherman of Amalfi; and under such circumstances of excitement, a glass of iced water might in itself become deleterious: but on the other hand the administration of a poisonous drug was no improbable project for the Viceroy; and men of his stamp, with whom a political end sanctions every crime, deserve to bear the full weight of that odium, which the eager credulity and instinctive dread of the multitude seldom fail to attach to such governors, where there is room for coupling a secret villainy with their known interests and wishes. But however this may have been, marks of insanity manifested themselves immediately after the voyage; his acts of justice became tinctured by a merciless severity; and his most ordinary actions were suddenly distinguished by wildness and incoherency. It was determined by the representatives of the people to send a deputation to the Viceroy, offering a return to obedience, provided the terms of capitulation were observed, and to depose Masaniello from his high office, and place him in confinement, surrounded by all the comforts of which his unhappy situation was susceptible. But the Viceroy had already resolved on a more summary procedure. On the night before the festival of *Our Lady of Mount Carmel*, Masaniello had become so outrageous, that he had been taken and bound; and this act of violence

having restored him to his senses, he was permitted on the following
day to attend divine service in the *Chiesa del Carmine*. He presented
himself to the people with an air of sadness and depression; they
received him with respect, and conducted him in silence to the church,
where the Cardinal, who officiated, came forward to receive him.
Masaniello returned his embrace, and placed paper in his hand – a
written paper directed to the Viceroy. It was his voluntary resignation.
In giving it, he observed 'that those whom he had saved, were about to
abandon him, that his career was over, and that after having made one
last tour of that city which he had preserved he would return to the
church, and await the death-blow which would now soon be struck'.
Then releasing himself from the arms of the Cardinal, who in vain
essayed to cheer him, he once more attempted to address the people,
and was recommending to them the care of their own liberties, when
he should no longer be there to protect them, but his strength and his
ideas suddenly failed him, and two monks of the convent, perceiving
his disorder, withdrew him from the tribune, and conducted him to
their dormitory. There, flinging himself on a mattress, he was sinking
into that deep repose he so much needed, when, roused by the vocifera-
tion of his own name, he started from his bed, hastily stepped forth,
and firmly but mildly asked, 'My people, do you seek me?' He was
answered by a discharge of fire-arms, and instantly fell at the feet of his
assassins, exclaiming *'Traditori! ingrati!'* His head was severed from his
body by a butcher, and sent to the Viceroy, who is said to have gazed on
it with a triumphant smile.

[26] ANOTHER VIEW OF MASANIELLO AND HIS REVOLT; FROM
PIETRO GIANNONE'S *ISTORIA CIVILE DEL REGNO DI NAPOLI*

Masaniello, in tatters and half naked, had a scaffold as a background
and a sword for a sceptre. There were 150,000 men at his back, armed
haphazardly but alarmingly enough, and they controlled the entire city.
As the instigator of sedition and leader of the insurrection, he moved

all motions, imposed silence, decided what was to be discussed and, as though everybody's destiny were in his power, killed with a nod or set fire to any house at which he glared. Heads were struck off, palaces burnt down. Through the Cardinal Archbishop's mediation, the Viceroy was induced to grant the edict of exemption which the mob had first demanded, and to accept a solemn agreement by which all taxes imposed since the time of Charles V were removed and no new ones levied. The commons and nobility were put on the same footing where voting was concerned. An amnesty was promised, and the rabble were to be allowed to continue to bear arms for the next three months until the King's consent had arrived. All this was ratified by a solemn oath in the church of the Carmelites, thus giving a short breathing-space. Masaniello, flattered excessively by the Viceroy, as was his wife by the Vicereine, grew excessively conceited, then disturbed in his mind, and finally, from lack of sleep and too much wine, delirious. Unacceptable even to his supporters and cruel to everybody, he was killed on the morning of 16 July in the friary of the Carmelites by people hired for the purpose; some of his most trusted followers shared his fate. The populace appeared not in the least concerned about his death; on the contrary, they seemed overjoyed at seeing his head on a pole. In consequence, general peace and calm were anticipated.

However, certain noblemen, with disastrous irresponsibility, snubbed some of the mob. On the following day, by extra-ordinary ill-judgement, the price of bread was raised. Rebellion immediately broke out again with such intensity that, after digging up Masaniello's body and re-uniting it with the head, his corpse lay in state in the Carmelites' church. The enormous throng bent on seeing it would never have dispersed if he had not been re-buried with the same solemn and regal ceremony as a Captain-General.

[27] THE CHURCH OF THE CARMINE ADJOINING THE PIAZZA DEL
MERCATO IN 1692; FROM CANON CARLO CELANO'S *NOTIZIE DEL
BELLO, DELL' ANTICO E DEL CURIOSO DELLA CITTÀ DI NAPOLI*.

The beautiful and venerated church of the Carmine was founded in the
following manner. There arrived at Naples some brethren called the
Order of the Blessed Virgin of Mount Carmel who, as soon as their rule
had been confirmed by Pope Honorius III in the year 1217, built a very
small church and convent just outside the city from alms given by the
Neapolitans. In it they placed a picture of the Blessed Virgin, known as
Santa Maria della Bruna, which they had brought with them. Some say
it was painted by St Luke the Evangelist.

When the Empress [Elizabeth], mother of the luckless King
Conradin, came to Naples to ransom her son from Charles I she found
that by order of the said Charles he was already dead, so she spent the
treasure she had brought in giving honourable burial to his royal bones
and in endowing chantries for his soul, since she was not allowed to
bear away his body; a great part went to the Carmelite brethren, and
out of her magnificent donation they built a new church and enlarged
their friary. Then, in the year 1269, to demonstrate his piety, Charles
gave the brothers a large field called the 'Moricino'. [Soon the city walls
were extended and enclosed the field, which became the Piazza del
Mercato.] . . .

We must now say something of the strange and beautiful things to
be seen in this church. Among the most important is the holy and
miraculous picture [of the Virgin], which is kept in the sanctuary
behind the High Altar. Beneath the sanctuary's pavement lie buried the
unfortunate King Conradin and also the Duke of Austria who was
beheaded with the said King . . .

Cardinal Ascanio Filomarino, by God's Grace Archbishop of Naples,
had a deep devotion to the holy picture; every Wednesday he would visit
it most devoutly and hear Mass. On the feastday he said Mass himself,
celebrating it with altar vessels of very rich plate including a splendid

chalice. This prelate thought it most improper that the acolytes who served the sanctuary, unveiling the picture or lighting the candles, could be seen over the top of the altar in consequence of the floor being almost as high as the altar itself. He therefore made the friars lower the floor so that people would not have to watch all the coming and going. While lowering it, by good fortune a leaden coffin some six palms long and two palms deep was discovered; on it were inscribed three letters, an R and two Cs, which were interpreted as signifying *Regis Conradini Corpus* [The body of King Conradin]. When opened, all the bones inside were found to be fleshless though the head still kept its teeth; clearly the skull of a young man, it had been placed on the breast. I gather that at the time the sword which was there too was all but intact; its blade shone bright and polished as the day it left the swordmaker. One could also see a few fragments of clothing, though as soon as they were touched they crumbled into dust. These relics were replaced, covered up again, and reinterred deeper down, where they remain to this day.

Close by, almost under the holy picture, another coffin was discovered. This was left undisturbed, but people believed that it contained the bones of the Duke of Austria. Some think that the coffins had been moved there when the church was altered during its enlargement by King Ferrante of Aragon.

Over the arch of the entrance to the gallery immediately opposite is placed a miraculous carved wooden crucifix held in deep and unfeigned veneration by all Neapolitans, a veneration demonstrated twice a year and whenever the city is suffering some affliction. It is well known that in AD 1439, when King Alfonso I of Aragon had closely invested the city, Don Pedro of Aragon, Infante of Castile, was shelling it with a great bombard brought from the town of Rieti, and had reduced the neighbourhood around the church to ruins – the place was bombarded to such an extent that part of the church itself was beginning to collapse. A cannonball of truly enormous size smashed through the gallery and was hurtling towards the crucifix, whereupon the sacred likeness on the cross turned its head away and the cannon ball did no more damage than to knock off its crown of thorns. So that the miracle should not be forgotten the head remained turned aside, as may be seen even now. A few days later, a shot fired from near the church smote off the head of that valiant Infante Don Pedro.

[28] THE EXECUTION IN THE PIAZZA DEL MERCATO OF ELEONORA DE FONSECA PIMENTEL, THE JACOBIN POETESS AND PROPAGANDIST WHO WAS A KEY FIGURE IN THE SHORT-LIVED PARTHENOPEAN REPUBLIC; FROM CONSTANCE GIGLIOLI'S *NAPLES IN 1799.*

Eleonora, who was of noble birth, and whose husband, Pasquale Tria de Solis, had been a Neapolitan officer and noble, demanded to be beheaded rather than hanged; but in these matters the Junta was extremely punctilious, and since by birth, although naturalized, she was Portuguese, her request was denied . . .

To this horrible death Eleonora Pimentel went forth serenely on August 20th, only asking for a cup of coffee before going, saying to her fellow sufferers and to those they were leaving behind: 'Forsan et haec olim meminisse juvabit!' [Perhaps one day it will be a pleasure to remember these sufferings.]

For the execution of August 20th, comprising as it did eight persons whose fate, for various reasons, aroused an intense excitement in the populace, the *Bianchi* [a religious confraternity dedicated to consoling condemned criminals] had petitioned that it might take place within the walls of the Carmine, 'representing that the sufferers, obliged to die in public, died in despair because of the insults of the populace'.

But petitions of this kind were never listened to, and the execution took place in the Mercato, the large, squalid piazza before the Church of the Carmine, where, notwithstanding the broiling heat, the concourse of people was enormous. The whole great square was surrounded by regular troops and *Sanfedisti*, besides two regiments of cavalry, and was commanded by the guns of the Carmine, within whose walls other troops in reserve stood under arms in case of any tumult.

Giuliano Colonna and Gennaro Serra were the first, and were beheaded. When Serra came out, blindfolded, from the guardroom of the Carmine, whence the prisoners issued one by one with the *Bianchi* as their turn came, and heard the cries of the mob all eager for the show, he said bitterly: 'I have always desired their welfare and they are rejoicing at my death!' . . .

The rest were hanged. Among them was Michele Natale, Bishop of Vico, on whose shoulders the hangman performed all sorts of antics, saying he might never again have the good luck to ride a bishop . . .

Eleonora's turn came last. As she came out of the guard-house the crowd tried in vain to make her cry, 'Viva il Re!' but the *Bianchi* by signs imposed something of silence. She was dressed in mourning, in a gown that clung close about her feet. She mounted the ladder without faltering, saluting as best she could her friends and companions – her fellow soldiers – who she knew were there dead around her. 'As she fell,' wrote De Nicola, 'the shouts of the populace went up to the very stars,' and were heard at the monastery of the Santi Apostoli, about a mile away.

The body hung there all day and until the next evening, and the people made ribald songs upon the woman.

[29] THE HANGING IN THE PIAZZA DEL MERCATO OF
THE WOULD-BE MURDERER OF KING FERDINAND II;
FROM CONSTANCE GIGLIOLI'S *NAPLES IN 1799*.

The present writer has heard, from an eye-witness, a description of the hanging of Agesilao Milano, the soldier who attempted to shoot Ferdinand II at a review in 1857. The gallows resembled those in the prints of the last century – a tall, upright 'tree' with one arm, from which the sufferer was suspended. To reach this there was a long ladder, and at the execution the hangman having bound the arms of his prisoner, blindfolded him and adjusted the rope round his neck, and then preceded him up the ladder, leading the prisoner by the rope, closely followed by the *tirapiedi* (literally, *pull-feet*), his assistant. On arriving near the top, the hangman scrambled up on to the cross-beam and made fast the rope; then, at a sign from him, the *tirapiedi* suddenly pushed the prisoner off the ladder, adroitly catching him by the feet as he fell, and swinging with him into space. At the same time the hangman from above scrambled down and seated himself astraddle on the shoulders of the victim, and the three swung to and fro in sight of an immense multitude, jamming, struggling, and pulling till life was gone. [*The lingering effects of the wound that Milano's bayonet inflicted on the King almost certainly contributed to Ferdinand's death two years later.*]

The Angevin churches: Santa Chiara, San Lorenzo Maggiore, Santa Maria Donnaregina, San Giovanni a Carbonara and the Incoronata

[30] CONDITIONS IMPOSED IN THE 1770S BY A DAUGHTER
OF THE NOBILITY ENTERING A CONVENT (ALMOST CERTAINLY
SANTA CHIARA); FROM MICHAEL KELLY'S *REMINISCENCES*.

(Michael Kelly (1764–1826) was an Irish singer, actor, composer and theatrical manager.)

The young and beautiful daughter of the Duke de Monteleone, the richest nobleman in Naples, was destined by her family to take the veil; she consented without a murmur to quit the world, provided the ceremony of her profession was performed with splendour; and a *sine qua non* was, that Cafarelli, the great soprano singer, should perform at it. It was represented to her that he had retired with a fine fortune to his estate, in the interior of Calabria, and had declared his determination never to sing again. Then said the reasonable young lady, 'I declare my *determination* never to take the veil unless he does. He sang six years ago, when my cousin was professed, and I had rather die, than it should be said, that she had the first singer in the world to sing for *her*, and that I had not!' The fair lady was firm, and her glorious obstinacy was such, that her father was obliged to take a journey into Calabria, when, with much entreaty, and very many *weighty* arguments, he prevailed on Cafarelli to return with him to Naples. He sang a *salve regina* at the ceremony; and the Signora having gained her point, cheerfully submitted to be led, like a lamb to the sacrifice, to eternal seclusion from the gay and wicked world.

[31] Royal tombs at Santa Chiara; from
Italian Sculptors by Charles Perkins.

The Angevin monuments at Santa Chiara are of rare historical interest, inasmuch as they commemorate that eventful epoch in Neapolitan annals which commenced with the reign of King Robert and ended with that of his grand-daughter, the too famous Queen Joanna [Giovanna] I. The most important among them is that of King Robert himself: *'signor savio ed espertissimo in pace ed in guerra, e riputato un altro Salomone dell' età sua.'* Passionately fond of books, which 'were always by his side by night and by day, sitting or walking, in war and in peace, in prosperity as in adversity', this rare monarch won the gratitude of the men of letters of his time by the esteem in which he held them, and their admiration by his personal attainments. Before Petrarch was crowned with laurel at Rome, he went to Naples and voluntarily submitted to be examined by King Robert, who gave him a diploma setting forth his titles to the honour about to be conferred upon him by the Roman senate, [and] bestowed upon him his royal mantle to wear at the ceremony . . .

Occupied in repeated and fruitless attempts to get possession of Sicily, and constantly obliged to reduce his turbulent barons to subjection by force, his public life was full of disquietude, while the death of his only son Duke Charles of Calabria, upon whose tried capacities for government he had counted in the future, clouded his private life with bitter disappointment and grief. The succession had by Duke Charles's death devolved upon his daughter Joanna, who had been married by King Robert to his nephew Andrea. Their unhappy union, and the character of the future queen, filled the old monarch with apprehension, and helped to bring down his grey hairs in sorrow to the grave. A few months after his death Queen Joanna announced by letter to her faithful subject Jacobus de Pactis, that she had commissioned the Florentine brothers Pancius (Sancius) and Johannes to erect a monument to her grandfather at Santa Chiara. These artists, who are otherwise unknown,

erected the imposing Gothic structure which surmounts the doorway
to the nuns' choir, towering above the high altar. Its Gothic canopy
rests upon double columns, decorated with well-draped statuettes of
the Virtues, some of which are very pleasing in sentiment. The gable is
adorned with a roundel supported by angels, containing a bas-relief of
the resurrection of Our Lord. Under this canopy is a recess shrouded by
curtains ornamented with golden lilies. Their heavy folds are held back
by angels who look down upon the dead king. Dressed as a Franciscan
monk, with a crown upon his head and across upon his breast, he lies
on top of a sarcophagus, whose front is decorated with a row of flat
niches, containing small figures in low relief of the king with his two
wives, Iolanthe and Sancia, and of his son Duke Charles with his wife
Maria of Austria, and their daughter Queen Joanna, relieved against a
deep blue background studded with golden lilies. Above this curtained
recess is a lofty tabernacle similarly decorated, containing a life-size
statue of the king seated and holding a globe and sceptre in his hands . . .

Giannone tells us that Duke Charles was the first member of the
royal family buried at Santa Chiara, but as he died long before the
church was completed, his body must have been deposited elsewhere
in the interim, and his monument may not have been made until after
that of King Robert. (When King Robert – says Giannone – asked Duke
Charles how he liked Santa Chiara, he replied that, being without tran-
septs and surrounded by many little low-roofed chapels which opened
out of it like stalls, it looked to him like a stable. Piqued by this answer,
or moved by a prophetic spirit, the King said, 'God grant, my son, that
you may not be the first one of us to eat in this stable.') The recumbent
effigy is draped in a royal mantle painted blue and decorated with
golden lilies, and the front of the sarcophagus is adorned with small
figures in relief representing the Duke, with a sceptre and a sword,
sitting in the midst of his counsellors and vassals, the first in their robes
of office, and the last in short doublets and cloaks. The wolf and the
lamb drinking out of the same cup, sculptured at his feet, symbolize the
wise and just conduct of affairs by which, while governing the kingdom

during his father's absence, he induced the turbulent nobles to live at peace with their inferiors . . . It is uncertain whether Marie de Valois, the second wife of Duke Charles, or his daughter Joanna I, lies buried in the monument next his own. The recumbent effigy draped in a long blue mantle lies on top of the sarcophagus, which rests upon female Caryatides standing on the backs of lions. The queen and her attendants are represented on the front of the sarcophagus, one end of which is decorated with well-draped figures of St Elizabeth and Santa Chiara in flat Gothic niches. In another Gothic tomb on the opposite side of the church lies Maria, the sister of Joanna and wife of her second cousin Charles, Duke of Durazzo.

[32] THE MUMMIFIED CORPSES BENEATH SANTA CHIARA IN 1825; FROM THE COUNTESS OF BLESSINGTON'S *THE IDLER IN ITALY*.

(Marguerite Power, Countess of Blessington (1789–1849) was an Irish novelist who was the mistress of the dandy, Alfred Count d'Orsay.)

The subterraneous chapels are guarded by soldiers. The altars are arranged in the usual style of those in Catholic chapels; innumerable torches illuminate the place; and an abundance of flowers and religious emblems decorate it. Ranged around the walls, stand the deceased unhappily disinterred for the occasion; and clothed in dresses so little suited to their present appearance, that they render death still more hideous. Their bodies are supported round the waist by cords, concealed beneath the outward dress; but this partial support, while it precludes the corpse from falling to the earth, does not prevent its assuming the most grotesque attitudes. Old and young, male and female, are here brought in juxta-position. The octogenarian, with his white locks still flowing from his temples, stands next a boy of six years old, whose ringlets have been curled for the occasion; and whose embroidered shirt-collar, and jacket with well-polished buttons, indicate the pains bestowed on his toilette. Those ringlets twine round a face resembling nothing human, a sort of mask of discoloured leather, with fallen jaws and distended lips; and the embroidered collar leaves disclosed the shrunken dark brown chest, once fair and full, where, perhaps, a fond mother's lips often were impressed; but which now looks fearful, contrasted with the snowy texture of this bit of finery. This faded image of what was once a fair child, has tied to its skeleton fingers a top, probably the last gift of affection; the hand, fallen on one side, leans towards the next disinterred corpse, whose head also, no longer capable of maintaining a perpendicular position, is turned, as if to ogle a female figure, whose ghastly and withered brow wreathed with roses, looks still more fearful from the contrast with their bright blue. Here the mature matron, her once voluminous person reduced to a sylph-like slightness, stands enveloped in the ample folds of the gaudy garb she wore in life. The youthful wife is attired in the delicate tinted drapery put on in happy days to charm a husband's eye: the virgin wears the robe of pure white, leaving only her throat bare: and the young men are clothed in the holiday suits of which they were vain in life; some with riding-whips, and others with canes attached to their bony hands. A figure I shall never forget, was that of a young woman, who died on the day of her wedding. Robed in her bridal vest, with the chaplet of orange flowers still twined round her head, her hair fell in masses over her face and shadowy form, half veiling the discoloured hue of the visage and neck, and sweeping over her, as if to conceal the fearful triumph of death over beauty . . .

Around several of the defunct, knelt friends, to whom in life they were dear, offering up prayers for the repose of their souls: while groups of persons, attracted merely by curiosity, sauntered through this motley assemblage of the deceased, pausing to comment on the appearance they presented.

'Why, bless me,' said a middle-aged woman, with a countenance indicative of more than usual self-complacency, 'here is poor Caterina Giustiniani: who could have thought that she would have been so sadly changed in so short a time?'

'Time changes us all sadly, even before death,' replied the person to whom she spoke.

'Not *all* of us,' rejoined the first speaker; 'why poor Caterina was not above five years my senior, and now I vow she looks any age.'

'Five years your senior! your junior, you mean.'

'I mean no such thing, and I can—'

Here the speakers moved away, and the rest of the dialogue was lost to me; but, from the tone of the latter part of it, and the looks of the parties, I was led to believe its conclusion was not amiable . . .

'Look at Nicolo Baldi,' said a man to his companion, pointing to a male corpse, somewhat more smartly dressed than the others, 'see how rakish he looks, with his head on one side, as if he were ogling the dead woman next to him.'

'Oh! yes, poor Nicolo always had an eye to the women,' replied the other. 'But see who is placed at the left side of him; no other than Bartolommeo Magatti, with whom he was always quarrelling.'

'Poor Nicolo must be dead, indeed, to stand quietly near one he so hated,' rejoined the first interlocutor.

[33] BOCCACCIO'S FIRST SIGHT OF FIAMMETTA AT SAN LORENZO ON 30 MARCH 1331; AND FIAMMETTA'S PARENTAGE; FROM *GIOVANNI BOCCACCIO* BY EDWARD HUTTON.

(The Florentine poet Giovanni Boccaccio (1313–75) is said to have composed his *Decameron* for Queen Giovanna I.)

He had gone to Mass, it seems, about ten o'clock in the morning, the fashionable hour of the day, rather to see the people than to attend the service, in the church of S. Lorenzo of the Franciscans. And there amid that great throng of all sorts and conditions of men he first caught sight of the woman who was so profoundly to influence his life and shape his work.

'I found myself,' he says, 'in a fine church of Naples, named after him who endured to be offered as a sacrifice upon the gridiron. And there,

there was a singing compact of sweetest melody. I was listening to the Holy Mass celebrated by a priest, successor to him who first girt himself humbly with the cord, exalting poverty and adopting it. Now while I stood there, the fourth hour of the day, according to my reckoning, having already passed down the eastern sky, there appeared to my eyes the wondrous beauty of a young woman, come thither to hear what I too heard attentively. I had no sooner seen her than my heart began to throb so strongly that I felt it in my slightest pulses; and not knowing why nor yet perceiving what had happened, I began to say, "Ohimè, what is this?" ' . . . When she saw that he continued to stare at her, she screened herself with her veil. But he changed his position and found a place by a column whence he could see her very well – '*dirittissimam-ente opposto . . . appoggiato ad una colonna marmorea*' – and there, while the priest sang the Office, '*con canto pieno di dolce melodia,*' he drank in her blonde beauty which the dark clothes made more splendid – the golden hair and the milk-white skin, the shining eyes and the mouth like a rose in a field of lilies. Once she looked at him, – '*Li occhi, con debita gravità elevati, in tra la moltitudine de' circostanti giovani, con acuto ragguardamento distesi.*' So he stayed where he was till the service was over, '*senza mutare luogo*'. Then he joined his companions, waiting with them at the door to see the girls pass out. And it was then, in the midst of other ladies, that he saw her for the second time, watching her pass out of S. Lorenzo on her way home. When she was gone he went back to his room with his friends, who remained a short time with him. These, as soon as might be, excusing himself, he sent away, and remained alone with his thoughts.

The morrow was Easter Day, and again he went to S. Lorenzo to see her only. And she was there indeed, '*di molto oro lucente* – adorned with gems and dressed in most fair green, beautiful both by nature and by art' . . .

It was not till February 2, 1313 that the king [Robert] opened the first general parliament in Naples after his coronation . . . Amid all this splendour Boccaccio describes the king's gaze passing over a host of beautiful women, to rest, always with new delight, on the beauty of the young wife of D'Aquino, who, since her husband belonged to the court, was naturally present. Well, to make a long story short, a little later the king seduced this lady, but as it seems, on or about the same night she slept also with her husband, so that when nine months later a daughter [Fiammetta] was born to her, both the king and her husband believed themselves to be the father. It is like a story out of the *Decameron*.

[34] PETRARCH, STAYING AT THE FRIARY OF SAN LORENZO, EXPERIENCES THE FAMOUS STORM OF 24 NOVEMBER 1343; FROM HIS LETTER TO CARDINAL COLONNA.

Curiously enough, rumours of impending disaster had been circulating for some days, started by the pious bishop of an island nearby who is an astrologer. Such forecasts are never quite accurate and he predicted an earthquake instead of a storm, saying Naples would be destroyed on 25 November 1343 His prediction caused so much alarm that a good number of Neapolitans made up their minds to repent and amend their way of life because of approaching death, abandoning all sorts of callings. On the other hand many mocked at their fears, especially as various other forecasts of disaster had been wrong about the dates and had demolished the prophet's credibility. I myself was neither panic-stricken nor altogether pessimistic, though I have to admit that I was mildly afraid since, in my experience, what one fears is more likely to happen than what one wants; also from spending the winter in cooler climes I am used to signs of foul weather, so I was inclined to be nervous and to a gloominess verging on superstition.

The night arrived, preceding a fateful day. Flocks of terrified women, whom danger had deprived of all self-control, began running through the streets and the piazzas, crowding tearfully into the churches to pray. Depressed by such signs of alarm everywhere around me, I went home about dusk. It was very still so, reassured, my servants retired to bed at the usual time. I myself decided to sit up and watch the moon setting as it was then, I believe, coming to the end of its first quarter. I stood by a window facing west until the moon was hidden by cloud, and the hill at the back finally obscured its pale face, some time before midnight. At last I went to bed, ready enough for my deferred slumber. I had only just closed my eyes when suddenly there was the most frightful noise; not only were the shutters rattling horribly but the actual walls themselves, built of hewn stone, were rocking on their foundations. My night-light, which I always keep burning when I sleep, had gone out. Everyone got up – fear of imminent death dispelled any desire for repose. While we were groping about, looking for one another in the darkness and trying to reassure ourselves with quavering voices by the light of a single lamp, led by the saintly Prior David – to his eternal credit – the friars in whose monastery we were staying and who had risen at their accustomed hour to sing Lauds, rushed into my room with candles, crosses and relics and in terror of some awful calamity began calling on God for mercy. I managed to pull myself together. We then spent the night in their church, shaking, suspecting we were about to die and that everything was collapsing in ruins about us.

I have not time to describe all the horrors of that hellish night, and even if I told no more than the truth, no-one would believe me. Heavens! What a deluge! What gales! What thunder and lightning! What bolts of fire! What earthquakes and what howling seas! And what dreadful screams. Eventually, even if by some evil spell the night had seemingly lasted twice as long as normal, dawn broke – yet we only knew from the time since there was no daylight whatever. The priests vested to say Mass, and we knelt round them on the cold wet ground, too afraid to look up. When it was obvious that, however dark, it really was day, the normal roar of voices in the city simply did not begin, except for around the seafront. As we could not find out what was happening, with the courage of despair – there are others who have experienced it – we climbed on to our horses and rode down to the bay to see, and perhaps to die.

Good God! Was there ever such a business? Even the very oldest sailors say they have never seen anything like it. There was a miserable, terrible, shipwreck going on in the very middle of the harbour; the wretched sailors had been hurled against the rocks, struggling in the waves and trying desperately to find some foothold, but being shattered like eggshells. The whole shore was littered with broken bodies, some of them still alive, from which brains and guts were protruding. Meanwhile men were yelling and women were shrieking as if they expected to shout down the noise of wind and waves. Houses were collapsing, many of them dashed from their foundations by the huge breakers. On such a day the sea would not obey the laws of nature, had no respect for either men or rocks. The great mole, built with so much costly toil, which as Virgil says, provided

'A haven with its jutting sides'

and the entire seafront quarter were swamped by the waves; the path one normally walks dryfoot was not only under water but became a hazard for navigators.

At least a thousand Neapolitan gentlemen were there on horseback, as though they had come to pay their country a last formal farewell. After I joined them I was a little less frightened, reflecting that if I died it would be in the best possible company. Then suddenly there was a fresh alarm. The very ground beneath us was being undermined by the breakers, so we hastily rode off to a vantage-point higher up. One hardly dared look – no human eye could bear the horrifying appearance of both the sea and the sky. There were thousands of gigantic waves between Naples and Capri; instead of being sky-blue, or black as it generally is in storms, the bay was a ghastly, foaming, white.

The younger of the two queens [Giovanna I], barefoot and not properly dressed, and accompanied by a gaggle of ladies whose self-respect had quite vanished from terror, came out of the palace and hastened to St Maria Maggiore to pray for God's forgiveness in this awful plight.

No doubt you are wondering how it all ended. Those of us on shore barely survived; nothing at sea could hope to live amid the waves, not even in the harbour. We watched three galleys from Marseilles, at anchor after a long voyage from Cyprus and planning to set sail for home the following morning, founder without a single soul from the complement being saved; no-one could help them, though everybody wept at the sight . . . .

That, briefly, is what happened yesterday . . . The birds can have the air and the fishes the sea, so far as I am concerned. I am a land animal and am determined to travel by land throughout the rest of my life.

[35] A VISIT TO SANTA MARIA DONNAREGINA IN
NOVEMBER 1770; FROM DR CHARLES BURNEY'S
MUSIC, MEN AND MANNERS IN FRANCE AND ITALY.

(Dr Charles Burney (1726–1814), musician and travel writer, was father of the novelist, Fanny Burney.)

We went to Mr Hamilton's to dine, but as he dined later than we had imagined, Mrs Hamilton proposed our going out to take a ride with her in the coach. Among other things we went to see, one was a great festival at the convent of La Donna Regina, *una bellissima fonzione*, at which were several bishops and a great deal of good company, with music, on account of two Turkish slaves who, being converted by loss of chains and gain of money, were this morning to be baptized. One was more than forty and the other upwards of thirty years old. They looked very silly (the only thing that could incline me not to suppose them knaves) and the *gens comme il faut* seemed to laugh in their sleeves. The nuns of the monastery were all at the grate except one whom Mrs Hamilton inquired after, but she was not allowed to come down, lest she should be the more confirmed in her repugnance to taking the veil into which her friends seem determined to tease her.

The dinner at Mrs Hamilton's was very comfortable as the company was select. After dinner came a fat friar to sing buffo songs, and Nasci to accompany him and to play some of his own music. Both were excellent, the former in humour and the latter in a graceful and easy manner of playing the violin.

[36] The church of San Giovanni a Carbonara; from *Cities of Southern Italy and Sicily* by Augustus Hare.

Proceeding eastward to the Strada Carbonara, and turning to the left down the Via Grillo, we find, on the left, the Church of S. Giovanni a Carbonara, built by Masuccio II for John of Alexandria in 1343, and enlarged by King Ladislaus in 1400 . . . On entering, the eye is at once arrested by the stupendous and magnificent tomb, erected by his sister Joanna [Giovanna] II to King Ladislaus, 1414, the masterpiece of Andrea Ciccione. It rises, above the door behind the choir, in three stages to the whole height of the church. In the first stage, four colossal statues of Temperance, Fortitude, Prudence, and Justice support the whole. Then, above an architrave with an inscription, are the seated figures of King Ladislaus and his mother, Margareta of Durazzo, with Loyalty, Charity, Faith, and Hope. In the third story, angels are drawing aside a curtain to display the sarcophagus which contains the king's body. On the summit is an equestrian figure of Ladislaus*, with his sword in his hand. He was three times married, but died without children in his thirty-seventh year. In the last year of his life, he had made the daughter of an apothecary at Perugia his mistress; she complained to her father that he was beginning to love her less, and by her father's advice she poisoned him.

In a beautiful octagonal Gothic chapel behind the high altar is the tomb, also by Ciccione, of Gian Caracciolo† (commonly called Ser Gianni), the handsome seneschal of Joanna II, who long vainly schemed

* See following extract for the character of Ladislaus.
† See page 51, for the murder of Caracciolo.

to secure his affections. One day she demanded of her courtiers what animal was most antipathetic to them. One said a toad, another a spider, Caracciolo declared that the creature he most dreaded was a rat. The next day, when he was going to his room, he met a servant with a cage full of rats. As he was trying to pass, the servant opened the cage door, and the rats rushed out. Caracciolo fled, and, trying all the doors in the passage, found only one open; it was that of the Queen's chamber. He was created Grand Seneschal, Duke of Avellino, and Lord of Capua. One day, in 1432 . . . he was found murdered in his room by men who summoned him to open, saying that the Queen was seized with apoplexy, and could not die without seeing him. He was buried in secret by four monks in the chapel he had built.

His statue is a standing coloured figure, grasping a dagger, stiff but very characteristic.

[37] THE DEATH AND CHARACTER OF KING LADISLAO; FROM PIETRO GIANNONE'S ISTORIA CIVILE DEL REGNO DI NAPOLI.

Discovering that King Ladislao was planning to attack Florence, the Florentine envoys resorted to treachery. It is said that having learnt that he was in the middle of an affair with the daughter of a physician from Perugia, with whom he was on quite familiar terms, they gave the man a huge bribe to poison him. It seems that the physician preferred money to his daughter's life. He persuaded her to anoint her privy parts with poison before she slept with the king, telling her that it was composed of medicines which would make him enjoy sleeping with her so much that he would fall even more deeply in love. By this means the King was struck down by an unknown and lingering disease . . .

He was generous to an extraordinary degree. He always admired a brave man and, taking part frequently in tournaments and being skilled in all martial arts, he was convinced that anyone who gave proof of similar skills in his presence could not be rewarded highly enough with honours and riches . . .

He was an unusually lustful prince. Besides his three wives he had many concubines. Among the latter in particular a daughter of the Duke of Sessa and another called Contessella whose family name is unknown. He kept these two in the Castel Nuovo from whence they never stirred, not even when he married the Princess of Taranto; however she was so offended by what she regarded as a deadly insult that he packed them off to the Castel dell' Ovo where another concubine, Maria Guindazzo, was already in residence. He kept others as well, both at Naples and at Gaeta. He employed pimps to procure especially beautiful and high-spirited women for him, like the Sultan of Egypt and the Ottoman Emperor in our own day. His sister Giovanna II was not going to have anyone say that she was her brother's inferior in this respect. No sooner had she been left a widow by the Duke of Austria than she took good care to provide herself with plenty of lovers. It is not too much to claim that King Charles III and Queen Margaret brought two monsters of lust and filthiness into the world.

[38] THE CARACCIOLO DI VICO CHAPEL AT SAN GIOVANNI A CARBONARA; FROM BENEDETTO CROCE'S *UN CALVINISTA ITALIANO, IL MARCHESE DI VICO GALEAZZO CARACCIOLO.*

(Benedetto Croce (1866–1952) settled in Naples when he was twenty, and first made his name as a local historian. He devoted the second half of his life to philosophy, in which he was partly influenced by his brilliant fellow Neapolitan and philosopher, Giambattista Vico.)

The Marchesi di Vico, a branch of the innumerable and very ancient Neapolitan family of Caracciolo, received their title in the sixteenth century. The ancestor of their line was a rugged baron, Gualtieri known as Viola, a supporter of King Ladislaus, of Giovanna II and of Rene of Anjou, who lost his lands in consequence of the victory of Alfonso of Aragon. Later his son Colantonio, nicknamed 'Scarface', joined the Aragonese party, which enabled him to better his condition; but the family only really re-established itself with his grandson Galeazzo, born from Colantonio's second marriage with Martuscella Piscicelli. Galeazzo served Ferrante of Aragon and his successors; in 1480 he commanded the fleet sent by the King of Naples to eject the Turks from Otranto, and he himself hoisted the royal standard on the walls of the town after it had been taken by storm; in 1495, during Charles VIII's occupation, he was busy organizing an army to fight for Ferrantino, and took part in the long campaign to reconquer the kingdom. The young King called him 'his dear comrade in arms', and it was then that Galeazzo acquired the estate of Vico, in the Capitanata.

The family had regained its wealth and position, and the son of this first Galeazzo, the second Colantonio, was not going to risk losing them again; while many Neapolitan barons (among them even some of the Caracciolo), short-sighted and badly advised, intrigued with the Angevin (or French) party and suffered ruin, exile, or death in consequence, he took better care of his own interests and remained faithful to the Spanish successors of the Aragonese kings. He did not allow himself to be swayed, as did so many others, by love of Naples and its liberty and independence. He thought only of the fortunes of his house . . . The Emperor [Charles V] had reason to hold him in esteem. Thanks to this, after the subjugation of Italy and of the Kingdom of Naples, on 8 August 1531 his estate of Vico was made a marquisate. He showed himself no less faithful to the despotic Viceroy Pedro de Toledo, whom he accompanied in August 1532 from Ratisbon, where the Imperial Court was then in residence, to Naples; his discussions with the Viceroy on the way home must surely, to judge from what was in store, have made Caracciolo realize that he was going to install his 'harsh and rigorous rule'. He was taken into Pedro of Toledo's trust and confidence, and was in the habit of playing cards with him every day . . .

In the matter of marriage he was no less quick and determined at seizing every opportunity, with the aim of bettering his family; and the way in which he acquired a wife and dowry filled all Naples with both scandal and envy. In 1515 his maternal uncle Luigi della Lagonessa died young; born of an ancient family of French origin, he was Lord of Telese, Finocchito, Palazzo, Iano and Vitulano; he left Giulia, an only daughter, scarcely more than a child who was heiress of all his lands. While the funeral was taking place and the widow, Beatrice Carafa, was in mourning and lamenting her husband's death, Colantonio pounced on the house, carried off his little cousin and, without waiting for either her mother's consent or a Papal dispensation, married her. He was liable to legal penalties for abducting a minor, and therefore stayed in a safe place for a considerable time; but the deed was done; neither wife nor mother-in-law wanted to see him punished; the business stopped there and, little by little, tempers cooled and in consequence Colantonio was able to return to Naples where, so the family historian tells us, he 'began to enjoy with great splendour the fruits of his boldness'.

Obviously he considered building to be a good way of demonstrating his magnificence. First he completed the family chapel, which had only just been started by his father: one can still see it in the church of San Giovanni a Carbonara, to the left of the High Altar. It is a large monument of richly carved white marble, circular in plan; there are eight Doric-Roman columns grouped in twos and joined by four arches; a bas-relief on the altar represents the Adoration of the Magi; on the left is Galeazzo's tomb with a statue of him as a warrior holding a sword and a jousting-spear. Colantonio's tomb, very similar, is on the right. Niches between the columns contain statues of the Apostles. To these, other tombs and statues were added later. The greatest Neapolitan sculptors of the period worked on this chapel; Giovanni da Nola and his pupils, the Ordoño, who were Spanish, and perhaps another Spaniard, Pedro de La Plata. In 1544 he had carved on the mausoleum which he was building the inscription which dedicates it to himself and to Giulia, his 'incomparable' wife.

[39] THE BUILDING OF THE INCORONATA BY QUEEN GIOVANNA I, IN 1352; FROM W. ST CLAIR BADDELEY'S *QUEEN JOANNA I.*

She had resolved, if she should live, to piously commemorate her union and coronation with Luigi. To this end she caused the ground upon which stood the old courts of justice to be cleared and publicly consecrated for the building of a Gothic church, to be named Santa Maria dell' Incoronata.

Under the eyes and hands (probably) of the pupils of Masuccio II, grew the beautiful edifice, nave and aisles, transept and tower . . .

Upon the spandrels of the groined vault, she ultimately caused her painters to illustrate for her, with all possible beauty of design and colour, the seven Sacraments of the Church. The various subjects depicted were treated according to the corresponding events and experiences of her own life; and in spite of the whips and scorns of time, these frescoes can still [1893] be studied in their original positions. 'Baptism' is represented by the Bishop of Cavaillon holding the infant Carlo Martello over the font of an octagonal baptistry; while 'Holy Orders' are typified by the consecration of the Queen's great-uncle, St Louis of Toulouse, by Boniface VIII. The design of 'Holy Communion' displays a group headed by the Queen herself, who is receiving the Sacrament from the Bishop. 'Confirmation' is described by the performance of that rite upon the children to whom the Queen had given birth; while 'Confession' reveals the Queen in the act of confessing to the priest. Some penitents being scourged by a friar are seen in the background. 'Matrimony', the most interesting, but most damaged, of the series, is rendered by the wedding of the Queen with Luigi of Taranto. The latter is shown in profile, bearded, crowned with leaves, and placing the ring on her finger, while brilliant groups of attendant knights and ladies stand by. Unfortunately, the entire upper portion of the Queen's figure has been obliterated. The last of the series illustrates 'Extreme Unction', as administered to King Luigi, which, consequently, must have been added after 1362, in which year he died.

[40] Luigi of Taranto, Giovanna I's second husband; from Pietro Giannone's *Istoria Civile del Regno di Napoli*.

Everyone thought it essential that the Queen should prepare to defend herself. She must first of all take a new husband who, by his personality and gifts, would be able to repel so powerful an enemy [as the King of Hungary]. Robert, Prince of Taranto, came to see her at Naples and suggested his brother Louis as a brave young nobleman in the prime of life. All the Queen's Council approved the proposal and since it was a year since King Andrew's death and because of the news of the King of Hungary's mobilization the marriage took place at once [in 1347] without waiting for the Pope's dispensation . . . in the year 1362 King Louis, being seized with a violent fever, died at the age of forty-one. He was an exceedingly handsome prince, sweet-tempered though no less courageous than his wife, but extraordinarily unlucky in everything he undertook.

Aragonese and Viceregal churches: Santa Anna dei Lombardi, San Domenico Maggiore, San Giacomo degli Spagnuoli, the Certosa di San Martino and the Gesù Nuovo

[41] THE CHARACTER OF ALFONSO II, DEPICTED KNEELING
IN PRAYER IN THE *PIETÀ* AT SANTA ANNA DEI LOMBARDI
(MONTEOLIVETO); FROM *MÉMOIRES* BY PHILIPPE DE COMMYNES.

(Messire Philippe de Commynes (d. 1511) was a Flemish nobleman who deserted Charles the Bold of Burgundy for Louis XI, and then accompanied Charles VIII during the French invasion of Italy in 1495.)

No man has been crueller than he [Alfonso], more vicious, more corrupt, more debauched. His father [Ferrante] was still more dangerous since no-one could ever tell what he was thinking . . . smiling in a friendly way he would seize and destroy people, as he did with Jacopo Piccinino . . . His near-relations and close acquaintances have informed me that he knew neither mercy nor compassion. Where money was concerned he never had pity or forbearance for his subjects. He turned everything in the country into goods for sale and merchandise. He had even time for pig-breeding, people being forced to mind his pigs for him; if they fattened, he sold them for his own profit – otherwise the people had to pay for the pigs themselves. In oil-producing districts like Apulia he and his son bought it at a fixed price which they dictated, and also corn before it ripened; then they forced up the prices and made the people buy all their oil and corn from them – so long as their own stocks lasted, no-one else's oil or corn was allowed to be put on the market. If a nobleman or a baron's estate prospered they would ask him for a loan and either take it with his agreement or else extort it by force. They confiscated everyone's stallions for their own use, so that in the end they had a herd which was far too large, stallions, mares and colts, keeping them all on their vassals' pastures, much to the latter's detriment. Both raped several women savagely. Indeed it was impossible for them to commit more evil crimes.

[42] ANOTHER SIDE OF KING ALFONSO II, BY A
NEAPOLITAN WHO REMEMBERED HIS REIGN; FROM A
LETTER OF 1525 FROM PIETRO SUMMONTE TO THE
VENETIAN ART HISTORIAN, MARCANTONIO MICHIEL.

(Pietro Summonte (1453–1526), a Neapolitan humanist, was born in Naples and spent his life there. He is one of the very few contemporary writers to have anything good to say of the Aragonese kings.)

In my time the Lord King Alfonso II, of most happy memory, was so fond of building and so anxious to create something genuinely magnificent, that, had not misfortune toppled him from his throne quite so soon, he would unquestionably have adorned this city very richly indeed. He intended to divert a far-off river along huge aqueducts to flow into the city, and when the new walls were finished – in large part already completed – he wanted to replan the principal thoroughfares so that they would run direct from one wall to the other, demolishing porches, awkward angles, and anything else that blocked the way, and at the same time straightening the roads which crossed them. The resulting symmetry of roads and streets, and the fact that it slopes naturally from north to south, would (besides giving it beautiful proportions) have turned our city into the cleanest and most elegant in Europe, not to mention other continents; the least shower of rain would have caused it to shine more brightly than a burnished silver coin. Moreover private houses were to be given fountains, and fountains and drinking taps were to be set up at crossroads and other spots, thus facilitating the watering of the streets and keeping them free of dust and clean after they were swept, winter or summer. In addition he was going to build a truly sumptuous church to hold the bones of the princes of the House of Aragon, together with a vast palace near the

Castel Nuovo in the Piazza dell' Incoronata, where the law courts were to be installed in various chambers; those engaged in legal matters would not have to go all over the place to conduct their business, but could have completed it without exposure to sun or rain, or unnecessary fatigue. By nature His Majesty was averse to leaving unfinished anything on which he had decided, and he was not a man to be deterred by the cost. Projects which incurred large expenditure pleased him best.

All these noble, sublime, schemes were halted and then brought to nothing by the sudden and barbaric invasion of King Charles VIII of France, who was responsible for driving the House of Aragon out of this realm.

[43] A PROTESTANT ENGLISHMAN'S IMPRESSION OF SAN DOMENICO
   MAGGIORE IN 1594; FROM FYNES MORYSON'S *AN ITINERARY* . . .

In the church of St Dominic is an altar which they say cost some 25,000 crowns, and in the vestry lie the bodies of nine kings in coffins of wood covered with pewter and having black velvet laid over them. Among these kings are Alfonso I, King of Aragon, and Ferdinand his son [Ferrante] and Ferdinand II [Ferrantino]. And in this place also the monks in like sort sing, or rather howl, rest to their souls. They show a crucifix which, they say, did speak to Thomas Aquinas in this manner: 'Thomas, thou hast written well of me, What reward dost thou ask?' And that Thomas should answer: 'No reward, Lord, but Thyself only.' I have heard that St Bernard, knowing the frauds and impostures of monks and not dissembling them, when the image of the Blessed Virgin did in like sort praise him, he did with much more piety and wisdom answer out of St Paul: 'Let women be silent in the church, for it is not permitted them to speak.'

[44] The church of San Domenico Maggiore; from
Cities of Southern Italy and Sicily by Augustus Hare.

The Church of S. Domenico Maggiore, which, in spite of alterations in
the fifteenth, seventeenth, and eighteenth centuries, and fearful gilding within, retains much of its noble original Gothic from designs of
1285, ascribed to Masuccio I. The western entrance, in a courtyard, has
a grand inlaid Gothic portal, with angels and lions. The interior has
three lofty aisles, with chapels full of tombs. An inscription records the
consecration of the church by Pope Alexander IV in person . . .

The Sacristy has a ceiling decorated with frescoes by Solimena. High
in the air, on a balustrade, are forty-five coffins of wood covered with
scarlet. Ten contain the remains of the Princes and Princesses of the
Aragonese dynasty, in whose time Neapolitan history attained its greatest glory. Here rest Ferdinand I, 1494; Ferdinand II, 1496; Isabella of
Aragon, wife of Giovanni Galeazzo Sforza the Younger, Duke of Milan,
1524; Mary of Aragon, Marchesa del Vasto, 1568; Antonio of Aragon,
second Duke of Montalto, and his two sons, Giovanni and Ferrante.
The coffin of Alfonso I, 1458, is here, but his remains were taken to
Spain in 1666. Many of the other illustrious dead have no inscription to
mark them. Some of the coffins are surmounted by portraits. The
mummy long shown as that of Antonello Petrucci, Minister of
Ferdinand I [Ferrante], beheaded for the 'Conspiracy of the Barons', is
in reality that of his son Giovanni Antonio, executed a few months
before his father. Above the coffin of Fernando Francesco d'Avalos,
Marchese de Pescara, are his portrait, his torn banner, and a short
sword, said to be that which was given up to him by Francis I at Pavia,
where he took a bloody revenge for his repulse when besieging
Marseilles . . .

The Convent of S. Domenico, which was a theological gymnasium of
the Middle Ages, became celebrated in 1272 from the lectures of S.
Thomas Aquinas . . . St Thomas was paid one ounce of gold, the equiva-
lent to £1 a month – '*Mercede unius unciae auri.*' The cell of the saint and

his pulpit are preserved. His lecture room is used for the meetings of the *Accademia Pontaniana*, founded in 1471 by Giovanni Pontano, secretary of state under Ferdinand I. There is no ground for the legend that the death of St Thomas was caused by poison.

[45] THE CHURCH OF SAN GIACOMO DEGLI SPAGNUOLI; FROM
AUGUSTUS HARE'S *CITIES OF SOUTHERN ITALY AND SICILY*.

On the left of the Strada S. Giacomo, the carriage should be stopped in front of a large building with a court used half for public offices, half as a kind of market. Here, on the left, an obscure door and passage will admit us to the Church of S Giacomo degli Spagnuoli built by the Viceroy Pietro di Toledo. On the right of the entrace is a Holy Family of Andrea del Sarto – 'a beautiful and genuine picture' (Burckhardt). Ill-seen in the choir is the magnificent tomb of Pietro di Toledo, 1553, by Giovanni Merliano da Nola, the son of a leather merchant, of whom we shall see numerous works at Naples. Statues of Justice, Prudence, Fortitude, and Temperance stand at the corners of the pedestal, which supports a sarcophagus, adorned with reliefs illustrative of the victories of the viceroy – 'over-crowded, ill-composed pictures in stone'. The whole is surmounted by kneeling statues of Don Pedro and his wife – the latter full of character and expression. Behind, with other monuments, is that of Walther von Hiernheim, 1557, counsellor and commander under Charles V and Philip II. The third chapel on the left contains a Descent from the Cross, by Gian Bernardo Lama.

[46] FANZAGO, ONE OF THE PRINCIPAL ARCHITECTS AND
DECORATORS OF THE CERTOSA DI SAN MARTINO; FROM *NEAPOLITAN
BAROQUE AND ROCOCO ARCHITECTURE* BY ANTHONY BLUNT.

Cosimo Fanzago was born in 1591 at Clusone near Bergamo. He came to Naples in 1608 with his mother, presumably after the death of his father, who is described in a document as *oppellaro*, which is probably intended to be *orpellaro* or gilder. His family had included a number of bronze founders and a maker of astronomical clocks. On arrival at Naples he went to live with an uncle, Pompeo Fanzago, who was an official in the tax office, but by 1612 he had moved to the house of the sculptor Geronimo D'Auria, son of Giovanni Domenico D'Auria, the most important Neapolitan sculptor of the later sixteenth century. In the same year he went into partnership with the Florentine sculptor and marble-worker Angelo Landi, whose daughter he married and with whom he collaborated till Landi's death, which probably occurred in 1620.

Except for a long stay in Rome about 1650 and short visits to Montecassino and Venice, Fanzago remained in Naples for the whole of his active life and died there in 1678. He established a great reputation as a sculptor, decorator, and architect, and received many commissions from churches, monasteries, and private patrons, but his methods of work were so peculiar that he found himself in increasing difficulties, which culminated in a lawsuit brought against him by the monks of S. Martino. This lawsuit darkened the latter years of his life and was continued against his heirs for many years after his death. From the documents connected with his activities at S. Martino it is clear that he was a difficult and violent man. In 1628 he attacked one of his masons, Nicola Botti, and according to one account murdered him two years later. In spite of this the monks continued to employ him, but eventually his malpractices as an architect became more than they could bear and they were forced to take action against him. It is not easy to find out from the documents exactly what had taken place, but it appears that Fanzago was extremely dilatory about finishing works in the time agreed and that, when he eventually delivered them, it was often found that they were not executed in accordance with the contract. He also played off one client against another, using for a chapel in S. Lorenzo sculptures prepared for S. Martino, taking marble which belonged to S. Martino to use for decoration of the Trinità delle Monache, and so on. Complaints of the same kind are to be found in connection with almost all the commissions of which records survive . . .

Fanzago's first commission was to complete the construction and decoration of the big cloister. It is clear from the documents that the lay-out of the cloister and the form of the arcade were settled before Fanzago came on the scene, but the decoration, which is recorded as being executed by him in a survey of 1631, is clearly of his own invention. It consists of relatively simple elements: white Carrara marble for the consoles, with little tongues of marble as keystones to the arches and for the fluted panels over the columns; grey marble for the frieze and the little decorative panels over the capitals and beside the consoles. In the contract of 1623 Fanzago undertook to finish this work in three years and, though in the event it was still not quite complete in 1631, there is no doubt that the design must have been made in 1623 . . .

The interior of S. Martino is one of the few cases in which a Gothic structure has been satisfactorily given a Baroque covering. It is not known exactly how Fanzago altered the original building, because no plans of it exist, but he must have accepted the structure of the old nave, because the present vault is composed of the original Gothic ribs . . . However, the remarkable feature is that the proportions of the nave – which must have been exceptionally wide for a fourteenth-century church – seem perfectly designed to take Baroque decoration, and there is no trace of the conflict so common in Gothic churches clothed in Baroque decoration, between the tall narrow proportions of the structure and the rich decoration which was conceived for a wider space . . .

The last years of Fanzago's life were a period of unhappiness and illness – in the end even senility – and he was reduced to a state close to poverty as the result of his lawsuit with the monks of S. Martino and disputes with other patrons.

[47] A LESS SEVERE PORTRAIT OF FANZAGO BY A NEAPOLITAN ART
HISTORIAN WRITING IN 1742; FROM BERNARDO DE DOMINICI'S
VITE DEI PITTORI, SCULTORI ED ARCHITETTI NAPOLETANI.

(Bernardo de Dominici (1648–1750) was born in Malta but spent his
life in Naples, and died there as a centenarian. Often unreliable, he
carries conviction in this case, for he very likely met people who had
known Fanzago, and he may even have met Fanzago himself.)

Finally he died in his eighty-seventh year, saddening the entire
community who had admired him for his rare talents; not many artists
can be compared to him, since he was both a truly excellent architect
and quite outstanding as a sculptor. His corpse, escorted by a host of
mourners, was taken for burial in the vault of the Servite fathers' church
of Santa Maria d'Ognibene, near where he used to live, and interred
there with much honour and everyone's tears on the 13th February in
the year 1678. In countenance Cosimo was striking, white-skinned but
high-coloured, wearing huge moustaches, with fine features and a
noble forehead and a jovial expression, very impressive to behold. He
had been well paid for his labours yet left little on account of entertaining his friends far too generously. A sincere man, he has since been
greatly maligned. He bequeathed a good name to his profession, doing
much to bring his art to a high degree of perfection and towards elevat-
ing it to an honoured place.

[48] THE CERTOSA DI SAN MARTINO IN 1688; FROM
NOUVEAU VOYAGE D'ITALIE BY MAXIMILIEN MISSON.

(Maximilien Misson (1650–1722) was a Huguenot refugee who settled
in London and earned his living by his pen.)

The great convent of the Carthusians at St Martin's is full of magnificent rarities. The monks who conducted us thither affirmed to us that

under one priorate there were laid out among them 500,000 ducats in silver plate, pictures and sculptures alone. Their church is none of the largest but every part of it deserves admiration. Nothing can be added either to the value of the matter, or excellence of the workmanship; the whole is of a finished beauty. *The Nativity of Christ* by Guido is an inestimable piece. The four pictures of the Lord's Supper, which are to be seen in the same place, were done by Spagnoletto [Ribera], Annibale Carracci, Paul Veronese, and Cavaliere Massimo; one has thought fit to represent Jesus Christ standing, giving the Sacrament to his Apostles and putting the Bread into their mouths, they being on their knees. There are a great many other pieces highly valued, too many to be here recited.

The cloister is one hundred paces square. All the pavement is of marble, inlaid with foliage and other ornaments of the like nature, and the four galleries are supported by sixty pillars each of one entire piece of fine white marble of Carrara. The monks are mighty well lodged, everyone having his own chamber, his closet, his library and his pretty garden; the Prior's apartment might well befit a prince. Among other things there they boast of the famous crucifix of Michelangelo drawn, as 'tis said, after the life from a certain peasant whom the painter crucified for the purpose. This story savours much of a fable and is so, I believe, but here it passes current for a certain truth. The picture is upon wood and is not above half a foot high. I observed that the crucifix holds his head exactly straight, which does not agree very well with the posture of a man expiring on a cross. They have also a *St Lawrence* by Titian and some designs of Rubens and Albert Dürer, which they prize very highly.

The various prospects which are discovered from there strike the beholder with admiration. You behold the sea and many islands, among which are Capreae, the famous seraglio of Tiberius. From thence you may distinctly view the greatness and ground plot of Naples with its castles, haven, mole and pharos. It is a pleasure to look on the gardens which surround it, and the fruitful hills which ascend to Campania the

Happy. If you cast your eyes on the other side along the sea-shore the small different bays, which mix alternately with the little capes washed by that peaceful sea, and the pretty villages with which the coast is strewed, make it a most charming object. A little further the air is thickened by the horrible smoke of Vesuvius and you may take a full view of this famous and terrible mountain.

[49] THE CERTOSA OF SAN MARTINO; FROM SIR SACHEVERELL SITWELL'S SOUTHERN BAROQUE ART.

(Sir Sacheverell Sitwell, writer, poet and aesthete, was born in 1897. His Southern Baroque Art appeared in 1924 and began the revival of interest in Baroque as a whole throughout the English-speaking world. He and his brother Sir Osbert were also among the first to revive interest in the Borboni.)

The traveller, Sir John [Henry] Swinburne, who visited Naples in 1779, tells us that in his time the annual income of the convent, though reduced, reached the total of £130,000 sterling. After providing, amply, for their own comfort, this sum was devoted by the monks to the benefit of the hundreds of beggars who infest and crawl about the rich suburb of Vomero. Even this could not exhaust their supplies of money, and the balance was applied to the benefit of the female relations of the monks. Sir John Swinburne says it was rumoured the Royal family intended shortly to inquire into and appropriate the surplus income of the convent. Swinburne's remarks are significant. A few years later, in 1799, the social ideas of the monks got the better of their political common sense. When the French had entered Naples, and proclaimed the Parthenopean republic, the monks, out of the church wardrobe, prepared the red, yellow and blue flag which the French soldiers hoisted on the Castel Sant' Elmo near by. But this was not all. When General Championnet arrived, they celebrated his coming by inviting a party of both sexes to the monastery. That evening the Carthusians gave a supper to about forty persons, male and female, and afterwards a dance was held in the prior's apartments. A printed memorial of the occasion remarks that the monks, full of joy and admiration, seeing such pretty smiling women dancing among them, could not help rejoicing, more than the rest, at the coming of Liberty. A water-colour drawing which accompanies these remarks shows the prior's apartments, richly hung with pictures, and filled with patriots of both sexes, who dance, under the delighted eyes of the monks, to the strains of a small and energetic orchestra.

This tarantella was overheard by the Royal authorities. On their return to Naples, in 1800, they dispersed the brothers among other charterhouses, leaving only five to perform the religious duties. In 1804 they were permitted to return. But the Bourbons had helped their supporters largely to the monastic funds, and the income was now only 57,000 ducats instead of the 95,000 of former years. Their subsequent adventures, how they were turned out by Napoleon in 1805, restored again by the Bourbons, and finally suppressed on the last day of the year 1866, were on a par with the fate they had precipitated upon themselves by their gay living.

[50] THE ORIGIN OF THE GESÙ NUOVO, FORMERLY THE PALACE
OF THE SANSEVERINO DUKES OF SALERNO; FROM ANTHONY
BLUNT'S *NEAPOLITAN BAROQUE AND ROCOCO ARCHITECTURE*.

An inscription, incorporated in the façade of the church, records that the palace was built in 1470, and that the architect was Novello da San Lucano, who is not otherwise recorded. There is no means of knowing the exact appearance of the original building, but it evidently belonged to the small group of palaces with façades composed of stones cut into diamond shapes . . . The original door of the Sanseverino palace, built in fine Florentine style, survives as the main door to the Gesù Nuovo, but is now surrounded by columns and a pediment with a cartouche superimposed on the lintel, dated 1597 . . .

[The Jesuits] finally decided, in 1584, to buy the Palazzo di Salerno, built by Roberto Sanseverino in 1470, and to pull it down, using the stones of the façade and some of the interior walls for the church, the Gesù Nuovo. The foundation stone was laid in the same year, but no actual building was done on it till 1593, though work then proceeded very fast. By 1595 the walls were finished, in 1596 the apse was vaulted, and in 1601 the church was consecrated. The decoration of the interior – one of the most splendid in the city – went on for many years; indeed the High Altar was not finished till 1854. In 1639 the church was badly damaged by fire and was restored under the direction of Cosimo Fanzago; but in 1688 an earthquake destroyed the dome, which was rebuilt by Arcangelo Guglielmelli. This dome in turn was taken down in 1774 on the grounds that it was unsafe and was replaced by the present low and unsatisfactory structure. Meanwhile the arches on either side of the High Altar had to be strengthened by the insertion of inner arches, probably to the design of Ferdinando Fuga . . .

When Valeriano [the architect and a Jesuit himself] died in 1596, the structure of the Gesù Nuovo was still unfinished and the existing marble decoration, which is among the richest of its kind in Naples, dates entirely from the seventeenth and later centuries. Valeriano unquestionably intended something much simpler, and . . . would have disapproved of the existing Baroque marbling and painting, but in fact the architects responsible for it seem to have taken great pains not to interfere with the grand lines of his design, and this is one of the rare cases in Naples where a sixteenth-century church has been clothed in Baroque trappings and has yet retained its own character as a spatial design.

The Cathedral of San Gennaro (the Duomo)

[51] THE STORY OF SAN GENNARO; FROM *THE LIVES OF THE FATHERS, MARTYRS AND OTHER PRINCIPAL SAINTS* BY ALBAN BUTLER.

(Alban Butler (1711–1773) was chaplain to the Duke of Norfolk, and the greatest British hagiographer.)

St Januarius, a native some say of Naples, others of Benevento, was bishop of the latter city when the persecution of Diocletian broke out [in AD 305] . . . St Januarius and his two companions, all these champions of Christ, were exposed to be devoured by the beasts in the amphitheatre, but none of these savage animals could be provoked to touch them. The people were amazed, but imputed their preservation to art-magic, and the martyrs were condemned to be beheaded . . .

Eruptions [of Vesuvius] which in the fifth and seventh centuries threatened this city [of Naples] with destruction by the clouds of ashes which they raised, are said to have darkened the sky as far as Constantinople, and struck terror into the inhabitants of that capital. The intercession of St Januarius was implored at Naples on these occasions, and divine mercy so wonderfully interposed in causing these dreadful evils to cease thereupon, especially in 685, Bennet II being pope, and Justinian the Younger emperor, that the Greeks instituted a feast in honour of St Januarius with two yearly solemn processions to return thanks to God. The protection of the city of Naples from this dreadful volcano by the same means was most remarkable in the years 1631 and 1707. In this last, whilst Cardinal Francis Pignatelli, with the clergy and people, devoutly followed the shrine of St Januarius in procession to a chapel at the foot of Mount Vesuvius, the fiery eruption ceased, the mist, which before was so thick that no-one could see another at the distance of three yards, was scattered, and at night the stars appeared in the sky.

The standing miracle, as it is called, by Baronius, of the blood of St Januarius liquefying and boiling up at the approach of the martyr's head is likewise very famous. In a rich chapel called the Treasury, in the great church at Naples, are preserved the blood, in two very old glass vials, and the head of St Januarius.

[52] The Cathedral Church of San Gennaro as it appeared to the Chevalier de Lalande in the 1760s; from his *Voyage d'un François en Italie*.

This cathedral is an old Gothic church, built on the ruins of a temple of Apollo, of which they found many traces when digging the foundations of the Treasury and in particular a column which the Theatines of St Paul have placed next to the side door of their own church. The present building was erected during the reigns of the first kings of the House of Anjou, Charles I and Charles II, about the year 1280, according to plans drawn by Nicholas of Pisa (whom we have mentioned several times in discussing Florence). The devotion which the populace have to San Gennaro supplied the money. After being very badly damaged and indeed all but demolished by the earthquake of 1485, the building was restored under Alfonso II through the piety of several noble families – Balzo, Ursina, Caracciolo, Pignatelli, Zurla and Dura – whose arms may be seen on the pillars. The great door was built at the expense of Cardinal Enrico Minutolo, Archbishop of Naples, as one reads in an inscription in Lombardic letters above it. It is ornamented by two porphyry columns bearing two lions from the ancient temple. Near the door they have placed three tombs, which were formerly next to the high altar, and which have since been renovated; they are those of Charles I, King of Naples; of Charles Martel, King of Hungary; and of Queen Clemency of Austria, his wife, daughter of the Emperor Rudolph I . . .

The crypt, which in Naples people call *Soccorpo*, is a little subterranean chapel with white marble walls and with Ionic marble columns which, it is claimed, are from the old temple of Apollo. The plan of the chapel is imaginative and unusual; the vaulting is decorated with bas-reliefs in the form of arabesques, very well done and in the antique taste. Here lies the body of San Gennaro, which used to be at another church outside the city; the Duke of Benevento, Sicone, having removed it, it was afterwards at the celebrated convent of Monte Vergine (of which we will speak later, and is some nine leagues to the east of Naples) from whence Cardinal Olivieri transported it to the cathedral and built the underground chapel. The cardinal's statue behind the altar is supposed to be by Michelangelo; it looks well enough but is not really well made . . .

The *Tesoro*, or chapel of San Gennaro, is the finest thing in the cathedral. It was built as a result of a vow made by the city of Naples during the plague of 1526, although the first stone was not laid until 1608. The architect was a Theatine priest called Grimaldi. The city paid for the chapel's construction, nominating two councillors as superintendents to it. The structure is circular, well proportioned, beautifully decorated, and surrounded by niches containing nineteen bronze statues of saints by Giulio Finelli, though these are of very mediocre quality. Below the niches are kept the actual relics of the saints in busts or little statues of silver; no doubt this is why the chapel has been given the name of *Il Tesoro*. It is certainly of the utmost richness. The pavement is of marble, the walls stucco with much gilt work. Indeed the ornamentation is so very lavish that one's eyes are quite dazzled.

The cupola is by Lanfranco. Originally it had been painted by Domenichino, about 1635, when that great artist, tired of his ill treatment at Rome, was trying to establish himself at Naples. It is said that fear of being poisoned had already persuaded Guido, Giuseppino and Gessi not to accept the commission. The jealousy of the Neapolitan artists, above all of Spagnoletto [Ribera], would not suffer any foreigner being given such an honour. When Domenichino arrived, the authorities removed the work already done by Belisario and others, which only served to fuel the anger of the Neapolitans. Domenichino had to endure ceaseless persecution. He fled to Rome, but then returned to Naples. His enemies bribed his assistants; the mason who prepared his chalks was suborned into mixing ash with them, so that the outline of what he was painting would crumble away. Fear of poison affected his mind to such an extent that he trusted no-one, not even his wife. Worry sapped his creative powers and the cupola was still not finished when, after working on it for three years, he died in 1641, not without suspicion of poison. His rivals soon had his designs effaced, after which it was repainted by Lanfranco. All that remains of Domenichino's work is on the angles of the cupola and some altar-pieces, which are hardly his best; the designs are good enough and well drawn, but the colour and the brushwork are very poor . . .

The treasure kept in this chapel and in the adjoining sacristy is immense. One may see there the superb gifts of the King and Queen of Spain on the occasion of their first visit, in particular a gold chalice studded with diamonds to the value of 100,000 francs. There are silver chandeliers ten or twelve feet long, forty-one bronze statues, thirty-six silver busts which are displayed on great feasts, and above all the bust of San Gennaro.

There is a niche with a silver door behind the altar. Here they keep a cherished reliquary in which are two ampullae, or phials, of glass; these contain the blood of San Gennaro picked up, so it is said, by a Neapolitan lady during his martyrdom. It is this blood which performs, several times a year, what is called in Naples the miracle of San Gennaro; normally hard and coagulated, it liquefies. On these occasions a city councillor brings one of the two keys to the shrine, and the master of the Archbishop's household brings the other. It is in honour of the miracle that the head of San Gennaro is displayed near the blood which is about to liquefy.

I was at this ceremony on 19 September 1765, at the side of the priest who was holding the reliquary. He held it against his chest while reciting the *Credo*, turning it over and over. After about eight minutes I actually saw the matter become fluid, without changing colour. The chapel was full of women calling on the saint with loud cries, and beating their breasts and tearing their hair, to hasten the miracle. When it

takes a little time, people generally suspect that it is because some heretic is present. On 24 November 1730 the miracle was delayed and the
delay was attributed to the English consul who was present; he was
asked politely to go and inspect the cathedral's other beauties, and he
dared not refuse. The congregation said that the miracle took place as
soon as the heretic went away . . .

However, even at Naples there are those who do not believe in it . . .
The Prince of San Severo had a monstrance or reliquary made, just like
that of San Gennaro, with phials or ampullae of the same shape. He
filled them with a compound of gold, mercury and cinnabar, whose
colour resembled that of the coagulated blood. He put liquid mercury
into hollow spaces in the frame surrounding the 'reliquary', which was
regulated by a valve. To make the compound liquefy he would then turn
the reliquary round and round until the valve opened and let some
mercury into the phial, whereupon it would become fluid and imitate
the miracle.

[53] SEVENTEENTH-CENTURY INTRIGUES OVER THE DECORATION
OF THE CHAPEL OF SAN GENNARO; FROM SIR HAROLD ACTON'S
PREFACE TO *PAINTING IN NAPLES FROM CARAVAGGIO TO GIORDANO*.

(Sir Harold Acton was born in 1904 of a distinguished Anglo-Neapolitan
family to which Sir John Acton, the Borbone Prime Minister, belonged.
He has written many books but is perhaps most famous for his two
studies of the Borboni (1956 and 1961), which have done so much to
re-establish the dynasty's name.)

The strength of Caravaggio's influence is most obvious in the work of
his follower Ribera, known as *lo Spagnoletto*, born near Valencia but
Neapolitan by adoption. Through Ribera and his patron, the viceroy
Monterrey, Italian and Spanish painters developed in the same direction. Velasquez was a friend of Ribera and he, too, seems to have been
affected by Caravaggio in *Los Borrachos* and *Vulcan's Forge*. Some fifteen

years younger than Caravaggio, whom he never met, Ribera soon
endeared himself to the viceroy as a compatriot of genius. The sadistic
martyrdoms he depicted with such gusto realized Monterrey's notions
of what religious painting should be, and Ribera became an arbiter of
taste at his court.

With Belisario Corenzio and Battistello Caracciolo – the former a
Greek, the latter a true-blue Neapolitan – Ribera formed a tyrannical
cabal. We know little that is nice about the personalities of this trium-
virate. Bernardo de Dominici, the Neapolitan version of Vasari, was
prone to embellish his anecdotes, but they undoubtedly contain a foundation of truth since they have been corroborated by others. According
to him, no painter could execute any major commission in Naples without the trio's consent. All the eminent artists who were invited from
Rome to decorate the chapel of S. Gennaro in the Cathedral were
driven away by their stubborn persecution. This Cappella del Tesoro, as
it was called, is Naples' holiest shrine, for it contains the patron saint's
skull and a phial of his blood which liquefies twice a year, so that the
intrusion of outsiders to decorate it was bitterly resented.

The trials of alien artists brave enough to accept the commission
were prolonged over the years. When Guido Reni came in 1621, his
assistant was so badly wounded that he hurried back to Rome; the
vindictive Corenzio was arrested on suspicion but released for lack of
evidence. After the indigenous Santafede failed to satisfy the commis-
sioners Corenzio was offered the job, but even he failed and his frescoes
were obliterated. Domenichino was then invited from Rome. This
highly sensitive artist accepted the challenge with misgiving, and soon
after his arrival he received a letter threatening his life unless he withdrew. He appealed to the viceroy for protection and though this was
promised with assurances for his safety, he hardly dared to leave his
lodging except to go to work. When the first of his frescoes was uncovered a year later he was so harassed by his local rivals, led by Ribera,
that 'he rode day and night almost without rest' to Cardinal
Aldobrandini's villa at Frascati in a state of collapse. It took him another

year to decide to finish the frescoes in Naples. By then he had lost favour with the viceroy and the painters redoubled their vexations. Poor Domenichino was reduced to such a state of nerves, as Passeri wrote, that his meals became a torment for fear of poison, and his nights for fear of the dagger. And when he died at Naples in 1641 his widow was convinced that he had indeed been poisoned.

Annibale Carracci was also reputed to have died as an indirect result of the cabal's harassment. Others were inveigled on board a galley which immediately weighed anchor and sailed for a mysterious destination. As we know from Benvenuto Cellini's autobiography, distinguished artists considered themselves above the law and even won respect for their arrogance. Caravaggio's brawls were essential to the image of *terribilità* he wished to impose. Ribera behaved despotically to his Neapolitan rivals. When Massimo Stanzione painted a dead Christ for the entrance to the Certosa di S. Martino which won general admiration, Ribera persuaded the monks to let him clean it under the pretext that it was too dark. In doing so he ruined it with a corrosive liquid.

[54] SAN GENNARO QUELLS AN ERUPTION OF VESUVIUS IN 1767; FROM SIR WILLIAM HAMILTON'S *CAMPI PHLEGRAEI*.

(Sir William Hamilton (1730–1803) is undeservedly best known on account of his marrying in 1791 Emma Hart – Nelson's future mistress. In fact he was a most distinguished diplomat and amateur of the arts and sciences, an antiquarian of international reputation and widely acclaimed for his observation of Vesuvius. He was British Minister at Naples for thirty-six years, and extremely popular – Gino Doria paid him the tribute of calling him a 'Neapolitanized Englishman'.)

The noise and smell of sulphur increasing, we removed from our villa to Naples and I thought it proper, as I passed by Portici, to inform the court of what I had seen and humbly offered my opinion that His Sicilian Majesty [Ferdinand IV] should leave the neighbourhood of the threatening mountain. However the court did not leave Portici till about twelve of the clock, when the lava was very near. I observed in my way to Naples, which was in less than two hours after I had left the mountain, that the lava had actually covered three miles of the very road through which we had retreated . . .

The confusion at Naples this night [Monday 19 October] cannot be described; His Sicilian Majesty's hasty retreat from Portici added to the alarm; all the churches were opened and filled; the streets were thronged with processions of saints. I shall avoid entering upon a description of the various ceremonies that were performed in this capital to quell the fury of the turbulent mountain . . .

During the confusion of this night [Tuesday 20 October] the prisoners in the public gaol attempted to escape, having wounded the gaoler, but were prevented by the troops. The mob also set fire to the Cardinal Archbishop's gate, because he refused to bring out the relics of St Januarius . . .

Thursday 22nd, about ten of the clock in the morning the same thundering noise began again, but with more violence than in the preceding days. The oldest men declared that they had never heard the like, and indeed it was very alarming; we were in expectation every moment of some dire calamity. The ashes, or rather small cinders, showered down so fast that the people in the streets were obliged to use umbrellas or flap their hats, these ashes being very offensive to the eyes. The tops of the houses and the balconies were covered above an inch thick with these cinders. Ships at sea twenty leagues from Naples were also covered with them, to the great astonishment of the sailors. In the midst of these horrors the mob, growing tumultuous and impatient, obliged the Cardinal to bring out the head of St Januarius and go with it in procession to the Ponte Maddalena, at the extremity of Naples towards Vesuvius; and it is well attested here that the eruption ceased the moment the Saint came in sight of the mountain.

[55] The liquefaction of San Gennaro's blood
as it appeared to the Irish singer Michael
Kelly in 1779; from his *Reminiscences*

I went ... to visit the miracle of St Gennaro or Januario, in the Cathedral; the King and Queen [Ferdinand IV and Maria Carolina], in state, attended his saintship. There were two immense orchestras erected in the church, and all good professors, vocal and instrumental, were engaged to perform upon these occasions. The Archbishop prays, or appears to pray, while the Te Deum is sung. He then displays a phial, which contains the congealed blood of St Gennaro; towards this he holds up a large wax taper, that the people may perceive it is congealed. The miracle consists, as everybody knows, in this blood dissolving before the congregation, and is supposed to be performed by the saint himself. As soon as it is liquefied, the Archbishop roars lustily, 'the miracle is accomplished!' The Te Deum is again sung, and the whole congregation prostrate themselves before the altar of the saint with gratitude and devotion, and every face beams with delight.

On one of these miraculous days, I witnessed a ludicrous scene. It happened by some accident, that the Archbishop could not make the miracle work. The Lazzaroni and old women loudly called on the Virgin for assistance. 'Dear Virgin Mary! Blessed Madonna! Pray use your influence with St Gennaro! Pray induce him to work the miracle! Do we not love him? Do we not worship him?' But when they found the Saint inexorable, they changed their note, and seemed resolved to abuse him into compliance. They all at once cried out, 'Porco di St Gennaro!' – 'You pig of a Saint!' – 'Barone maladetto!' – 'You cursed rascal!' – 'Cane faccia gialutta!' – 'You yellow-faced dog!' In the midst of this, the blood (thanks to the heat of the Archbishop's hand) dissolved. They again threw themselves on their knees, and tearing their hair, (the old ladies particularly), with streaming eyes, cried, 'Oh! most holy Saint, forgive us this once, and never more will we doubt your goodness!'

[56] JOHN HENRY NEWMAN'S VIEWS ON THE
MIRACLE, IN SEPTEMBER 1847; FROM WILFRID
WARD'S *LIFE OF CARDINAL NEWMAN*.

I understand that Sir H. Davy attended every day, and it was this
extreme variety of the phenomenon which convinced him that nothing
physical would account for it. Yet there is this remarkable fact that
liquefactions of blood are common at Naples – and unless it is irrever-
ent to the Great Author of Miracle to be obstinate in the inquiry, the
question certainly rises whether there is something in the air. Mind, I
don't believe there is – and, speaking humbly, and without having seen
it, think it a true miracle.

[57] THE CONSECRATION* OF FRANCIS II AS LAST KING OF
THE TWO SICILIES, AT THE CATHEDRAL OF SAN GENNARO IN
1859; FROM RAFFAELE DE CESARE'S *LA FINE DI UN REGNO*.

(Raffaele de Cesare (1845–1918), journalist, politician and Italian
senator, came from near Bari and did much to salvage the reputation of
the Borboni in this book, which was published in 1894.)

All Naples was en fête, and for three nights there were splendid illuminations and fireworks. The first and most important ceremony was
of course the sovereign's visit to the chapel of San Gennaro, which took
place with great pomp on the morning of 24 June. At ten a.m. a salvo
from the guns of the forts and of the battleships in the bay, the latter
flying bunting, announced the departure from the royal palace of the
King and Court, with ten running footmen carrying flaming torches,
everyone in full dress, on their way to the Duomo, amidst columns of
troops and to the cheers of the crowd. The carriages went almost at a
walk, so that all were able to admire Maria Sophia, who was wearing a

---

* There was no longer a coronation, in consequence of the crown's having been lost at
sea in 1806 during the royal family's flight to Sicily after the French invasion.

particularly striking dress and looked very lovely indeed. Alighting, the King and Queen entered through the cathedral's main door, under a canopy carried by city councillors, and were received inside by Archbishop Riario Sforza and the canons of the metropolitan chapter. Laying aside his mitre and crozier, the Archbishop gave them a crucifix to kiss and then blessed them with holy water. The Duomo was decorated in the most costly fashion; rich silken hangings ornamented the walls while the chapel's windows were covered with beautiful lace curtains. The royal throne had been erected before the High Altar at the Gospel side, with two seats, two prie-dieux and two cushions; there was a gallery at the Epistle side for the royal princes; and in the nave there were two stands, one for the diplomatic corps and the other for the high aristocracy of the *libra d'oro*. The King's seat and cushion were covered in a special satin given by the Prince of Bisignano [Master of the Household and head of the Sanseverino, the greatest family in the kingdom]. The music was directed by Maestro Parisi during the pontifical Mass celebrated by the Cardinal Archbishop. The latter intoned at the top of his voice, '*Domine salvum fac Regem nostrum Franciscum Secundum et Reginam nostram Marianm Sophiam*'. At the end of Mass the *Te Deum* was sung. After the final blessing, according to ancient custom, Riario Sforza presented the sovereign and the princes with bouquets of flowers, with which they proceeded to the chapel of San Gennaro. Although the saint's head was still on the High Altar, the blood in the phial liquefied immediately; 'something which has never happened before', says the official account, 'in the memory of man; of which everyone learnt with the most devout satisfaction and which was with reason regarded as a truly auspicious omen.' The sovereign then rode back to the Royal Palace with his court, where he reviewed his troops before they marched back to their barracks.

Palazzo Reale

[58] FONTANA AND CAVAGNA, THE ARCHITECT AND WOULD-BE ARCHITECT OF THE PALAZZO REALE; FROM ANTHONY BLUNT'S *NEAPOLITAN BAROQUE AND ROCOCO ARCHITECTURE*.

Domenico Fontana . . . is first recorded in Naples in 1594, settled there in 1596, and stayed there till his death in 1607. His reason for leaving Rome was a simple one: during the Pontificate of Sixtus V he had been all-powerful, but when the Pope died in 1590 he lost his position as papal architect, and he had enough enemies to make his prospects in Rome hopeless. The invitation from the Viceroy was therefore welcome. He was appointed Royal Architect on his arrival, and his activities were entirely devoted to work for the Viceroy. Much of this was of a practical kind; widening streets, draining marshes, and constructing aqueducts, a type of work for which he was admirably equipped and on which his reputation in Rome had been largely based; he also designed two major official buildings: the Royal Palace and the Palazzo degli Studi [now the Museo Archaeologico].

Fontana was an architect with a limited supply of ideas, and for the design of the Palazzo Reale, begun in 1602, he simply took the elevation which he had used for the Villa Peretti, designed for Sixtus V when he was a cardinal, and expanded it from five bays to twenty-one, producing inevitably an effect of monotony, broken only by three doors. The appearance of the palace today is affected by the fact that the loggia was altered in the eighteenth century, when for reasons of structural safety alternate arches had to be blocked up, but even allowing for this altera-tion the Palazzo Reale has all the dryness which marks Fontana's Roman works without their saving grace, the feeling of mass, which makes both the Lateran and the block added to the Vatican by Sixtus V impres-sive even if not distinguished. The court is somewhat more interesting. Fontana used for it the type of double loggia which he employed at the Lateran, but made the arches wider, thus giving a more airy effect to the whole building. He also broke the monotonous repetition of the bays by making the central bay on each side even wider than the others, so that it had to be covered by a depressed arch . . .

Giovanni Battista Cavagna . . . should be treated as one of the visiting architects, since he was almost certainly born in Rome, but he spent many years in Naples, and his architecture has a clear local character. He is recorded in Naples from 1572 till 1577, and then again from 1591 to 1605. His most important work is the Monte di Pietà, but he also built the choir of Monteoliveto and collaborated with Vincenzo della Monica in the construction of the church of S. Gregorio Armeno . . . Cavagna's career in Naples ended unhappily. When the Viceroy announced his intention of building a new royal palace, Cavagna put forward plans which were rejected and he was evidently bitterly disappointed that this highly profitable commission should have been given to Domenico Fontana. He poured forth his anger in a long but unfinished memorandum, attacking both the character and the designs of his rival and, though the tone is one of exasperation, some of the criticisms were valid. He particularly attacks Fontana for his choice of site, which involved the destruction of the old palace and its fine park, which was right on the outskirts of the town and faced on a square so small that a visitor could never see the façade at a proper distance. The loggia was useless and only served to harbour beggars; it also made the rooms in the mezzanine so dark that they were more suitable for criminals than for officials. And so on. But it was too late; the palace was already built in great part and Fontana was installed in favour of the Viceroy. Cavagna thought it wiser to get out, and in 1605 he withdrew to Loretto.

[59] Entertainment at the Palazzo Reale by
a Spanish viceroy, the Duke of Osuna (1616–
20); from Alfred von Reumont's *Die Carafa von
Maddaloni. Neapel unter spanischer Herrschaft*

On one evening a hundred and twenty ladies were invited to supper
and were waited on by none but their relations. The Viceroy did not
appear till after the dessert, but watched through a little window. Then
he entered splendidly dressed, the casements were flung open, and the
lavish remains of the banquet were thrown down into the arsenal
courtyard. The *piano nobile* was magnificently illuminated and a ball
commenced, continuing into the small hours of the morning.

During the carnival of 1618 there was a great masquerade at the
palace: a Turkish ship 'sailed' through the great hall, man after man
leaping from its deck, and then there was a tournament; the evening
ended with a ball and a banquet. Never before had Naples seen such
entertainments as those given by Osuna, and they were not restricted
to the carnival but took place throughout the entire year.

On the feast of San Lorenzo in 1619 the Duchess of Osuna gave a great
ball; there was one dance by twelve young ladies of very high rank indeed,
who wore under-garments of white satin edged with gold lace and match-
ing petticoats which reached to their knees; they carried silver brocade
trains over their arms and had white crowns with herons' plumes on their
heads. The cost of this raiment was met by the Viceroy himself, being not
less than 600 ducats each. Everything they wore was paid for by him,
down to their shoes. When the orchestra struck up, they came forward
two by two, each one carrying a lighted torch in her right hand, and as
they danced they curtsied to His Excellency. Other dances followed,
including a galliard. After dishes of fruit had been served, of grapes and
melons (the customary refreshment of rich and poor, high and low alike),
there was a special torch dance by the daughter of the Duke of Monteleone-
Pignatelli, which the Viceroy was formally invited to watch, since it was in
his honour. The ball continued until five o'clock in the morning.

[60] THE ENTRY OF THE FIRST BORBONE KING, CHARLES
III, INTO NAPLES IN 1734; FROM PIETRO COLLETTA'S
STORIA DEL REALME DI NAPOLI DAL 1734 AL 1825.

(Pietro Colletta (1775–1831), perhaps the most famous of Neapolitan
historians after Giannone, was a native of the city. A soldier from the
age of twenty-one, originally in the Borbone service, he rose to the rank
of General in the armies of Joseph Bonaparte and Marshal Murat. He
was Minister for War in the Carbonari government of 1820 and spent
two years in prison in consequence. His *Storia* did not appear until
1834.)

Now that the capital had been freed of all traces of the previous regime,
the Infante entered it with royal pomp on 10 May. The people greeted
him with wild enthusiasm, since they had high hopes of their new
sovereign, and their rejoicing became almost ecstatic when his equer-
ries scattered large amounts of gold and silver coin in all the main
streets. In the morning he made his solemn entrance through the
Capuan Gate, but wishing to first of all give thanks to God for his victories he dismounted at the church of San Francesco on the outskirts,
staying in the monastery till 4 o'clock in the afternoon. He then continued his entrance into the city, riding a fine charger, magnificently
dressed and wearing splendid jewels. He took care to go first to the
cathedral to receive Cardinal Pignatelli's blessing and to take part with
due devotion in the ceremony of thanksgiving, and also to hang a rich
collar of rubies and diamonds round the neck of San Gennaro's bust.
When these pious duties were over, he proceeded to the palace. As he
was passing the prisons of the Vicaria and San Giacomo, their keys
were presented to him in homage to his sovereignty, whereupon he
gave orders for the cell doors to be opened and to release all the prisoners, an act of foolish generosity. The city was entirely given over to
celebrations – its militia lined the streets and provided the guards at
the palace, while the fireworks and illuminations went on all night . . .

On 15 June 1734 he published an edict of Philip V of Spain, in which the latter bestowed his ancient but newly established claim to The Two Sicilies, once again united in an independent king, on his son Charles, born of his blessed marriage to Elizabeth Farnese. The new King had himself proclaimed 'Charles, by the Grace of God, King of The Two Sicilies and Jerusalem, Infante of Spain, Duke of Parma, Piacenza and Castro, and Hereditary Grand Prince of Tuscany'. He changed the royal coat of arms, adding to the national arms of The Two Sicilies the golden lilies of the House of Spain, the azure lilies of Parma, and the red balls of the Medici. The city renewed its public rejoicing and the priests continued to offer services of thanksgiving. The King introduced a new entertainment to the festivities. This was the *Cocagna*, a huge construction supposed to depict the Garden of the Hesperides, from which were hung costly gifts for which anyone was allowed to compete, though they were deliberately hung high up and very hard to reach – the object was to arouse the mob's greed and encourage it to show its agility. From the palace roof Charles watched the competition with boyish amusement, thoroughly enjoying the spectacle of such an amusing game. Suddenly part of the *Cocagna*'s scaffolding, insecurely constructed and over-loaded with people, collapsed, pulling everything down with it and crushing those underneath. Many were killed and hundreds more injured. Very soon the piazza in front of the palace was deserted. The King at once issued an edict which forbade any repetition of this type of entertainment.

[61] CHARLES III AND QUEEN MARIA AMALIA AT THE ROYAL PALACE IN 1739; FROM *LETTRES HISTORIQUES ET CRITIQUES SUR L'ITALIE* BY CHARLES DE BROSSES.

(Charles de Brosses (1709–1777), Principal President of the Parlement of Burgundy, was a lawyer, dilettante and man of letters. His Italian letters were not published until 1799.)

*　　*　　*

When we arrived, the King and Queen were at Portici, a country house at the foot of Vesuvius; it is their Fontainebleau. He returned the same day and that evening we were presented to him. There was a grand Court gala because of the King's birthday, and he had his hand kissed by all his nobles. These lords were dressed with the utmost splendour, while His Majesty was adorned by an old suit of brown drugget with brass buttons. He has a long, thin, narrow face, with a very prominent nose, a gloomy, vacant expression, and a mediocre and unhealthy physique. He does little business, never speaks, and is only interested in hunting; ironically, there is not much to satisfy him at the latter since the countryside has long been despoiled of any game by the peasants or the *lazzaroni* who are free to shoot everywhere, so much so that His Majesty returns in high good humour when he has killed a brace of thrushes and two brace of sparrows. Because of the birthday the Queen also gave her hand to be kissed, which to my mind was more of an honour than a favour. They both dined in public and were served according to Spanish etiquette which is observed to the letter at this Court, the King by a Gentleman of the Chamber, and the Queen by the Comtesse de Charny ... They kneel to serve wine to the King and Queen and only rise when the glasses are returned to them. I was therefore a little irritated by the Queen who, greatly to the detriment of the divine Charny's knees, spent half an hour making a Canary wine soup in her glass. She has an air of malice, this worthy Princess, with a nose like a ball, a face like a crayfish, and the voice of a magpie. People say she was pretty when she arrived from Saxony, but she has just had smallpox. She is still very young and somewhat girlish. (She has certainly slept with her husband; at the time when I was writing this at Naples she was a month or five weeks gone with child, and the birth took place before there was any outward sign of pregnancy.) After dinner we all watched troops parade in the great piazza in front of the palace, which went on for quite long enough.

[62] A Court ball at the Palazzo Reale in 1769,
given by the eighteen-year-old King Ferdinand IV, as
experienced by his brother-in-law, the Emperor Joseph
II; from *The Bourbons of Naples* by Sir Harold Acton.

The King gave me a great salute with all his might on my behind at the
moment I least expected it, in the presence of more than four people.
For an age I had the honour of carrying him on my back, and more than
twenty times he came and put his arms over my shoulders, slackening
his whole body so that it dragged after me. When I got rid of him he
prowled round the hall with two of his favourites, clutching them by
the collar or by the breeches, laughing and joking with them but notic-
ing nobody else. Our departure for this ball was truly singular. We
proceeded in great ceremony to the ante-chamber, where all the courtiers and high officials were waiting for us. The march began with solem-
nity and good order, the King and Queen both accompanied by two
chamberlains with lights, but apparently the King was bored with this
procession, for he began to shout like the postillions and kick bottoms
lustily, right and left, which seemed the signal to start galloping. The
whole Court, big and small, ministers, old men, galloped away while
the King chased them in front of him, always shouting at the top of his
voice. The French Ambassador Choiseul unhappily found himself in
the King's path and received a punch in passing. Weak as he is, his nose
collided with the wall. In this manner they passed the first and second
ante-chambers, saloon and corridor, while I remained with the Queen
on my arm, leading the ladies. I had almost lost sight of the galloping
troop, when we finally met them at our normal pace at the door of the
theatre, which was packed with a dense crowd; owing to the ticklings
and cries it was appallingly noisy. I asked what the ladies usually did on
these occasions, and they assured me that when the King gallops they
gallop too, so that all these good old dames follow the procession out of
breath.

[63] Sir William Hamilton's account of King
Ferdinand IV and I's mad brother and his behaviour
at the Palazzo Reale; from Sir Nathaniel
Wraxall's *Historical Memoirs of my own time*.

I have frequently seen the unfortunate Duke of Calabria, who has only
been dead a few years, and who, by his birth, was heir to the Spanish
monarchy. He attained to manhood, and was treated with certain
distinctions, having chamberlains placed about him in constant attendance, who watched him with unremitting attention, as otherwise he
would have committed a thousand excesses. Care was particularly
taken to keep him from having any communication with the other sex,
for which he manifested the strongest propensity; but it became at last
impossible to prevent him altogether from attempting to emancipate
himself in this respect. He has many times eluded the vigilance of his
keepers, and on seeing ladies pass through the apartments of the palace,
would attack them with the same impetuosity as Pan or the satyrs are
described by Ovid when pursuing the nymphs, and with the same
intentions. More than one lady of the court has been critically rescued
from his embraces. On particular days of the year he was allowed to
hold a sort of court or levée, when the foreign Ministers repaired to his
apartments to pay their compliments to him; but his greatest amusement consisted in having his hand held up by his attendants, while
gloves were put on it, one larger than another, to the number of fifteen
or sixteen.

[64] The death of Ferdinand IV and I's mad elder brother,
the Duke of Calabria, in 1777; from *The Courts of Europe
at the Close of the Last Century* by Henry Swinburne.

(Henry Swinburne (1743–1803) was a Northumbrian squire and would-
be diplomat.)

*   *   *

The small-pox has declared itself on the fool Don Philip, the king's elder brother, and the whole court is in alarm. There seemed to be great debates about what was to be done; at last it was arranged for the royal family (except the sick man) to set out for Santa Lucia . . .

The Infant Don Philip, an idiot, died upon the 17th instant, and four days after his body was carried in a coach, preceded by twenty-four servants with flambeaux, and the judge of the court on horse-back, to Santa Chiara, to be exposed on a Catafalqua. The troops lined the road. The Catafalqua had this inscription on it – *Raptus est, mutat ne malitiam intellectus ejus* [He has been taken, lest his mind should turn to evil].

All is in gala, and there are no signs of a funeral ceremony.

[65] QUEEN MARIA CAROLINA, IN THE PALAZZO REALE,
HEARS OF THE EXECUTION OF HER SISTER; FROM SIR
HAROLD ACTON'S *THE BOURBONS OF NAPLES*.

Throughout 1793 the fate of Marie Antoinette had preyed constantly on her mind. She had been preparing for the catastrophe, as her letters to Gallo show. In July she wrote: 'They have taken away my unfortunate sister's son and moved him into the apartments of his late father with a certain Simon, a shoe-maker, and his wife. This blow must have been terrible for my unfortunate sister. I could have wished it to end her life. For a long time I have been wishing her a natural death as the best thing that could happen to her. But Providence has decreed otherwise and we shall have to submit. Certain it is that she is made to suffer all the sharpest pangs, at such intervals as to drain the full bitterness of each. And just when time and resignation seem to have formed a protecting crust, her wounds are torn open again.' In August: 'I am increasingly anxious about the fate of my wretched sister and long for it to be over; my imagination always anticipates reality. I do not know what to hope or fear for her and her family. What I wish is that France could be pulverised with all its inhabitants.'

The news of her execution prostrated her nonetheless. Pale and weeping, she led her children to the palace chapel, where they repeated her sobbing prayers with tremulous voices. A yearning for vengeance was mingled with her grief, and left a permanent scar on her character. Under a picture of Marie Antoinette in her study she inscribed: *'Je poursuiverai ma vengeance jusqu' au tombeau.'*

[66] THE LAST HOURS OF MURAT – 'KING GIOACCHINO NAPOLEONE' – AT THE PALAZZO REALE IN 1815, AFTER HIS DEFEAT AT TOLENTINO; FROM A. HILLIARD ATTERIDGE'S *MARSHAL MURAT*.

He entered his capital for the last time at five in the afternoon of 18 May, escorted by four Polish lancers.

In the streets the people cheered him as if he were a victor. But at the palace [Queen] Caroline, who had tried to dissuade him from his desperate venture, received him with chilling coldness in this hour of failure. 'Madame,' he said, in bitter disappointment, 'do not be surprised at seeing me alive. I have done all I could to meet death.' A number of nobles and officers came to greet him, and were astonished at the calmness that he showed in the midst of disaster.

Next morning there was disappointing news from San Gallo. Bianchi, the Austrian commander, had refused to hear of armistice or negotiations. He declared that he was now master of the kingdom of Naples, and would not recognise King Joachim. All that he would agree to would be a military convention with General Carascosa, from the advantages of which 'Marshal Murat' must be excluded.

An English squadron lay in sight of Naples, and Caroline had averted a threatened bombardment of the capital only by surrendering the few armed vessels that flew the Neapolitan flag. Gaeta still held out. Murat announced his intention of going there and sharing the fate of its garrison. But would Gaeta venture to resist the Austrians? and even if it did, a capitulation must come sooner or later. His friends persuaded him that his best course would be to try to reach France.

On 19 May he spent his last day in his palace at Naples, preparing for his flight. It could not be long delayed, for there were already signs of a revolutionary movement among the fickle people, and rumours of a hostile landing from the British squadron. It was decided that, to prevent his departure being at once discovered, Caroline should for the present remain at Naples, and rejoin him later in France. It was thought that she could always count on a safe-conduct and free passage even from the Allies.

After nightfall, with his diamonds and some 300,000 francs in banknotes, and some gold sewn into his clothes and belt, he dressed in civilian costume and rode out of Naples. He was accompanied and immediately followed by his two nephews, the Bonnafous, his aide-de-camp, Colonel de Beauffremont, the Polish colonel, Malchewsky, the Duke of Roccaromana, the Marchese Giulano, his secretary, de Coussy, and his valet, Leblanc. At the coast village of Miniscola the fugitives hired and embarked in two fishing-boats and put to sea in the darkness.

[*Eventually Murat reached France, but Napoleon refused to receive him. After the Hundred Days he led a tragi-comic expedition to Calabria to recover the throne; he was arrested by peasants at the 'little town of Pizzo, handed over to the military, court-martialled, and shot on 13 October 1815.*]

[67] THE BUILDING OF THE CHURCH OF SAN FRANCESCO DI PAOLA
OPPOSITE THE PALAZZO REALE BY FERDINAND IV AND I; FROM
PIETRO COLLETTA'S *STORIA DEL REALME DI NAPOLI DEL 1734 AL 1825.*

The King fulfilled an oath he had sworn when a refugee in Sicily. He had been told that the church of San Francesco di Paola at Naples was to be pulled down in order to enlarge the piazza in front of the royal palace and to provide the space for a pantheon; he vowed that if God should see fit to restore to him the lost half of his kingdom he would build the church anew, and much more magnificent than before. His wish came true in 1815. He gave orders for the church to be rebuilt, inviting architects throughout Italy to enter a competition for the contract; the plans of Fazio and Peruta, both Neapolitans, were selected, but while they were waiting for their reward and anticipating the fame they would acquire, the contract was given instead to another architect, a certain Bianchi from Lugano who was completely unknown to them and indeed to anyone else. The foundation stone was laid personally by the King on 17 June 1816 with great pomp and the ceremonies of the Church, the most famous painters and sculptors in Naples assisting in the reconstruction. Landi and Cammuccini, names known not only in Italy but across the Alps, contributed two paintings on themes from the New Testament. At the time I write [1825–30] the church is still unfinished.

[68] THE CARBONARI'S REVOLUTION OF 1820; FROM
THE HON. KEPPEL CRAVEN'S *A TOUR THROUGH THE
SOUTHERN PROVINCES OF THE KINGDOM OF NAPLES.*

The sect of the Carbonari, an association founded in imitation of free-masonry, and which had been proscribed and persecuted with equal rigour by the usurping and legitimate sovereigns, was avowedly the principal agent and operator of the changes which had been effected in the government . . .

They came in on Sunday the 9th of July, at about midday, and proceeding by the Strada Toledo, defiled before the Duke of Calabria [the future King Francis I], who stood at the window of the royal palace, and admitted their leader to the honour of an audience; after which he was granted the additional favour of kissing the King's hand.

The regular troops, headed by General Napolitano, opened the march, and were followed by the mass of provincial militia, walking rapidly without any order, conducted by General G. Pepe, and a priest of the name of Menichini, who may be looked upon as the principal mover of all the secret springs which had set the revolution in motion. This intelligent and indefatigable man attracted full as much notice, and by far more curiosity than his companion; he is said to have passed several years in England and to have been in Spain since the change which has taken place in that Kingdom.

The constitution itself, in a palpable shape, made its appearance in the procession, conveyed in a common hackney one-horse chair called a curriculo. The spectacle displayed by the bands of provincial militia was singular in the extreme; as, though they were all most formidably armed, their weapons varied as much as their accoutrements: a very small proportion of them were clad in military uniform, the majority being habited according to the different costumes of their respective districts, which at the same time bore a very warlike aspect.

It must be acknowledged that the cartridge belt, the sandalled legs, the broad stiletto, short musket, and grey peaked hats, so peculiarly adapted by painters to the representation of banditti, seemed here to realize all the ideas which the inhabitants of the north have formed of such beings; and the sunburnt complexions and dark bushy hair and whiskers of the wearer greatly contributed to render this resemblance more striking.

A strange contrast was exhibited by the more opulent classes of these same legions who, though equally well provided with arms of all descriptions marched among the ranks of their picturesque companions, attired in the full extreme of modern French and English fashions. All bore the Carbonari colours at their breast, while scarves of the same, or different medals and emblems tied to their waistcoat, denoted the rank they severally held in the sect. Banners with inscriptions in honour of this patriotic association were also carried by them. [The Carbonari emblems were a hatchet, a hammer, a *vanga* (a kind of spade) and other instruments used by the real *carbonari* – charcoal workers.] . . .

That evening [12 July] the great theatre of San Carlo was illuminated and opened to the provincial troops gratis, who availed themselves of this licence to fill it in a degree unparalleled on any former occasion. The sight presented by the seats of the pit, occupied by so motley an assemblage, many of which were armed cap-à-pie, was not one of the least remarkable exhibitions among those witnessed by the public in the short space of twelve days. The Duke of Calabria and his family were present at the representation, and more than divided the applause bestowed on the performers.

[*Unfortunately the revolution was out of control by the end of the year. Ferdinand I and the Princes were prisoners in the Royal Palace and the tricolour flew everywhere; the Carbonari ruled instead of the new Parliament; the treasury's reserves were squandered; soldiers would not obey their officers, and there was general anarchy. In December 1820 the King fled in a warship placed at his disposal by the British government, leaving the Duke of Calabria as Regent, and took refuge in Austria. In March 1821 Austrian troops marched into The Two Sicilies, the Carbonari army and their leaders ran away, and Ferdinand was restored for the third time, to the cheers of ordinary Neapolitans.*]

[69] THE DEATH OF FRANCIS I IN NOVEMBER 1830 AND HIS LYING-IN-STATE AT THE ROYAL PALACE; FROM SIR HAROLD ACTON'S *THE LAST BOURBONS OF NAPLES*.

The King received Extreme Unction on November 8 and took an affectionate leave of his sobbing family. 'I am detached from everything mundane,' he murmured. 'I do not wish my sufferings to cease, but to suffer more in order to atone for my sins.' Then he asked for some water, but he could not swallow and seemed about to suffocate. Fervently clutching a holy image given him by Pius VII, he said: 'I wish to join Jesus Christ with my heart and soul.' Beckoning to Ferdinand, he told him: 'I have come to the fatal moment when time ends and eternity begins. My power and glory on earth are finished; these honours, this Court will vanish like a dream. You will soon ascend the throne, my son: listen to your dying father . . . Be good and just before God; do not let yourself be seduced by power and pleasure. Bear these words in mind: all is vanity in this world, all is a dream, a passing shadow.' Dominicans, Theatines, and monks of other Orders came to bring him plenary indulgences, and he welcomed them all with a smile. Seeing that he was in pain while clasping a crucifix, Monsignor Giunta bent over to relieve him. As if he feared that the crucifix might be removed, he clutched it convulsively with both his withered hands. Then he made signs for a holy candle to be lighted beside his bed. His articulation became blurred as he tried to repeat the prayers of his confessor; then his voice was silent. These details are gleaned from an account published by a witness. Ulloa adds that the King made a gesture as if to bless his children, but his arm dropped languidly. 'Oh Naples!' he murmured with a sigh, and fell back dead.

None could deny that the King's death had been edifying. Indeed – 'Nothing in his life became him like the leaving it.' For all his religious zeal, his meticulous attention to State affairs, he had never endeared himself to the Neapolitan people. He might have been admired in the eighteenth century, but the times were against him and he was against the times. He left a large family: six sons and seven daughters; and Ferdinand, his heir, was a youth of unusual promise. The royal corpse was exposed for three days before the funeral in Santa Chiara. On the third night the two bodyguards on duty beside the elaborate catafalque were startled by a sinister thud. They scampered off in a panic. One of the dead King's arms had fallen on the floor because his corpse had been embalmed too hastily.

[70] GENERAL GUGLIELMO PEPE VISITS FERDINAND II AT THE PALAZZO REALE IN 1848; FROM *NARRATIVE OF SCENES AND EVENTS IN ITALY FROM 1847 TO 1849* BY GUGLIELMO PEPE.

(Guglielmo Pepe (1783–1855), a Calabrian, enlisted in the army of the Parthenopean Republic and later served in Murat's forces, rising to the rank of General. He commanded the Carbonari troops in 1821 and in consequence spent the next twenty-seven years in exile. In 1848 Ferdinand II allowed him home and gave him command of the 'Constitutionalist' expedition in aid of the Venetians.)

*   *   *

Since I had quitted Naples, many improvements had been made in the royal habitation. On entering the room appropriated to the officers on duty, I was saluted as a person of high position, and immediately introduced to the King. He retained no trace of the boy of ten years old, whose beauty I had then admired; with added years he had become colossal, and his countenance did not indicate tenderness of heart. Yet his manner to me was only too gracious . . .

Accordingly I repaired to the palace in my morning costume, and was conducted by the King to a very small cabinet, where I was seated opposite him, without knowing the motive. I felt we were descending, and I then perceived that we were in a machine constructed to descend and ascend, in order to avoid the fatigue of mounting the lofty stairs . . .

We soon arrived at the quarters of the 12th of the line in the Santa Petito, the greater number of whom were Sicilians. Scarcely had the drums beat, when, in an instant, the soldiers, while running, took their knapsacks and placed themselves in order of battle. The King commanded the manœuvre, and everything was performed to perfection. There was no flattery in my warm congratulations, nor in telling him that I had never seen troops move better on the drilling-ground, and that, though the English might excel them in precision, they were certainly inferior in agility. This exercise was scarcely terminated, when a crowd of soldiers, subaltern officers, and women, presented themselves to the King, each loudly supplicating for some favour; and he appeared pleased with this. That my readers may understand the nature of these petitions, I will repeat one of them. A woman presented herself, saying, 'Majesty, I am the wife of Sergeant –, we have two children, maidens, but *real* maidens; you have promised to give them husbands; I beseech you not to forget the promise, to avoid the sin to which they are exposed, the virtuous young girls!' The King replied, 'I will not forget my promise.'

[71] THE EXILED POPE PIUS IX VISITS NAPLES;
FROM *THE TIMES* OF 27 SEPTEMBER 1849.

(Pius IX – Pope from 1846 to 1878 – had granted a parliamentary constitution in the Papal States, but the Romans had nonetheless revolted and forced him to take refuge in The Two Sicilies in 1850.)

A circumstance occurred here yesterday [16 September] which, if not got up by the police – a supposition hardly credible – proves that either the person of the King [Ferdinand II] or of the Pope, or probably of both, was then destined for assassination. It having been announced that Pius the Ninth would give his benediction from the grand balcony of the Palace, overlooking the large square of San Francisco, a great crowd commenced assembling as early as 11 o'clock, though the hour named for the ceremony was noon. Suddenly, the report of a pistol was heard in the midst of a group collected in front of the places to be occupied by the King and the Supreme Pontiff, and of course the greatest sensation was excited among the people and respectable persons who had already taken their seats in the adjoining balconies. Two men at the same instant were arrested, on one of whom a pistol just discharged was found, and on the other a hand-grenade or small shell. The pistol had exploded by accident, probably the hair trigger, not having been secured, being acted on by the pressure of the crowd. No-one was hurt by the discharge; and if, on examination, it can be shown that the weapon was not loaded, the affair was possibly got up by the police; but of the fact of a shot being fired, of a pistol just discharged being found in the pocket of one prisoner, and of a hand-grenade on the person of the other, his companion, there is no doubt; and it will be for those men to show why they came thus armed into a position which immediately commanded the Royal and Papal balcony. During the night inflammatory bills directed against the King, not the Pope, were posted on the walls of the Palace, and a large parcel of the same placards was found on each of the prisoners. This circumstance is most important as, whilst it explains in a direct manner the nature of the business in which these rascals were engaged, it may probably lead to the discovery of the persons by whom they were employed. It is well known that a secret society, affiliated with those of the Red Republic in other parts of Italy and in France, exists at Naples, though hitherto its members have escaped the researches of the police. Many an innocent man has been arrested on suspicion of belonging to that society, but as yet the slightest clue to the chiefs has not been obtained, and it will be truly fortunate if this circumstance leads to a discovery of them. The prisoners were carried, after having been promenaded through the town, to the Castello del Ovo . . .

If the benediction of Pio Nono can do a people good, those of Naples have had almost a surfeit of it. Early in the week the Pope went to the church of Pie de Grotto to offer up his devotions at the same altar before which on the 8th, the King knelt, and, though he came by steamer from Portici, a certain number of the faithful were present. It was amusing to see the Lazzaroni, who crowd that vicinity, rushing into the water to receive him, and to hear their cheers of '*Viva il Re!*' – that of Pio Nono having the odour of last year's movement fresh upon it. Almost every day has been devoted to a similar purpose, and not a charity, church, convent, or nunnery, that has not had its turn. Yesterday, however, was the grand day, in which it was announced that the Supreme Pontiff would give his benediction to the whole population of Naples at 12 o'clock, from the grand balcony of the Royal palace. The hour was ill chosen, as the sun has full play on the great square, where the people had to stand uncovered, and one's appreciation of the blessing must be very great to induce one to risk a *coup de soleil*; but still the place was well thronged, though in nothing like the manner in which would have been if an hour in the afternoon, close on sundown, had been named.

The Pope, the King, and the numerous personages composing the suites of both, were protected by crimson awnings stretched over the balconies, and the nobility who occupied the palace of the Prince of Salerno were in the shade, but the bulk of the people were exposed to the action of a mid-day sun, which would have roasted an egg in five minutes. I had a reserved place, under the shelter of the cupola of the church of San Francisco, and there, quite at ease, I looked down on the gridiron of fried heads that was displayed beneath me. How many went home and died I cannot say, but certainly the spectacle was very brilliant, and I must say that the costumes of the women, and their fanciful dresses, made in the bright sun a very pretty display. The general effect was heightened by the elegant costumes and graceful persons of the Neapolitan ladies, who filled the neighbouring windows and balconies. The whole formed a rich and billowing picture, which assumed a tone of sublimity at the moment when the Pope raised his hands and the multitude knelt down to receive the blessing which he called from Heaven upon them.

[72] THE LAST BALLS AT THE PALAZZO REALE; FROM
RAFFAELE DE CESARE'S *LA FINE DI UN REGNO*.

One of the last great entertainments at the Royal Palace was a magnificent costume ball on 26 February 1854, which is not yet forgotten even now [1894]. Those who attended went in seventeenth-century cavalier dress, the royal party in the style of Louis XIII. King Ferdinand wore a suit of grey velvet, the Count of Aquila was in black velvet, and the Count of Trapani in sky-blue velvet. As for their Spanish Carlist kinsmen, the Count of Montemolin wore light tawny velvet, Prince Sebastian dark tawny velvet and the Infante Don Ferdinand dark-blue velvet. There were also some German princes accompanied by their retinues, so that the palace was resplendent with rich fabrics and glittering jewels. Only the very highest of the Neapolitan aristocracy had been invited to the ball. Among them was Giovanni del Balzo who came as a Calabrian brigand, his costume owing more to fancy than reality. He was ordered to leave by the King, who called Major Yunghi – a Swiss officer dressed as a miller – and told him, 'Tell Giovanni he must learn how to behave.' Del Balzo left, without knowing why he had been sent away; when he came to make his excuses to the King two or three days later, Ferdinand II said, 'Remember, brigands are never allowed into my house, not even fancy-dress brigands.' The very last ball at the palace was held on 23 January 1856, with 2,000 guests. Another was planned for January 1857, but it did not take place because of a calamity which some people blamed on the Duke of Ventignano. The following conversation between the King and the Duke of Ascoli reveals a curious side to the former's character. He was reading through the previous year's guest list, striking out the names of those who had died or whose politics were in doubt and possessed progressive tendencies. Eventually they reached the name of the Duke of Ventignano, as he had asked for an invitation. Ferdinand II knew that he must invite the Duke, a man of considerable gifts and proven loyalty. However, he told Ascoli, 'You know the things people say about him. Personally, I don't credit them. I will invite him, but I can tell you now that the party will never take place.' In fact the King believed firmly in the Evil Eye, as was only too evident on a number of occasions, though in each case he tried not to show it. The Duke was included in the guest list. A week after the invitations were sent out, Agesilao Milano tried to assassinate the King and the ball had to be cancelled.

[73] The attempt to murder Ferdinand II in 1856; from Sir Harold Acton's *The Last Bourbons of Naples*.

At the annual review in honour of the Immaculate Conception on December 8 a private soldier named Agesilao Milano stepped out of the ranks during the march past and aimed a violent bayonet thrust at Ferdinand on horseback. This would have been fatal had not the pistol-case at the saddle turned the weapon aside, which glancing off inflicted a slight wound. Before Milano could make his second lunge Major Latour galloped up and knocked him down: he was hustled away. Few noticed what had really happened. The King remained perfectly calm. To his brother-in-law Don Carlos, Count of Montemolino, who rushed to his aid, he whispered: 'Stand back and keep silent!' His admirable presence of mind probably saved the country from civil war. The commander of the Swiss regiments confirmed Nisco's statement that if the attempt had been noticed by many it would have been imputed to a military plot, and the Swiss would have been ordered by their officers to fire on the Neapolitan troops. Perhaps this was what Milano had hoped for, as the army was known to be loyal.

The King sat on his horse until the review was over; then he was quickly driven back to the palace and his private physician was summoned. Fearing that the bayonet might have been poisoned, the Queen knelt down and sucked the wound herself. Fortunately it did not seem serious, but as the King was overexcited the doctor prescribed a sedative. In the afternoon he drove out with his family through the most crowded streets to show that he was unhurt . . .

Within less than a month two other incidents intensified the King's alarm. On December 17 a powder magazine in the arsenal near the royal palace exploded, causing many casualties and breaking every window and street lamp in the vicinity . . . Two weeks later, on January 4, 1857, the steam frigate *Carlo Terzo*, which was to carry a great quantity of arms and ammunition to Palermo, blew up with a terrific explosion at 11 p.m., causing the death of most of her crew . . .

Two such powerful explosions at such short intervals in the same area were scarcely due to coincidence. They shook Ferdinand's faith in his army . . . He took refuge in ambitious schemes of road building and land reclamation as well as in works of charity. He spent more time at Caserta than in Naples; for once he would not attend the gala performance at the San Carlo for his birthday on January 12, and the Court ball which was to have been given the same month was deferred.

[74] OFFICERS OF THE ROYAL HOUSEHOLD OF THE TWO
SICILIES IN 1858; FROM THE *ALMANACK DE GOTHA*.

Master of the Household and High Steward: Pietrantonio Sanseverino,
Prince of Bisignano.

Master of the Horse: The Marquis Michele Imperiale.

Grand Butler (Major Domo): Sebastiano Marulli, Duke of Ascoli.

Captain of the Bodyguard: Brigadier-General Vincenzo Ruffo, Prince
della Scaletta.

Grand Almoner: Monsignor Pietro Naselli de Alliata, Archbishop of Leucosia.

Master of the Court Ceremonies: Don Alfonso d'Avalos, Marquis of
Pescara and Vasto.

Knight of Honour to the Queen: Onorato Gaetani, Duke of Laurenzano.

Lady of Honour: The Princess of Bisignano.

Principal Equerry: Don Troiano Spinelli, Duke of Laurino.

Private Secretary to the King: Brigadier-General Francesco d'Agostino.

Assistant Private Secretary: Major Augusto Severino.

Aides-de-camp General to the King: HRH Vice-Admiral the Count of
Aquila; Lieutenant-General the Prince of Ischitella; Lieutenant-
General the Prince of Castelcicala; Brigadier-General Ricardo, Duke
of Sangro; HRH Brigadier-General the Count of Trapani; Counter-
Admiral Frederico Roberti; Brigadier-General of Marines Leopoldo
del Re; and Colonel Count François de la Tour.

Officer in waiting on the King: Brigadier-General the Duke Alessandro
Nunziante*.

[75] FAREWELL TO FERDINAND II; FROM *THE*
ILLUSTRATED LONDON NEWS OF 18 JUNE 1859.

For twenty-hours after the death of the King [on 22 May] his body lay
upon his bed in the Royal apartment of Caserta, guarded day and night

---

* who was to betray King Francis II.

by gentlemen of the bedchamber and other attendants, dressed in full uniform and deep mourning. At the end of twenty-hours the body was dressed by the same attendants, and was placed on a table, covered with crimson velvet fringed with gold, in the middle of the room in which his deceased Majesty usually slept. Each of the attendants then kissed the hand of the King. They then placed the body in a coffin furnished with eight handles, and carried it to the door of the chamber, where it was received by the chief officers of the Court, by the Commander of the Royal Body Guard, and others, all bearing lighted torches, and was thence conducted, being at the same time accompanied by the clergy of the palace, to the place where it was consigned to the physicians and surgeons of the Court appointed to inspect and embalm it.

On the Saturday night, at midnight, the body of the late King was brought into Naples privately, and deposited in the Hall of the Viceroys, on a bier, underneath a Royal canopy. Four altars were erected in this chamber, and the bier was decorated with the emblems of sovereignty. The body was guarded day and night by four chief officers of the Court, by the gentlemen of the bedchamber, by the Royal Body Guard, and other attendants, in turn, as during the life of the late King. On Sunday, Monday, and Tuesday mornings Mass was performed by the priests appointed by the Cappellano and Maggiore; and in the afternoon of Sunday and Monday, and the morning of Tuesday, the '*Libera*' was sung by the four mendicant orders. On the first two days on which the body was exposed the public were admitted from ten a.m. until six p.m.; and on Tuesday from eight a.m. until midday. Sunday being a holiday, crowds flocked in from all the country round Naples, and added sensibly to the already dense population of the capital. The palace had the appearance of a strong place besieged. Inside the iron rails which surround it were troops, and cannon were placed there specially for this occasion; whilst outside the gates were a number of mounted hussars, who, with drawn swords, rode up and down, and had immense difficulty in keeping off the thousands who pressed towards the entrance. No distinction of persons was observed in admitting people, so that Lazarus and Dives went in together, and rags and silks rustled side by side . . .

On the afternoon of the 31st of May the body of the late King was removed from the Palace to the Church of Santa Chiara. The body lay in state in the church during the remainder of Tuesday, and on Wednesday morning the last funeral rites were performed. The Royal carriages returned to the church, and the service was commenced by the chanting of the 'Libera' by the four mendicant orders – the Dominicans, Franciscans, Augustines, and Carmelites. At ten o'clock the forts and the shipping renewed the firing every two minutes. Four battalions of the Royal Guard were ranged from the church along the street to Monteoliveto, and during the ceremony they fired three salvos – one at the beginning of the Mass, another at the elevation of the Host, and the last when the Royal remains were deposited in the vault. At the same time the forts, ceasing to fire their minute guns, also fired three salvos. As soon as the Mass had been said the body was placed on a table near the high altar, surrounded by the Corporation, the Prefect of Police, the King-at-Arms, the Ministers of State, and the clergy. The coffin having been opened, a third recognition of it was made, and the Minister of Ecclesiastical Affairs demanded, 'Is this the body of H.M. Ferdinand II, King of The Two Sicilies?' An officer replied, 'It is.' The Comptroller of the Household then closed the coffin and delivered the keys to the Master of the Court Ceremonies, who gave them to the Major Domo, the Commander of the Royal Guard, and the Head Chaplain. Accompanied by the distinguished persons present, the body was then borne to the Royal vault, where the Padre Guardian of the monastery, having given a receipt for it, placed it, with the aid of the members of his confraternity, in a copper coffin, locked also with three keys, which were given up to three several officers, who finally consigned them to the King. As soon as the function was over the diplomatic body and others went to compliment the new King at

Capodimonte. And so ended the days appointed for the funeral of the deceased King Ferdinand II.

[76] Francis II's first public audience at the Palazzo Reale in 1859; from Raffaele de Cesare's *La Fine di un Regno*.

On 25 June there was a solemn *baciamano*, conducted according to the strictest Court etiquette. This was an important event for the world of officialdom and for the aristocracy, since a *baciamano* had not been held for many years. The sovereign and his consort stood under a *baldacchino* in the throne-room, surrounded by the princes of the blood, high dignitaries, bishops, and ladies-in-waiting; as was his custom the King was in the uniform of a colonel of Hussars, while the Queen wore a royal tiara and mantle. The appearance of the room, filled with a host of great personages, in splendid uniforms and wearing orders and decorations from all over the world, who were pacing up and down and bowing graciously to each other, was imposing in the extreme. However in one part of the vast room amidst all this glittering colour, a long streak of black began to be seen, emerging from the doorway and moving slowly towards the throne. It was the judicature in hats and cloaks like those of Don Basilio in *The Barber of Seville*. The oddity of the contrast and the comic spectacle it afforded caused Maria Sophia to break into peals of girlish laughter in which everyone present joined, especially the princes. The laughter was infectious and difficult to restrain; people could not keep their faces straight nor disguise their laughing as coughing. It turned the ceremony into a gay and cheerful occasion. All the councillors and corporation of the city of Naples attended this first *baciamano* and exercised their ancient privilege of remaining covered in the sovereign's presence.

[77] FRANCIS II IN 1860, AGED TWENTY-THREE, FROM *FRANCESCO II DI BORBONE, L'ULTIMO RE DI NAPOLI* BY PIER GIUSTO JAEGER.

That Spanish etiquette which insisted on accompanying every mention of the sovereign spoken or written with the formulas D.G. (*Dio guardi* – 'God preserve him') or N.S. (*Nostroo Signore* – 'Our Lord'), besides everybody's all but religious obsequiousness, did not save Francis from becoming the object of open criticism and from being considered as of little or no account by the old nobility (some of whom at once left the kingdom when a constitution was granted) and by those who came into contact with him in the course of duty. The reference in the *Gattopardo* to 'a seminarist dressed up as a general', even if only a novelist's invention, may well be how he actually appeared to a great Sicilian or Neapolitan nobleman of 1860. The most charitable view was that the education young Francis received from his tyrannical and authoritarian father [Ferdinand II] – whose personality crushed him down to the very end – had left him altogether in the dark about matters of state (the late King's motto, like that of many other monarchs, having been that Borboni should 'reign one at a time'). His personal religion, influenced by stories about his mother, Christina of Savoy, who had died shortly after his birth – the 'Holy Queen' in the eyes of the people – verged on superstition, with an elaborate cult in the Neapolitan popular tradition of relics and statues, and had formed what was left of his character.

Yet his correspondence with Filangieri shows that Francis was at least deeply concerned with military matters, paying scrupulous attention to them. What he really lacked – and what made him ill-fitted for coping with such a grave crisis – was personal authority and the ability to take decisions; and there was no-one in whom he could confide (apart from Queen Maria Sophia who, after all, was only nineteen) . . .

On visiting him, the English Admiral Mundy found a well-built young man, quite tall, with dark hair cut very short and an olive complexion, wearing a plain, tight-fitting uniform with the Order of San Gennaro as his sole decoration. Mundy noted that, while the King's manner was dignified, during their conversation he seemed hesitant and confused, so badly informed as to ask if the Admiral's ships had come from Malta: everybody else knew that the English fleet had just returned from witnessing the Borbone humiliation at the surrender of Palermo.

From the King's private papers one has a very strong impression that he was making a pathetic attempt to model himself on his father. With foreigners, however, he always made a pretence of being in sympathy with popular opinion. Nothing during this crucial period gave any indication of just what he would show the world that he was capable of during those last hundred days at Gaeta. When confronted by real adversity his character changed almost unbelievably; the hesitant Francis II became a rousing orator and something of a hero.

[78] FRANCIS II LEAVES THE PALAZZO REALE FOR THE LAST TIME ON 6 SEPTEMBER 1860; FROM *GARIBALDI AND THE MAKING OF ITALY* BY THE PRO-RISORGIMENTO HISTORIAN, G.M. TREVELYAN.

On the same day he and his brave Bavarian Queen went for their last drive in the streets of Naples. They sat in an open carriage, like simple private citizens, and the passers-by, who took off their hats to them in silence, observed that they were laughing and talking together as usual. The clumsy shyness of the King's demeanour to his wife, which had distressed her in the early months of their marriage, had now to a large extent passed away. A few yards from the Palace, at the busy entrance of the Chiaia, their equipage was brought to a stand by a block in the traffic, and they were forced to wait some moments close to a gang of workmen who were taking down the Bourbon lilies from over the shop front of the Chemist to the Royal Family. Francis pointed out to Maria Sophia the too significant nature of the men's task, and husband and wife turned to each other and laughed.

Next morning, September 6, the walls of Naples were placarded with the King's proclamation of farewell to his people. In restrained and dignified language he protested against the way in which he was being driven from his Capital, in spite of his constitutional concessions, and announced that he hoped to return if the luck of war and politics favoured his claims. In the course of the day the main part of the army marched out of the town by the Capua road, indignantly refusing D'Ayala's invitation to fraternise with the National Guard and desert to the side of Italy. A garrison of six or ten thousand was left behind to guard the fortresses of the Capital, but their commanding officers were strictly ordered by Francis II to remain neutral and to shed no blood. Nothing was said to them about surrender or evacuation, although if they were attacked they could only hold the forts by shedding blood, which would transgress both the letter and the spirit of the King's commands. It is probable that he had not clearly thought out what he wished them to do. But it may fairly be said that he adhered in an honourable manner to his decision not to inflict the horrors of war on Naples, and the rumour that he ordered the castles to bombard the town, after he had gone, was pure fiction.

At four in the afternoon the constitutional Ministers were summoned to the Palace to take their leave of the King. There was no party in the State that wished them to accompany him to Gaeta. They found him courteous and cheerful, buoyed up by excitement at a great change and by relief after long tension. He said to Don Liborio, half in jest, half in earnest, 'Don Libò, look out for your head,' referring no doubt to his own prospective return. 'Sire,' was the unabashed reply, 'I will do my best to keep it on my shoulders.' The Ministers were not invited to say farewell to the Queen.

Shortly before six in the evening Francis and Maria Sophia walked down arm-in-arm from the Palace to the dock which lay close under their windows. Both were composed and cheerful. The Queen left her wardrobe behind, saying to her maids, 'We shall come back again.' The hundreds of Neapolitan grandees and officials who had fattened on the

Court for twenty years past, were notable by their absence. But the faithful Captain Criscuolo received his sovereigns on board the *Messaggero*, a small ship of 160 horse-power and four guns. As she steamed through the crowded port of Naples, she ran up a signal for the rest of the fleet to follow, but not one vessel stirred. The captains were already in league with Persano.

The Teatro San Carlo

King Charles wanted a new theatre, as the capital had very few and they were of poor quality. To make it not just magnificent but impressive as well, he gave orders for it to be made the biggest in Europe and to be built as quickly as possible. The plans were once again drawn up by Medrano, but the actual construction was entrusted to Angelo Carasale, a man of humble origins who had grown famous on account of his talents as an architect and several large and imaginative buildings. He chose the site next to the palace and demolished a large number of houses on it, thus adding a large area so that the rear of the stage could be extended for presentations of battles, chariots and cavalry in the background. He began work in March 1737, finishing in October the same year; on 4 November, Charles's feast day, the first performance took place. The theatre's interior was illuminated by countless candles reflected in almost as many looking-glasses, producing so much light as to make the fable of Olympus come true. A huge and lavishly decorated box was included for the royal family. When Charles entered the new theatre he was amazed by its grandeur and its beauty, and congratulated the architect warmly – while the audience cheered the King for having created all this splendour.

Everyone was delighted. Charles summoned Carasale so that he could thank him in full view of the world, placing his hand on his shoulder in token of friendship and patronage. Carasale, not normally the most modest of men, in turn thanked the King both verbally and by repeated bows. When the mutual congratulations were over, Charles said that since the theatre stood next to the palace, it would have been much more convenient had the royal family been able to go from one to the other by an internal passageway. The builder looked abashed. Saying, 'We will think about it,' the King thereupon dismissed him.

When the performance was over, Carasale was waiting for Charles; he asked the King to return to his palace by way of the passage for which he had given orders. In no more than three hours, by demolishing thick walls, constructing a scaffolding of beams and framework, hiding the roughness of the work with tapestry and carpets, and using curtains, mirrors and lighting, Carasale had somehow succeeded in creating a corridor which was both beautiful and spectacular.

[80] THE SAN CARLO, CHARLES III, AND MUSIC
AT NAPLES IN 1739; FROM *LETTRES HISTORIQUES ET
CRITIQUES SUR L'ITALIE*, BY CHARLES DE BROSSES.

That evening they opened the great palace theatre for the first performance of Domenico Sarro's opera, *Parthenope*. The King came. He talked throughout half the opera and slept during the rest of it – for a certainty, the man doesn't like music. He has his box in the second tier, facing the actors; it is much too far away since the room is so enormous that in one part people can scarcely see anything, and in another they hear nothing at all . . . This was the first important opera we had seen. It was composed by Sarro, an accomplished musician, yet was dull and boring and not at all good. On the other hand it was perfectly performed. The celebrated Senesino sang the chief role and I was enchanted by the quality of both his singing and his acting. I was therefore astonished to see that the Neapolitans were very far from being satisfied – they complained that he was singing in too old-fashioned a way. One should explain that musical fashion here changes every ten years. All the applause was reserved for la Baratti, a new actress, pretty and very self-confident, who took the part of a man; an interesting touch, which no doubt contributed not a little to her popularity. She really deserved it, though, even when playing the part of a girl. The enthusiasm with which she is applauded is so great that her performances have become more and more frequent and at the time I left she was being paid 180 sequins for each production . . . They are careful to cater for the tastes of the simpler sort of person. No opera can hope to please unless it contains, among other essentials, an imaginary battle; 200 errand-boys on either side play this, though care is taken to place a number of bravos in the first row who know how to use weapons. This cannot fail to give pleasure, and at least it is not so ridiculous as our duels between Cadmus and Theseus, who slay each other while dancing. In the opera of *Parthenope* there was a most impressive cavalry action which entertained me greatly; the two generals sang a duet in perfect harmony on horseback before attacking each other, and were obviously capable of doing justice to the long harangues of the heroes in the *Iliad*. There are four operas on at the same time at four different theatres. After having tried them all, I soon abandoned three in order not to miss a single performance of *Fresquatana*, a comedy in dialect with music by Leo . . .

Naples is the capital of the musical world. It is from its numerous conservatories where they instruct youth in the art that most of the famous composers emerge; Scarlatti, Vinci, that musical god Leo, Rimaldo, Latilla and my charming Pergolesi . . .

You realize of course that the transition is quite natural, and the passage almost unnoticeable, from opera to courtesans. They are here, people claim, in even greater numbers than in Venice. They say that it is not so much the fault of the girls as of the climate, as it has been since antiquity.

[81] MUSIC AND THE SAN CARLO IN THE 1760S AND 1770S, ACCORDING TO THE CHEVALIER DE LALANDE; FROM HIS *VOYAGE D'UN FRANÇOIS EN ITALIE*.

Music is the Neapolitans' triumph. Apparently eardrums are more sensitive, more attuned to harmony, more sonorous, in this country than in the rest of Europe; the entire nation sings; gestures, inflections of voice, the way each syllable is emphasized, conversation itself, all show and manifest a sense of harmony and music. Naples is the principal source of Italian music, of great composers, and of excellent operas . . .

There are five theatres at Naples; the San Carlo, the Fiorentini, the Teatro Nuovo, the San Carlino – which is where the *opera buffa* is performed – and the Teatro del Fondo.

The San Carlo theatre adjoins the palace and is outstanding for its size among all modern Italian theatres; it has been built more or less in the taste of Turin, with Medrano as architect and Carasale as contractor . . . There is a passage to the royal palace, so that the king may go there under cover. The public reach it by large and most convenient staircases and along fine corridors . . . There are six rows of boxes which are big enough to play cards and receive visits in; there are twenty-four boxes in the first row and twenty-six in the ones above. The auditorium is so large and so high that one cannot hear some of the music . . . The theatre was beautifully decorated for the King's marriage; besides gilding and painting, the front of each box has been embellished with a looking-glass of about two feet by five. Before each of these are two candlesticks, and the candles are lit when the King is present on gala days. The partitions separating the boxes have on them mirrors four feet tall and eighteen inches wide – when it is illuminated, the room astonishes one by its magnificence . . .

In my time the leading composers at Naples were Piccinni, Sacchini, Francesco di Maio, Traetta, Guglielmi, Caffaro, Ferradini, Jommelli. The dramatic side of Italian operas accords very well with the beauty of the music, especially in the verses of Apostolo Zeno and Metastasio; the latter is the most sought-after, and no year goes by without his setting a poem to some new music, since musicians are far commoner in Italy than great poets and one may have whatever one wants in the way of music . . .

La Gabrielli, who shone at Naples in 1765, was supposed to have the finest voice in Italy. She had been at Vienna for some time, but was obliged to leave; in 1765 she was invited to Petersburg, Berlin, Genoa, Parma, and Florence, but her fees were so exorbitant and she made herself so difficult that in the end she stayed at Naples, where in any case she wanted to spend the year. She was accustomed to wear on her bosom, like some order of chivalry, the monogram in diamonds of a young nobleman with whom she was having an affair, and whom she loved to distraction. (Incidentally, at Naples one is not allowed to maintain an actress openly, nor even to go to the theatre when she is performing; if one keeps a mistress, it costs far less than it does at Paris.) At the moment la Balducci is supposed to have the finest voice, as Marchesini is among the *castrati*.

[82] THE BURNING OF THE SAN CARLO IN 1816; FROM PIETRO COLLETTA'S *STORIA DEL REALME DI NAPOLI DAL 1734 AL 1825*.

One night the magnificent theatre of the San Carlo caught fire, by accident. The few people who were there – rehearsing a play – fled in panic and their shouts and the clouds of smoke rising from the building gave the alarm. A crowd gathered from all over the city, but it was too late. The flames spread and the King and the royal family hurriedly left the palace next to the theatre. The fire took hold of the vast roof, the lurid, crackling flames being reflected up on St Elmo and in the sea down below. The spectators watched in horrified amazement. Then the sky, hitherto calm, grew overcast and flames were blown by the wind towards Castel Nuovo and actually reached its walls. Luckily the danger did not last long, since the theatre was burnt to the ground within two hours. The shortsightedness of having disbanded the fire brigade was now generally admitted, though even then the mistake was not put right.

The following day I went to see the ruins. They reminded me of ancient Rome or Paestum, though I found the spectacle still sadder because of my recent memories of Niccolini's fine painting and Rossini's music. Marble and granite burnt to powder, melted-down glass and metal, lay about everywhere.

The King [Ferdinand IV and I] gave orders for the theatre to be rebuilt as quickly as possible. In a mere four months it rose again, even more beautiful, and people could not decide which of the two monarchs had built better, father or son.

[83] NAPLES AND THE SAN CARLO IN 1817; FROM
ROME, NAPLES ET FLORENCE, BY STENDHAL.

(The novelist Stendhal (Henri Beyle, 1783–1842) had a lifelong love affair with Italy and Italian music.)

9 February. A grandiose approach: for an hour we descended down to the sea along a broad road carved out of the soft rock of which the city is built. Thickness of the walls. First building, the Albergo de' Poveri. It is very impressive indeed, much more than that loudly praised chocolate-box at Rome called the Porta del Popolo.

Here we are at the Palazzo degli Studi; turn to the left and there's Via Toledo. One of the principal objects of my journey, it is the busiest and the gayest street in the world. But would you believe it? We were running round looking for a hotel for an entire five hours; it seems that there are two or three thousand English visitors here; I am installed at last, on the seventh floor, but it's opposite the San Carlo and I can see Vesuvius and the sea.

The San Carlo not being open this evening, we hastened to the Fiorentini, a little theatre shaped like an elongated horse-shoe, with excellent music – it rather resembles the Salle Louvois in Paris. Tickets are numbered here, as at Rome, and all the front rows were taken. They were playing *Paolo e Virginia*, an opera of the moment by Guglielmi; I paid double and got a place in the second row. There was a glittering audience, all the boxes full and the ladies wearing much jewellery, and as at Milan there is a central chandelier . . .

12 February. At last, the great day when the [just rebuilt] San Carlo opens. Delightful madness, hordes of people, a dazzling audience. One had to put up with – and return – some rude pushes and shoves. I had promised myself that I would keep my temper and I managed to do so, but I lost both my coat tails. My seat in the pit cost me thirty-two carlini (fourteen francs), and my tenth share of a box in the third tier five sequins . . .

15 March. A charming ball at the Royal Palace. One had to be in fancy-dress, but soon took off one's mask. I enjoyed myself enormously from eight at night until four in the morning. All London was there; to me it seemed that the English ladies looked the most beautiful. Nonetheless there were some really lovely Neapolitans, among them that poor little Countess N. . ., who goes to see her lover at Terracina once a month. The master of the feast does not deserve those pompous phrases à la Tacitus bestowed on him throughout Europe; he is simply Squire Western in *Tom Jones* – a prince more interested in boar-hunting than in death sentences . . .

20 March. This evening, as I was going in to the San Carlo, a gend'arme ran after me to tell me to take my hat off. In a theatre four times as big as the *Paris Opéra* I had failed to notice who knows what prince.

Paris is the capital of the world, because one is never noticed there, and the court is simply an interesting spectacle.

At Naples the San Carlo opens only three times a week; already it has become no more than an unfailing meeting-place for businessmen, like la Scala. Going down the galleries, splendid titles written on the box doors tell you in large script that you are a mere atom which can be annihilated by an Excellency. If you come in wearing a hat, a hero of Tolentino will harry you. Perhaps la Conti enchants you so that you want to clap – the King's presence makes your applause sacrilege. When you want to leave your seat in the pit, you bump into some *grand seigneur* laden with orders and entangle your watch-chain with his chamberlain's key (as happened to me yesterday), and he mutters that you lack respect. Weary of so much grandeur, you go out and ask for

your conveyance; some princess's six steeds will block the gateway for
an hour, while you wait and catch a cold . . .

[84] THE FIRST PERFORMANCE OF ROSSINI'S MOSÈ IN EGITTO AT
THE SAN CARLO IN 1818; FROM STENDHAL'S LA VIE DE ROSSINI.

I have to admit that I went off to the San Carlo with strong prejudices
against the plagues of Egypt . . . The opera opens with the Plague of
Darkness, a plague which is dangerously easy for producers and on that
account ridiculous; all that is needed is to lower the footlights and dim
the lamps. I burst out laughing when the curtain went up – the
wretched Egyptians were dotted in tiny groups all over the vast stage,
deep in prayer. But I had heard a mere twenty bars of the superb introduction when all I could see was a mighty people plunged into deep
affliction, like the Marseillais praying during the plague of 1720.
Pharaoh, tamed by his people's lamentations, cries out

Venga Mosè!

Benedetti, who took the part of Moses, came on to the stage in a
sublimely simple costume which had been copied from Michelangelo's
statue in the church of San Pietro in Vincoli at Rome; he had not
addressed twenty words to the Almighty before I was overcome by
emotion; I no longer saw an old charlatan turning his rod into a serpent
and playing tricks on a fool, but a great minister of the All Powerful
making a vile tyrant tremble upon his throne. I still recall the effect of
these words:

Eterno, immenso, incomprensibil Dio!

. . . The second half of this first act went easily enough; it was the
Plague of Fire, represented by a few little fireworks. The second act,
which is about I simply don't know what plague, was very well received,

a magnificent duet being applauded to the skies; shouts of *bravo maestro, evviva Rossini*! rang out in every part of the theatre. The Crown Prince, the Pharaoh's son, is secretly in love with a young Jewess; when Moses is about to lead his people out of Egypt, the Jewish maiden comes to bid her lover farewell. Nature has never provided a better theme for a duet. If Rossini has not quite risen to the occasion with his

Principessa avventurata . . .

his attempt nonetheless reaches the listener's very soul. Mademoiselle Colbran and Nozzari sang with great verve and skill, though like the composer there was a certain lack of emotion and pathos.

In the third act, I really cannot understand why, the librettist Totola introduced the Crossing of the Red Sea without realizing that the crossing was not so easy to stage as the Plague of Darkness. Because of the shape of the auditorium in any theatre, it is only possible to depict the sea on a back-cloth, but in this case it was indispensable to produce a sea in front since the crossing had to be shown. The chief technician of the San Carlo, determined to solve an insoluble challenge, had come up with a ludicrous solution. The pit saw the 'sea' rising into the air some five or six feet higher than its 'shores'; those in the boxes, soaring above the 'waves', could see only too clearly the little *lazzaroni* who were dividing the waters at Moses' command. No-one would even have noticed at Paris: however at Naples, where *décor* is frequently splendid, there is a heightened awareness of this aspect of stage production and audiences refuse to tolerate absurdities which are too blatant and have a keen sense of the ridiculous. People laughed a great deal; their amusement was so good hearted that no-one grew angry or hissed. But no-one listened to the rest of the opera – everybody was talking about that superb introduction . . .

The following season, I am told, Moses was revived, the first act being greeted with the same enthusiasm and the Crossing of the Red Sea with the same roars of laughter. I was not there. However I found myself in Naples when a third revival was planned. The evening before this third production a friend of mine called on Rossini at about midnight, to find him lounging on his bed as usual and surrounded by at least a score of friends when, to everybody's joy, the librettist Totola burst in. Ignoring the entire company, he shouted, '*Maestro! maestro! ho salvato l'atto terzo!*' '*E che hai fatto . . .?*' [But what the devil could *you* do?] Rossini responded, imitating the man of letters' half burlesque, half pedantic manner – 'People will go on laughing at us as they always do.' 'But, *maestro*, I've written a prayer for the Jews for before the Crossing of the Red Sea.' Then the wretched librettist pulled a huge bundle of paper folded like a legal document out of his pocket and handed it to Rossini, who began to read various scribbles in the margin of the front page. While he was reading the poor librettist went round shaking hands, muttering all the time, '*Maestro, è lavoro d'un' ora.*' Rossini scowled at him: '*E lavoro d'un' ora, he!*' The unhappy librettist, trembling with fear and more than ever frightened of having a joke played on him, looked as though he wanted to sink into the ground and answered with a forced laugh, '*Si, signor, si, signor maestro!*' 'All right then, if it only took you an hour to write your prayer, it will only take me a quarter of an hour to write the music!' So saying, Rossini jumped out of bed, sat down at a desk in his nightshirt, and composed the music for Moses's Prayer in eight or ten minutes at most, with no piano and while his friends went on talking at the top of their voices as everyone does in Italy. 'Here you are, here's your music,' he said to the librettist, who vanished. Rossini jumped into bed, joining in our laughter at Totola's terror. Next day I made a point of going to the San Carlo. There was the same applause for the first act, and the same jokes and barely restrained laughter when the Crossing of the Red Sea began in the third. Indeed the pit was already starting to laugh out loud, when the audience suddenly realized that Moses was singing an entirely new aria:

Dal tuo Stella to soglio . . .

The Jews sang the chorus with Moses. Taken by surprise, the pit began to listen and the laughter stopped altogether. The chorus, which is very beautiful, is in the minor key. Then Aaron takes up the prayer and in turn the Jews sing the chorus with him. Finally Elcia, the Jewish maiden, appeals to heaven with the same supplications and again the people echo the chorus, throwing themselves on their knees and repeating the prayer fervently; the miracle is worked, the waters dividing to make a crossing for the people of the Lord. The last section is in the major key. You cannot imagine the thunder-claps which echoed throughout the entire theatre – it is amazing that it did not collapse. Those in the boxes stood up and leant out to applaud, shouting till they were hoarse. '*Bello! Bello! O che bello!*' I have never seen such a furore, nor such a triumph. It was all the greater because everyone had come prepared to laugh and make fun of the work. (*Gioacchino Rossini (1792– 1868) had nine other operas first performed at the San Carlo*).

[85] MUSIC AT THE SAN CARLO UNDER THE LATER BORBONI; FROM SIR HAROLD ACTON'S *THE LAST BOURBONS OF NAPLES*.

Compared with the eighteenth century the nineteenth was dull from an artistic point of view: except music, the fine arts suffered, as elsewhere, from the frequent political upheavals, especially from those of 1848. Literary romanticism had flowed into Rossini's *La Donna del Lago* (1819) and Donizetti's *Lucia di Lammermoor* (1835), both inspired by Sir Walter Scott, and it continued to flow with increasing fervour into the operas of the short-lived Bellini and the long-lived Verdi, whose whole career was a crescendo of masterpieces, the most popular of which, *Rigoletto, Il Trovatore* and *La Traviata*, were produced during Ferdinand II's reign. None of these composers were Neapolitans, but Bellini and Donizetti both studied and won their early plaudits in the capital. Giovanni Pacini, a Sicilian like Bellini, and the Calabrian Saverio Mercadante, were the best-known composers who settled at Naples and swayed the San Carlo audiences during Ferdinand's reign. But who now remembers *La Vestale*, once highly admired as Mercadante's masterpiece, or Pacini's *La Stella di Napoli*? Perhaps Glyndebourne will revive them in the right spirit. Enrico Petrella kept up the tradition of Paisiello and Cimarosa: he too has been forgotten, whereas *Santa Lucia* and other popular songs of the period are still universal favourites.

[86] THE REBUILT SAN CARLO OPERA-HOUSE ATTENDED BY
FERDINAND IV AND I AND THE ROYAL FAMILY IN AUGUST 1823;
FROM *THE IDLER IN ITALY* BY THE COUNTESS OF BLESSINGTON.

San Carlo is a magnificent theatre, both in size and decoration. The boxes are roomy and well ventilated, and the parterre is all divided into stalls. The royal box is in the centre of the house, and forms a very strik-ing and ornamental object. It projects considerably, is supported on gilded palm trees, and is surmounted by a large crown; from which descends, on each side, a mass of drapery, apparently of metal painted and gilt, to resemble cloth of gold, which is held up by figures of Fame. The interior is cased with panels of looking-glass; and fitted up with crimson velvet, trimmed with bullion fringe. This box is seldom occu-pied by its royal owner, or any of his family. His Majesty sits in a large private box, near the stage, attended by two officers of state. The Hereditary Prince and Princess, with their family, which is very numer-ous, occupy a very large box near that of the King. The Princess Christine looked exceedingly pretty last night; and many a furtive glance was cast towards her – a homage that did not seem offensive to her feelings, if one might judge by her countenance, although it is strongly disapproved by the elders of the royal family. Curious stories are told on this subject at Naples; and it is asserted, that more than one young noble has been advised to travel for his health, because detected in looking too often towards the pretty Christine.
(*The Princess married her cousin, Ferdinand VII of Spain, and became the mother of Queen Isabella II*).

[87] THE FIRST NIGHT OF BELLINI'S FIRST OPERA AT THE SAN
CARLO; FROM HERBERT WEINSTOCK'S *VINCENZO BELLINI*.

The first performance of *Bianca e Gernando* finally took place at the San
Carlo on May 30, 1826. The hereditary prince, Ferdinando [the future
Ferdinand II], in whose honour the grand gala was being offered, was
present, as were other members of his family, including his mother,
Queen Maria Isabella – but not his father, Francesco I, who was conva-
lescing from an illness so lingering that it had threatened to cause a
second postponement of this première. The icy Spanish etiquette that
surrounded the Bourbons required audiences not to applaud in the
sovereign's presence unless he applauded first. Florimo specified that
on the first night of *Bianca e Gernando*, applause broke out after the
section of the Bianca-Gernando duet beginning '*Deh! fa ch'io possa
intendere*' after the king had given the signal, but as the king was not
present, the applause must have been begun by either the queen or the
hereditary prince. *Bianca e Gernando* was greeted with less inhibited
enthusiasm at its next performance, and as more repetitions took place,
its tall, handsome twenty-five-year-old composer became a lion in the
Neapolitan salons. From Milan on August 4, 1828, Bellini himself
would write to Florimo: 'I remember very well, and you can too, that
Bianca made all the homes in Naples want me . . .'

(*Bellini, a Sicilian, is better known for such operas as* La Sonnambula,
Norma *and* I Puritani.)

[88] A VERDI FIRST NIGHT AT THE SAN CARLO;
FROM *GREAT OPERA HOUSES* BY S. HUGHES.

The first performance of *Luisa Miller* at the San Carlo was planned for
November 1849. Verdi was very much against going to Naples to super-
vise production; he had not enjoyed his first visit to the city and he did
not consider a second one to be necessary. Cammarano and Flauto
nevertheless persuaded him to change his mind, and Verdi set off. He

was held up in Rome, however, by a quarantine imposed owing to the spread of a cholera epidemic in many parts of Italy, and the delay postponed the production of *Luisa Miller* by a month. When at last he did arrive in Naples Verdi found the San Carlo in a very shaky financial state and one of the first things Cammarano did was to tip off the composer to make certain of being paid his three thousand ducats advance at once. Verdi demanded his advance with the clearly implied threat that if he did not receive it he would take his score and go home. This was countered by a member of the management of the theatre, the Duke of Ventignano, who sought to intimidate Verdi into giving up the score by threatening to refuse the composer a visa to leave the Kingdom of Naples. His authority for this was an unrevoked eighteenth-century law which forbade all 'artists' to leave Naples without the government's permission. Verdi, who in any case resented being classed as a comedian or a singer within the meaning of the Act, thereupon announced that, in that case, he would immediately collect himself, his opera and his belongings and take refuge on board a French warship which was in the harbour. With which the incident closed and the production of *Luisa Miller* began.

But even now the irritations and distractions did not end. There was frequently to be encountered in Naples at that time an amateur composer called Capecelatro who, though he was a great admirer of Verdi's, was nevertheless believed to possess the Evil Eye, and whose influence was considered quite definitely by Verdi's friends to have brought about the failure of *Alzira* at the San Carlo four years before. This time, however, they were determined to guard Verdi against a possible recurrence of the disaster and during his entire stay formed a human shield against the approach of *the jettatore* Capecelatro – in the streets, at the theatre, in the restaurants, up to the very door of the composer's hotel bedroom.

It seemed that the precautions taken against the Evil Eye had succeeded, for the première of *Luisa Miller* on the 8th of December, 1849, took place without incident until, when the composer was taking his bows on the stage after the second act and the bodyguard was relaxed, Capecelatro managed to break through the defence. A little while later one of the pieces of scenery fell and narrowly missed Verdi as he stood in the wings. It was also suggested that this break-through of the *jettatore* during the last interval was responsible for the comparative lack of success of the final act which followed, but evidently, like a drug or an anaesthetic, the effect of the Evil Eye wore off; on the second night and at every subsequent performance *Luisa Miller* was received with immense enthusiasm.

[89] THE LAST SEASON AT THE SAN CARLO UNDER THE BORBONI, 1859–60; FROM RAFFAELE DE CESARE'S *LA FINE DI UN REGNO*.

The season at the San Carlo began in September 1859 with *Semiramide* and also a new ballet, *Elzebel*, which was not a success. There followed *Il Trovatore* and *La Traviata*, the by now innumerable performances of which were – if the critics may be believed – starting to irritate even those with posteriors of cast iron. *Norma* did better since la Steffenoni gave still more pleasure than had la della Spezia, being equally majestic but with a far finer voice, while Negrini was a perfect Pollio. The production of an advertised new opera was advanced, though in the event Petrella's *Duca di Scilla* did not appear until 31 March. It had had great success in Milan. Hopes were high, but were not realized; not because of the singing, however, which had been entrusted to la Steffenoni, Negrini, la Paganini and Guicciardi. After running for only a single night the opera was moved to the Teatro Nuovo where it went on until May, with scarcely more success. This opera, which has been totally forgotten by the historians of music, was by a composer gifted with remarkable facility but insufficient inspiration. It has been said with truth that Petrella was always in a hurry whatever he was writing, just as he has been reproached for a Bohemian way of life which eventually led to his financial ruin and death in Genoa as a pauper. Yet his operas were full of fresh and cheerful tunes which are still alive and popular. Neither he nor Mercadante ever achieved genuine musical distinction, though occasionally they approached it. In some ways the music of both was typically Neapolitan . . .

Meanwhile there were more new ballets, *Ida di Badoero* and *Benvenuto Cellini*, in which Guglielma Salvioni made her début, so beautiful that she turned the heads of all the San Carlo's habitués until she was completely overshadowed by la Boschetti, whose performance in the ballet *Loretta l'Indovina* (choreography by Costa) was frenziedly applauded by the Neapolitans. *Loretta* was repeated again and again, and la Boschetti was recognized as the prima ballerina of the day . . . Signora Amina was then still at the height of her career; graceful, full of vivacity and charm, for more than twenty years she held sway over many hearts – in particular, it was rumoured, over that of the Count of Aquila [Francis II's uncle and a much respected admiral in the navy of The Two Sicilies].

Via Toledo and the Palace of Capodimonte

[90] THE CREATOR OF THE VIA TOLEDO, AND HIS REFORMS;
FROM L. COLLISON-MORLEY'S NAPLES THROUGH THE CENTURIES.

The most famous of all the viceroys, the Great Viceroy, as he is always
called, was Don Pedro de Toledo, Marchese di Villa-franca (1532–54).
He has left as permanent a mark upon the city as any of the kings, and
his name is commemorated in the Toledo, the Via Roma, as it is offi-
cially called to-day, still the principal street of Naples and long one of
the finest and most famous in Europe. . . .

The chief interest of Toledo's rule in Naples lies in the great reforms
he carried out in the city itself, reforms hardly less sweeping than the
'risanamento' of our own day, and far more remarkable considering the
time at which they were executed. The taxes on salt meat and fish with
which he proposed to raise the necessary funds produced riots, doubtless fomented in no small degree by the nobility, which became so serious that they were put down with difficulty, the ringleader being
executed. But Toledo was not to be daunted and soon substituted a still
heavier tax. The streets were narrow enough in all conscience, and, with
their tall buildings, seemed to have been expressly built to keep out the
sun, as is often the case in hot countries. On February 6, 1533, a decree
was issued that all balconies, permanent awnings and fixed stalls in
front of shops, which not only blocked the way and made the streets
impassable, but also afforded shelter to evil-doers, should be removed
under penalty of a heavy fine. The benefit of the change was instantane-
ous. The Viceroy himself rode in state in the sun through districts into
which it had never before penetrated. Streets were widened and straight-
ened as far as possible, while the square in front of the Castel Nuovo was
broadened and the castle walls strengthened and repaired. The whole
city was paved with lava blocks in place of the old cobbles.

More important were the new walls, which, including the sea-wall
by the Marina, were completed within two years. The old wall ran by

the Strada de' Fossi, now Gesare Rosaroll, from the Porta Capuana encircling the Duchesca, Alfonso II's charming villa. Toledo's wall then followed the Via Foria, where we still have the Porta S. Gennaro, to the neighbourhood of the Museum and to the old Porta Reale on the Toledo, where it dipped to the Largo Santo Spirito, past the existing Porta Alba. Here it turned west to the Castel S. Elmo, whence it ran south along the Pizzofalcone, enclosing S. Lucia and the Arsenal and carrying on till it reached the Castel Nuovo. It was Toledo who built the Castel S. Elmo, the bridle of the city as Evelyn calls it, well stored and garrisoned with native Spaniards, in 1537, in place of the old Angevin fort of Belforte, making it almost impregnable for those days. The water tank is almost as large as the Piscina Mirabile at Baia.

In forty years this whole new quarter was built over. Indeed, by the middle of the seventeenth century the population had risen from 50,000 to 200,000 [in reality 300,000], an increase which testified rather to the unsatisfactory condition of the provinces than to the pros- perity of the capital and which was not relished by the Viceroys, since it made the city more difficult to control. Lastly Toledo built the hand- some broad Via Toledo from the Palazzo Reale to the Largo Santo Spirito 'with a faire and large pavement to walk upon' raised on each side, as Moryson notes. The nobles slowly began to move west from the older quarters to the Toledo and the Pizzofalcone, though many still remained in their old palaces. A later Viceroy built the first bridge over the cleft in the Pizzofalcone, through which runs the Strada di Chiaia, the main artery between old and new Naples . . .

But perhaps we feel nearest the Great Viceroy in the church of S. Giacomo degli Spagnuoli by the Municipio, which he built for his coun- trymen, and dedicated to St Iago. It was the chapel of the Knights of St Iago [de Compostella] in Naples. He had the reverence of the typical Spaniard of the day and insisted upon the churches being well kept up. Some of the Viceroys even made it a practice to join in a procession if they chanced to meet the Host being carried through the streets. Here is Don Pedro's cenotaph, erected during his lifetime . . .

It was Toledo who first collected all the courts into the Castel Capuano, the Vicaria Nuova or the Vicaria as it is called . . . The old name still lingers in the '*managgia la Vicaria vecchia*' of the Neapolitan who is cursing his inability to take vengeance as he would like, a striking testimony to the terror it inspired. Here were installed the healthiest and most up-to-date prisons of the day for all classes, the dungeons of the noble being at that time, of course, very different from those for the lower orders.

[91] THE GROWTH OF THE SPANISH QUARTER AND THE ORIGINS OF THE *CAMORRA*; FROM GINO DORIA'S *STORIA DI UNA CAPITALE*.

Until the beginning of the sixteenth century Naples and the Neapolitans were very different from what evolved during the vice-royalty and still exists today [1935]. Despite continuing demolition, rebuilding, extension, adornment and decoration, the city we now see was born between 1500 and 1600; looked at as a whole, from that time forward the life of its inhabitants was much the same under the Viceroys and the Borboni, and in appearance they were much the same as we are today . . .

Partly for reasons of space, partly for work and employment, and perhaps a little from a taste of novelty, the ordinary people moved out of the traditional lower-class warrens into the new districts created during the enlargement of the city under the Viceroy Pedro de Toledo and quickly swarmed into these suburbs, despite repeated attempts to deter them. In the hilly area at the top of the new Toledo street, which was soon covered by houses and became even more crowded and dangerous than the city, they began to live in close proximity to the new rulers' soldiery, which had its headquarters and barracks there, till the neighbourhood came to be called 'The Quarter', as it is still known vulgarly today. One cannot say that the people lived altogether harmoniously with these troops, of whose ill manners, overbearing ways, and consequently well-deserved unpopularity there is plenty of evidence, frequently attested in the Spaniards' own picaresque romances;

willingly or unwillingly, they had to exist side by side, however much more the military may have taken than they contributed. (One may cite the somewhat exaggerated note struck by Traiano Boccaline in *Bilancia Politico* – 'Every vile Spanish soldier who arrives barefoot in Naples goes away clad in silk and cloth of gold.') . . . The bodies of Spanish soldiers were frequently found at the crossroads, knifed in the back, and it was very difficult to catch the culprits since, as will be seen, that *omertà* had developed which, with the criminal fraternity's secret rituals, would make the reputation (owing a good deal to legend and folk tale) of what is now the *camorra**. Such killings – carried out at night under cover of pitch darkness and in an impenetrable labyrinth formed by certain streets – were vendettas to avenge insults or affronts to family honour rather than inspired by patriotism.

[92] THE EFFECTS OF THE GREAT PLAGUE OF 1656, SEEN IN THE VIA TOLEDO; FROM *JOHN INGLESANT*, A NOVEL BY J.H. SHORTHOUSE.

(Joseph Shorthouse (1834–1903) was a chemical industrialist by profession. *John Inglesant*, published in 1881, was one of W.E. Gladstone's favourite books.)

As he entered the city, and passed through the Largo into the Strada Toledo, the sight that met his eyes was one never to be forgotten.

The streets were full of people, – more so, indeed, than is usual even in Naples; for business was at a stand, the houses were full of infection, and a terrible restlessness drove every one here and there. The stately rows of houses and palaces, and the lofty churches, looked down on a changing, fleeting, restless crowd, – unoccupied, speaking little, walking hither and thither with no aim, every few minutes turning back and retracing their steps. Every quarter of an hour or thereabouts a confused procession of priests and laymen, singing doleful and despairing

* See also page 252.

misereres, and bearing the sacred Host with canopy and crosses, came from one of the side streets, or out of one of the churches, and proceeded along the Strada. As these processions passed, every one prostrated themselves, with an excess and desperate earnestness of devotion, and many followed the Host; but in a moment or two those who knelt or those who followed rose or turned away with gestures of despair or distraction, as though incapable of sustained action, or of confidence in any remedy. And at this there could be no wonder, since this crowd of people were picking their way amid a mass of dead corruption on every side of them under their feet. On the stone pavement of the stately Strada, on the palace stairs, on the steps before the churches, lay corpses in every variety of contortion at which death can arrive. Sick people upon beds and heaps of linen – some delicate and costly, some filthy and decayed – lay mingled with the dead; they had been turned out of the houses, or had deserted them to avoid being left to die alone; and every now and then some one of those who walked apparently in health would lie down, stricken by the heat or by the plague, and join this prostrate throng, for whom there was no longer in this world any hope of revival.

This sight, which would have been terrible anywhere, was unutterably distressing and ghastly in Naples, the city of thoughtless pleasure and of reckless mirth, a city lying under a blue and cloudless sky, by an azure sea, glowing in the unsurpassable brilliancy and splendour of the sun . . .

Sick and dizzy with horror, and choked with the deadly smell and malaria, Inglesant turned into several osteria, but could find no host in any. In several he saw sights which chilled his blood. At last he gave up the search, and, weary as he was, sought the hospitals. The approaches to some of these were so blocked up by the dead and the dying who had vainly sought admission, that entrance was impossible. In others the galley slaves were at work. In every open spot of ground where the earth could be disturbed without cutting off the water pipes which ran through the city, trenches had been dug, and the bodies which were collected from the streets and hospitals were thrown hastily into them, and covered with lime and earth. Inglesant strayed into the 'Monte della Misericordia' which had recently been cleared of the dead. A few sick persons lay in the beds; but the house seemed wonderfully clean and sweet, and the rooms cool and fresh. The floors were soaked with vinegar, and the place was full of the scent of juniper, bay berries, and rosemary, which were burning in every room. It seemed to Inglesant like a little heaven, and he sank exhausted upon one of the beds. They brought him some wine, and presently the Signore di Mauro, one of the physicians appointed by the city, who still remained bravely at his post, came and spoke to him.

'I perceive that you are a stranger in Naples and untouched by the disease,' he said. 'I am at a loss to account for your presence here. This house is indeed cleared for a moment, but it is the last time we can expect help. The supply of galley slaves is failing, and when it stops entirely, which it must in a few days, I see nothing in the future but the general extirpation of all the inhabitants of this fated city . . .'

Shortly after he was gone, the crowd thronging in one direction before Inglesant's window caused him to rise and follow. He came to one of the slopes of the hill of Santo Martino, above the city. Here a crowd, composed of every class, from a noble down to the lowest lazzaroni, were engaged in the clear morning light, in building a small house. Some were making bricks, some drawing along stones, some carrying timber. A nun had dreamed that were a hermitage erected for her order the plague would cease, and the people set to work, with desperate earnestness, to finish the building. By the wayside up the ascent were set empty barrels, into which the wealthier citizens dropped gold and jewels to assist the work. As Inglesant was standing by, watching the work, he was accosted by a dignified, highly bred old gentleman, in a velvet coat and Venice lace, who seemed less absorbed in the general panic than the rest.

'This is a strange sight,' he said; 'what the tyranny of the Spaniards was not able to do, the plague has done. When the Spaniard was storming the gates, the gentleman of the Borgo Santa Maria and the lazzaroni fought each other in the streets, and the gentlemen avowed that they preferred any degree of foreign tyranny to acknowledging or associating with the common people. With this deadly enemy not only at the gates but in the very midst of us, gentlemen and lazzaroni toil together without a thought of suspicion or contempt . . .'

[Inglesant] inquired how it was that he remained so calm and unconcerned amidst the general consternation.

'I am too old for the plague,' he replied; 'nothing can touch me but death itself. I am also,' he continued with a peculiar smile, 'the fortunate possessor of a true piece of the holy Cross; so that you see I am doubly safe.'

Inglesant went at once to the harbour, musing on the way on these last words, and wondering whether they were spoken in good faith or irony.

The scenes on the streets seemed more terrible even than on the preceding day. The slaves were engaged here and there in removing the bodies, but the task was far beyond their strength. Cries of pain and terror were heard on all sides, and every now and then a maddened wretch would throw himself from a window, or would rush naked perhaps, from a house, and, stumbling and leaping over the corpses and the dying, like the demoniac among the tombs, would fling himself in desperation into the waters of the harbour, or over the walls into the moats. One of these maniacs, passing close to Inglesant, attempted to embrace a passer-by, who coolly ran him through the body with his sword, the bystanders applauding the act.

[93] PALACES IN AND NEAR THE VIA TOLEDO; FROM SIR
SACHEVERELL SITWELL'S *SOUTHERN BAROQUE ART.*

The chief palaces of Naples are in the Piazza of San Domenico, and here is the gloomy and terrible Palazzo Sansevero . . . This palace was the scene, in 1590, of a drama that should be of interest to students of music. In that year Carlo Gesualdo, third Prince of Venosa and the nephew of San Carlo Borromeo, who was then living in this palace, discovering his second wife in the act of adultery, killed her and her lover on the spot. He then fled to his castle of Gesualdo and there murdered his only son, in whose features he fancied that he recognized a resemblance to the seducer of his wife. In expiation of this deed he founded two monasteries at Gesualdo, one for Dominicans and one for Capuchins. In the church of the latter there still exists a large painting representing this double tragedy. The Prince died in Naples and is buried in the Gesù Nuovo in a chapel built at his expense from the designs of Fanzago. Ever since this sinister story the palace has been associated with bad fortune to its occupants. It is a magnificent and substantial building, and has many rooms decorated with frescoes by Belisario Corenzio; but in spite of the solidity of its appearance quite half of the building collapsed in the eighteenth century, burying many victims in its fall, and the lurid sequence was brought down to modern times by the last Duchess of Sansevero, who, while watching a procession through the square in 1878, fell from a balcony and was dashed to pieces on the paving-stones beneath. The Palazzo Maddaloni in the Toledo, now used as a bank, is the finest of this period in Naples, and has splendid frescoes by Micco Spadaro, Giacomo del Po and Francesco di Mura, for every building in these streets is a palace of some once powerful family, and their crumbling cornices and shuttered and apparently deserted interiors are in the strangest contrast to the appalling slums which are crowded into this small area of Naples. The chief streets leading round and towards the square, the Strada dei Tribunali and the Strada Trinità, have also the same huge family palaces, where in some instances, the framework of the classical entrance doors rises higher than the second floor of the mean houses on the opposite side of the street. One palace there is in particular, that of the Roccella family, where the doorway, with faun caryatides upholding its cornice, has, on either side, a fabulous monster in stone, waiting with open mouth for the letters that it should carry to the family upstairs, for they are too mythical to venture further afield than their own threshold. As if to verify this guess at their habits, from inside the court you can see another pair of monsters at the foot of the stairs, and then the staircase itself growing more fantastic at every turn, until it disappears on the lowest landing, at which level they find it possible to live safe from the crowds outside.

[94] KING FERDINAND II PUTS DOWN THE INSURRECTION
OF 15 MAY 1848 IN THE VIA TOLEDO; FROM SIR
HAROLD ACTON'S *THE LAST BOURBONS OF NAPLES.*

But already there were signs of rebellion in the streets. Barricades were being erected along the Toledo.

'These barricades were the first preparations for the funeral of liberty,' wrote General Guglielmo Pepe. 'Positive data are wanting as to their first authors, which proves that they could not have been persons of note.' The evidence points towards La Cecilia and Mileti, combined with the republican deputies and their provincial henchmen, who were most conspicuous in the ensuing struggle. They had long been itching to imitate the Parisian pioneers. Those who remonstrated with them were branded as cowards and traitors, beginning with Gabriele Pepe, commander of the national guard. Mattresses were dragged on to street balconies, doors were bolted and barred; there was a babel of shouting and hammering, digging, slamming of shutters, accompanied by drums and bugles: booths, church confessionals, chairs and stools, carts, tables, shop-signs were piled together with earth, paving stones, tiles and mortar on top of them. Several deputies ran to implore the people to pull down the barricades, but they were not listened to. The Prince of San Giacomo was forced to abandon his splendid carriage and many other proud family coaches were reduced to shambles.

The King had agreed to suppress the oath of allegiance, but he foresaw the end of his reign if he allowed himself to be blackmailed by barricades. The Princes of Ischitella and San Giacomo urged him to send troops to demolish them, but he was determined to avoid bloodshed if possible. Hence the troops were confined to barracks while the barricades increased, and it was rumoured that thousands of armed rebels were marching on the capital from Salerno. The King summoned Colonel Piccolellis of the national guard and said: 'I have discarded the oath and withdrawn the troops, yet they are still building barricades. What more do they want?' The colonel did not know what to answer, except that his efforts to restore calm had failed. Another colonel, Letizia, and the mayor Antonio Noya, asked for a few soldiers to accompany them, but the King repeated: 'No soldiers, no uniforms! The citizens themselves must do the job.' The mayor and the colonel went off again and exhausted every argument. The barricades kept on shouting: 'These are our safeguards against betrayal.' When this was reported to the King, he still refused to order the troops out. 'There is greater courage in command than in obedience,' he said, and sent word to the assembly that the opening of Parliament depended on the removal of the barricades. It was already long past midnight. All the royal family spent a sleepless night in the King's study. A ship was anchored in the bay in case they should have to escape . . .

Soon after 11 a.m. the firing began. Two shots rang out near the royal palace. One of the royal guards was killed, another fell wounded. There was a loud clapping of hands, and Mileti shouted: 'Now we're in for it, brothers. At last we can fight for ourselves and the fatherland.' Without waiting for orders, the troops camping on the square started firing at the rebels, who fired back to renewed applause from neighbouring balconies. It took half an hour to destroy the first and most solid barricade, whose defenders withdrew into the adjacent Cirella palace to discharge their weapons from padded windows. The inmates, who had felt so safe behind their mattresses, were very indignant when it was their turn to be slaughtered. The palace had seemed impregnable. Firing on the troops had been such fun while it lasted. This was not playing the game. Then the fort of Sant'Elmo thundered thrice, but only with powder, and hoisted the red flag, a signal for the garrison to take up arms. General Roberti, the commander of the fort, had refused to obey orders, preferring to lose his post, as Guglielmo Pepe wrote, 'rather than commit an infamous fratricide'; Major Zanetti obeyed in his stead. 'What are you doing?' the general asked him. 'My duty,' answered the major. But it was the general who won the plaudits of the historians. The red banner was not hoisted a moment too soon. The King, who had been watching the castle anxiously in fear of betrayal, heaved a sigh of relief . . .

The diplomatic corps had had considerable difficulty in reaching the royal palace on foot. The Spanish ambassador, acting as their spokesman, offered the King sympathy and moral support, and the King, thanking him with his hand on his heart, called Heaven to witness that all this was happening in spite of himself. 'God only knows what I suffer!' he exclaimed. This was visible in his features, for he looked haggard and worn and his hair had turned quite grey. Nobody would have suspected that he was only thirty-eight. He paced up and down the room with elephantine tread. 'From time to time Ferdinand stopped and said to those who were about him, or to such of the corps of foreign diplomatists as kept arriving – "Gentlemen, I did not expect this! I have not deserved this of my people! I have granted the Constitution, and I intend faithfully to maintain it! I have granted everything – I have done everything to avoid bloodshed; and now they blockade me and my family in my own house." When the troops moved, and the firing began at the great barricade at the end of the Toledo, scarcely two hundred yards from the palace, he was still more agitated, though evidently not by personal fear, for which there was not, during the whole day, the slightest ground. To a general officer who came up for instructions, he said, in the hearing of hundreds – 'Spare my misguided people! Make prisoners! Do not kill! Make prisoners!' A little later, when the signal-guns were first beginning to roar in the streets, a superior officer came in and asked permission to take military possession of that great pile of building . . . containing the War and Finance offices, and nearly all the public offices of state (Palazzo San Giacomo, on Piazza Municipio).

'With that building well filled with troops,' said the officer, 'I promise Your Majesty that we will soon reduce this canaille (*canaglia*) to reason.' The King stepped up to him, and putting his hand on his shoulder, said, 'Be calm, sir, and do not call the people *canaglia*! They are Neapolitans – they are my countrymen and subjects! They are misguided by a few bad men; but they are still my people!' And when the officer was taking his departure with the necessary order, Ferdinand called him back and again said, 'Be calm! If you allow yourself to be transported with passion there will be great slaughter, and this I would by all means avoid! Take prisoners, but do not kill! There are many now in the streets who by to-morrow will repent of their error!' . . .

One of the last heavy barricades stood before the fine sixteenth-century Gravina palace near Monteoliveto. This belonged to the radical deputy Giuseppe Ricciardi and served as the headquarters of the rebellious opposition. It was defended by volleys of musketry from the upper storey windows, so that when the Swiss and royal guards under Major Alessandro Nunziante were able to penetrate the courtyard they were in a vindictive mood. All the inmates caught with muskets hot in their hands were slaughtered and over fifty were arrested, though many escaped through secret passages or climbed over walls at the back as the troops entered in front. The roof caught fire – some said because the inmates had been burning seditious publications, others because the lazzaroni had thrown a fire-brand into one of the attics – and the flames destroyed the whole top floor before the troops were able to extinguish them. The smoke drifted into the hall where the deputies were sitting, some still hopeful, but most of them too bewildered to decide what to do next . . .

Most of the deputies lingered on in the hall of Monteoliveto until an officer presented himself in the King's name and ordered them to dissolve. It was about seven o'clock in the evening. They were quietly escorted to their houses by gend-armes, except the round dozen who sought asylum on French ships. Saliceti fled to Rome. The flight of these deputies seemed a spontaneous confession of guilt . . . Outside

Monteoliveto the struggle also went on till evening, when the troops laid down their arms and bivouacked along the Toledo and on various public squares. About six hundred prisoners had been taken to three frigates in the bay for their own safety; they were soon pardoned and released. The most prominent rebels had scuttled; those who remained went into hiding, shaved their long whiskers and disguised themselves as royalists. As soon as it was possible to protect property against plunder this was done, but it had been impossible to prevent pillage in the heart of attack, and the houses of prominent radicals fell a natural prey to what Pepe called 'the dregs of the populace' . . .

According to the official *Journal of the Two Sicilies*, about one hundred and thirty people were killed, but this is too conservative an estimate. A Swiss officer calculated that there were more than 1,900 victims on both sides. There were many more wounded, especially at the barricades and in the houses attacked by the Swiss, but a large number of these were treated by private doctors in great secrecy. There is no truth in the legend that the King turned to the lazzaroni and said: 'Naples is yours!' Undoubtedly the lazzaroni, who loved their King almost as much as San Gennaro, took this patriotic perquisite for granted and helped themselves . . .

When Major Nunziante reported to the King that all resistance was over, he is said to have embraced the Queen and exclaimed: 'Let us go at once and thank the Holy Virgin of the Carmine. I shall give tokens of my gratitude to all those who fought for me.' He had gained far more than he had lost on this tragic day. Since January 29 he had granted concession after concession; in spite of his private reservations he had given the liberals their chance, and what had they done with it? Owing to the mess they had made, a steady tide of opinion had turned in his favour. More and more of his subjects agreed that it would be better to restore his absolute authority.

[95] Charles III begins the Palace of Capodimonte
in 1738; from Pietro Colletta's Storia del
Realme di Napoli dal 1734 al 1825.

The King planned to build a new villa on a hill overlooking the city,
called Capodimonte, simply because he had heard that the little game-
birds known as *beccafichi* were especially plentiful there during the
month of August. The designer of the palace of Capodimonte was the
famous architect Medrano. However, when it was half built it was
found that there were vast caves below it, which had been dug long ago
to quarry tufo and rock; in consequence enormous sums had to be
spent on filling them in to prevent the building on top from collapsing,
an expenditure three times that of the work above ground. The King
grew tired of the business. There was no proper road to the palace and
the plan for constructing one was abandoned. The palace was left
unfinished. Capodimonte then seemed like some ancient monument
when seen from the city, since the half-constructed buildings looked
like a ruin. Nonetheless, the time would come when this unfinished
palace took the fancy of other kings.

[96] Dr Charles Burney visits Capodimonte in October
1770; from his *Music, Men, and Manners in France and Italy*.

In the afternoon I went with the same company [the Hamiltons] as in
the morning to Capodimonte – it was so far and so high that we went
in three calêches. It is a palace of the King of The Two Sicilies not
finished, but contains the greatest number of fine pictures I ever saw in
one collection. The cameos, too, medals, intaglios and other antiques,
are innumerable. All these belonged to the House of Farnese and came
by succession to Don Carlos [Charles III] by the Treaty of Vienna, who
brought them from the Duchy of Parma to Naples. They have not been
long here as no account of them is to be found in the old books which
describe Naples. The palace was begun in 1738. The library here is one

of the best in the kingdom, under the care of Padre della Torre, to whom I had a letter, but unluckily he is still out of town. There is on the first floor a suite of twenty-four rooms all full of excellent paintings by the first rate masters such as Raphael, Correggio, Titian, Michelangelo, Guilio Romano, P. Veronese, Albano, Parmigiano, Caracci, Guido etc. There are more Correggios and Parmigianos in this collection than in any other in the world – for which it is not difficult to account, as they were brought here from Parma . . .

The prospect of town and country at descending the stairs [is] most rich and beautiful – the fields now begin again to be green as in spring. This fine day after so much rain makes everything appear charming.

[97] OTHER RESIDENTS AT CAPODIMONTE; FROM *TRAVELS IN THE TWO SICILIES* BY HENRY SWINBURNE.

When the rainy season sets in, it commonly lasts several successive weeks, falling, not in such showers as we are acquainted with in England, where we have rain more or less every month of the year, but by pailfuls, an absolute waterspout, that carries all before it, and almost drowns the unfortunate passenger who is caught out of doors by the storm. The quantity of rain at Naples is much more considerable than that which falls on the same space of ground in England. Whole months of drought are compensated by the deluge of a day: and besides, the south winds are frequently so boisterous in winter, as to burst open the bolts of both doors and windows. At that rainy time of the year, few are so wretched and helpless as to lie in the street, but most of the vagrants resort to the caves under Capodi Monte, where they sleep in crowds like sheep in a pinfold. As they are thus provided with a dwelling, for which no rent is exacted, they also procure food without the trouble of cooking or keeping house: the markets and principal streets are lined with sellers of macaroni, fried and boiled fish, puddings, cakes and vegetables of all sorts; where, for a very small sum, which he may earn by a little labour, running of errands, or picking of pockets, the lazaro finds a ready meal at all hours: the flagon hanging out at every corner invites him to quench his thirst with wine; or if he prefers water, as most of them do, there are stalls in all the thoroughfares, where lemonade and iced water are sold.

The Seafront: the harbour, Santa Lucia, the Chiaia, Piedigrotta, and the Bay

[98] NAPLES IS BESIEGED IN 1284 BY THE GRAND ADMIRAL OF SICILY, ROGER OF LAURIA, WHO CAPTURES THE FUTURE CHARLES II; FROM SIR STEVEN RUNCIMAN'S *THE SICILIAN VESPERS*.

In May Roger took his main fleet to the Bay of Naples. The Angevins had been unable to recover Capri or Ischia. Roger used the islands as a base for raids into the bay. He occupied the little island of Nisida, off Posillipo, and anchored a squadron under its shelter, with which he could blockade the harbour. Any Neapolitan boat that ventured out into the bay was promptly captured or sunk. The blockade infuriated the Neapolitans. They demanded that the government should take action, and when it delayed they murmured of revolt. Charles of Salerno was uncertain what to do. His father, of whom he was in awe, had forbidden him to attack the enemy. The papal legate, Cardinal Gerard, who was always by his side, kept repeating his father's advice. He himself was a diffident young man. An accident in early childhood had left him lame and conscious of his weakness. He was deeply worried about the effects of the blockade. He did not know when his father would arrive. It may be, too, that he was anxious to prove to the world and to himself that despite his lameness he could fight gallantly and well.

King Charles and his fleet left Provence at the end of May 1284; but his son did not know of it. In early June, in spite of the legate's disapproval, Charles of Salerno armed the galleys that his shipyards had just completed. On Monday, 5 June he embarked with a large suite of knights, and sailed out of the harbour. He seems to have believed that Roger of Lauria's main fleet was away raiding down the coast and that he would destroy the squadron based on Nisida. But Roger, who knew that King Charles was approaching, had concentrated his forces to be ready for him. The Prince of Salerno led his ships into an enemy fleet far superior to his in numbers and in arms. The battle was brief and decisive. The Prince and comrades fought bravely, and for a moment, when they first attacked, they had some success. But they were quickly surrounded. One or two Angevin galleys were sunk; the majority were captured with their crews, and amongst them the Prince himself.

When the news of his defeat and capture was known in Naples, riots broke out. Frenchmen found in the streets were massacred and their houses were pillaged and burnt. The legate and the members of the government who had not been captured with the prince took refuge in the citadel. Other cities down the coast followed the example of Naples. Roger of Lauria, knowing that Queen Constance was anxious to secure the release of her half-sister Beatrice, Manfred's daughter by his Greek wife, sent a message to the Princess of Salerno to say that he could not answer for the prince's life unless she were handed over to him. The Princess had to comply; and Beatrice was sent on board, to enjoy her freedom after her eighteen years of imprisonment . . .

King Charles arrived with his fleet at Gaeta, the northern-most port of the Kingdom, on 6 June, the day after the disaster off Naples. He soon heard the news; and his first reaction was fury with his son. 'Who loses a fool loses nothing,' he said, and added bitterly: 'Why is he not dead for disobeying us?'

[99] THE PORT OF NAPLES IN ELIZABETHAN TIMES; FROM FYNES MORYSON'S *AN ITINERARY* . . .

Towards the south side is the haven, and beyond the bay of Naples lies firm land; for the sea coming in from the west makes this bay. Upon this side is a fortification for the safety of the haven, which is called *Il Molo* and it drives off the waves of the sea and makes the haven like a half moon, and therein at this time were twenty galleys and ten small ships. The Armoury [Arsenal] lies upon the sea, from whence the galleys and ships and land forces are armed; and among other things there is kept the rich armour (yet without any ornament of gold) of the

French king Francis I, which he did wear when he was taken prisoner at Pavia. Thereby lies a large market place, in which is a fair fountain with many images casting out water. Also there is a tower where they set light by night, to guide seamen into the haven. In the said market place is a stone upon which many play away their liberty at dice, the King's officers lending them money, which when they have lost and cannot repay, they are drawn into the galleys for the Spaniards have slaves of both sexes.

[100] THE PORT OF NAPLES IN THE LAST HALF OF THE
EIGHTEENTH CENTURY; FROM *VOYAGE D'UN FRANÇOIS
EN ITALIE* BY THE CHEVALIER DE LALANDE.

The port of Naples, which is at the eastern end of the town, is defended by a long mole which encloses it on the west and on the south, and by a short mole which defends it to the north. At the end of the mole there is a little fort called *fortozo San Gennaro*; the little mole, or *Braccio nuovo*, was built in Charles III's time, and it too is defended by a little fort. These two forts were constructed after Admiral Byng had threatened the city of Naples during the war of 1745, and had forced the ministery to sign a treaty of neutrality without allowing it time to consider the matter. The lantern or lighthouse of the port is at the entrance to the mole. The promenade along the mole is most agreeable and is much frequented after ten o'clock at night and especially at dusk. A pavilion and a fountain have been built there, with a statue holding a cornucopia.

This port can hold up to four four-decker ships of the line, but in 1765 there were only two frigates in it, together with some tartans loaded with grain. There were also two galleys in the floating-dock, the other galleys being at sea. A Genoese shipwright was about to build a ship of 70 guns at Naples, and since I was there Mr Acton has been busy strengthening the King of Naples's navy; however, at that date it consisted of one ship of the line of sixty guns, two frigates of thirty and twenty guns respectively, five galleys (of which three were off Sicily and two in the old floating-dock in Naples), four galliots or semigalleys which were in Sicilian waters, six xebecs of from eighteen to twenty guns, unusual vessels which have oars and both square and lateen rigged sails, and finally a little *galiotella* of thirty-two oars captured from the Turks. In 1784 there were two ships of the line, three frigates, eight xebecs, three brigantines and eight galliots, and they were building another frigate and another brigantine. They sent the King of Spain, for his expedition against Algiers, both ships of the line, two frigates, two xebecs and the royal galleys which normally patrol the Sicilian coast.

They are now building a large number of barges armed with cannon at Castellamare, and these will be used to defend the coast. They should be more effective than the redoubts which are much too far apart.

The Marine Academy, established at Portici some time ago, has aroused the enthusiasm of many noblemen, and the first families in the kingdom seek to place their sons there.

For merchant purposes I have only seen tartans of twenty-four feet built at Naples, which can only carry comparatively small cargoes of wheat. They use the local sycamore, masts being imported from Marseilles and Leghorn; however they build larger tartans as well, which can carry much bigger cargoes. The reason that they build so few ships, and that there are so few at Naples, is that trade there is far from considerable. Nevertheless there is such a large population and so many idle people in this great capital, that one is surprised not to see more traffic and activity. No doubt the peaceful nature, simple needs, warm climate, and fertility of the country are the basic reasons for such indolence.

The port of Naples is small, but the roadstead off Santa Lucia is very good indeed, between Castel Nuovo and the Castel dell' Ovo.

This port was never more impressive than in 1759 at the embarkation of the King of Spain [Charles III, the former King of The Two Sicilies, who had just inherited the Spanish throne]. He went on board a ship of ninety guns and was escorted by forty others, without taking

into account all the merchant vessels who took part in the farewell and
gave his departure the air of a triumph.

[101] SANTA LUCIA IN 1849; THE WORDS OF THE SONG
BY ENRICO COSSOVICH (A DALMATIAN SEA-CAPTAIN),
SET TO MUSIC BY TEODORO COTTRAU.

Il Barcaiuolo di Santa Lucia

1

Sul mare luccica
L'astro d'argento,
Placida e l'onda
Prospero e il vento.
Venite all'agile
Barchetta mia
Santa Lucia!
Santa Lucia!

2

Con questo Zeffiro
Cosi soave
Oh! com' e bello
Star su la nave!
Su passaggiere
Venite via
Santa Lucia!
Santa Lucia!

3

In fra le tende
Bandir la cena
In una sera
Cosi serena
Chi non domanda
Chi non desia?
Santa Lucia!
Santa Lucia!

4

Mare si placido
Vento si caro
Secondar far i triboli
Al marinaro
E na gridando
Con allegria
Santa Lucia!
Santa Lucia!

5

O! dolce Napoli,
O! suol beato
Ove sorridere
Volle il creato,

6

Or che tardate
Bella e la sera
Spira un auretta
Fresca e leggiera:

Tu sei l'impero   Venite all' agile
Dell' armonia!   Barchetta mia!
Santa Lucia!   Santa Lucia!
Santa Lucia!   Santa Lucia!

[102] THE ORIGIN AND AMENITIES OF THE CHIAIA; FROM
VOYAGE D'UN FRANÇOIS EN ITALIE BY CHEVALIER DE LALANDE.

The Chiaia is a still more agreeable quayside [than Platamone, adjoining and near Santa Lucia], much bigger, wider and longer; it was paved
in 1697, during the time of the Duke of Medina Celi as one reads on an
inscription. In 1779 there were planted there three rows of trees with
palings round them, protected by parapets and grilles, and embellished
by fountains, statues, trellises, lawns, flowerbeds and orange trees;
there have also been built terraces, casinos, cafés, billiard-rooms; and it
is one of the finest promenades in the whole world. The main road,
which is at the right, is for carriages. The July fair, which used to be held
on the square in front of the Castle, has been moved to the Chiaia,
where there are fireworks and music . . .

There are some very large palaces and several churches along the
road, which was once part of the quayside and where there are occasionally horse-races, as in Via Toledo.

[103] THE CHARMS OF THE CHIAIA IN THE 1790S, AS SEEN BY A
PROFESSIONAL ARTIST; FROM *SOUVENIRS* BY MME VIGÉE-LEBRUN.

(Mme Vigée-Lebrun (1755–1842), was a portrait painter and the friend
of Marie Antoinette.)

The 'quai de Chiaja' was always so lively that it never ceased to offer me
any number of amusing spectacles, whether lazzaroni coming to refresh
themselves at a beautiful fountain in front of my windows, or young
laundresses washing their linen there. On Sundays young peasants in

their best clothes danced the tarantella in front of my house, beating a little drum, and every evening I could see fishermen, the flames from their torches reflected in the sea. Behind my bedroom there was an open gallery which looked on to a garden filled with orange-trees and lemon-trees in flower. However, as with everything, there were inconveniences to my room and I had to take notice of one in particular. For several hours each morning I dared not open my windows over the quay, since an itinerant kitchen had been set up below me, where women cooked tripe in great cauldrons with bad oil, whose odour ascended. I was therefore reduced to looking at the sea through my shutters. But how beautiful it is, the sea at Naples. Often I spent whole hours watching it during the night, when the waves were calm, silvery in the splendid moonlight. Often too I used to take a boat for an excursion and enjoy the magnificent spectacle presented by this city which one always sees in its entirety, like some amphitheatre. Sir William Hamilton had a little cottage on the shore, where I sometimes dined. Small boys came and dived into the sea for several minutes for a halfpenny, and just at the moment when I began to be afraid for them, would surface with the halfpennies in their mouths.

At the Chiaia there is the Villa Reale, a public garden by the side of the sea which is delicious to walk in during the evening. The Farnese Hercules had been placed in the garden; as the statue's original legs had been discovered, they had been put back instead of the replacements made by Michaelangelo. However the latter had been left by the side of the statue so that one could compare them and acknowledge the sublime superiority of the Antique over even Michaelangelo . . .

I had to leave my beloved Hôtel de Maroc, because although one had so much to admire from it during the day, it was very different at night and impossible for me to close my eyes. Carriages went to and fro along the Ghiaia to the Grotto at Posillipo where there were disreputable supper parties in the taverns. The noise, which I had to suffer every night, at last made me leave my hôtel. I moved to a pretty little cottage lapped by the sea, whose waves broke beneath my windows. I was enchanted; this smooth, gentle noise lulled me to sleep deliciously. Alas, a week later there was the most dreadful storm, a tempest so violent that the wild waves actually poured into my room. I was swamped, and fear of a recurrence made me leave my charming cottage, much to my regret. Moreover between the sea wall and my house there was a space where elegant carriages, the same vehicles which had prevented me from sleeping over the Chiaia, used to park for what one calls at Naples 'faire heure'.

[104] SIR WILLIAM HAMILTON AND EMMA HART AT THE PALAZZO SESSA IN CAPPELLA VECCHIA A CHIAIA, IN THE SPRING OF 1787; FROM *ITALIÄNISCHE REISE* BY WOLFGANG GOETHE.

(Wolfgang Goethe (1749–1832), one of the greatest European writers, left in his *Italian Journey* a vivid testimony to the cultural impact of Naples on late-eighteenth-century visitors – whether they were addicts of the Neo-Classical or forerunners of the Romantic.)

Sir William Hamilton, who is still here as the English Minister, has finally, after a life devoted to art and scholarship, discovered one of the greatest of nature-lovers and of art-lovers in the person of a beautiful young woman. She lives with him, an English girl of about twenty. She is very beautiful, with a lovely figure. The old gentleman has had an ancient Greek dress made for her, which suits her remarkably well. Robed in this, letting down her hair, and taking two shawls in her hands, she adopts every conceivable pose, attitude, and facial expression, until those who watch her all but think themselves in a dream. One sees in her everything that the greatest artists have delighted in portraying, whether in movement or aspect, and to perfection. Standing, on her knees, sitting, reclining, sad and serious, playful, joyful, penitent, lascivious, threatening, anxious – each mood succeeds the other in quick succession. With exquisite taste she adapts the shape of her veil to each mood, and turns it into every conceivable sort of head covering. The old gentleman holds up a lamp for her, joining in the performance with total enthusiasm. He professes to detect a resemblance in her to every celebrated antique, including the lovely profiles on Sicilian coins and even the Apollo Belvedere. At any rate, it is certainly unique as an entertainment. We spent two whole evenings watching it and thoroughly enjoyed ourselves. Tischbein is busy painting her today . . .

Sir William Hamilton has succeeded in living in this city for many years and now, in the evening of his life, is reaping a rich reward for it. His rooms, which he has furnished in the English fashion, are quite delightful and the vista from a room at the corner of the palace is unsurpassed. Below is the sea, with Capri and Posilippo on the right and the promenade along the Villa Reale between one and the Grotto: on the left is an old convent which once belonged to the Jesuits and after that the coast from Sorrento to Cape Minerva . . . Hamilton is a man of the most consummate taste, and after exploring everything created has at last discovered a masterpiece of nature in the shape of a lovely woman . . .

Hamilton and his beautiful companion continue to be most friendly. I dined with them and Miss Hart showed off her playing and singing in the evening light.

Through Hackert's good offices – his kindness towards me increases every day and he would like me to see everything worth while – Hamilton took us into his secret store-room. There was an amazing mixture of objects there, the artefacts of every age heaped one on top of the other, heads, busts, vases, bronzes, various types of lamps of Sicilian agate, even an entire small chapel, sculpted and painted, and many other things which had come into his possession by haphazard buying. Seeing a long packing case on the floor with its lid unfastened, I was curious enough to open it and found two splendid bronze candelabra. I discreetly drew Hackert's attention to it and whispered that they looked exactly like some at Portici.

[105] THE FEAST OF PIEDIGROTTA, ONE OF THE GREAT ROYAL
SPECTACLES OF NAPLES, AS SEEN BY THE CHEVALIER DE LALANDE
IN 1765; FROM HIS *VOYAGE D'UN FRANÇOIS EN ITALIE*.

The church of Santa Maria di Piedigrotta is situated in the Strada di
Pozzuoli, so called because it is near the famous grotto cut through
the mountain to reach Pozzuoli; this church is occupied by canons
regular of St John Lateran; it was built in 1351 through the piety of
three people who were convinced that they had had a miraculous
vision on 8 September, in which they had been commanded to build
the church.

Every year, on the same day, there is a procession there which is
one of the most celebrated in Naples. I watched it on 8 September
1765. It was a very fine day and everything helped to enhance the
feast's splendour; they had suspended Court mourning so that jewels
and dress would make the festivity still more brilliant. There were
10,000 men under arms. The King [Ferdinand IV and I], preceded by
a dozen state coaches, arrived in ceremony two hours before sunset to
attend the church of Piedigrotta and pay homage to the Virgin. All the
balconies were hung with carpets and the whole of the shore of the
Ghiaia was crowded with people. One cannot conceive a setting more
suited for so immense a multitude of spectators and soldiers; ships
standing just off the shore, flying their pennants and firing their
cannon, contributed to the striking impression. Everybody is anxious
to watch the ceremony; there are apartments which are let for 200
livres for that day, which otherwise cost no more than 300 for the
entire year. People of quality who do not live at the Ghiaia give dinner
parties in rented apartments, and it is even claimed in Naples that
country menfolk sometimes have a clause inserted in their marriage
contracts that they are to take their wives to Naples on the day. A
glimpse of the spectacle is well worth putting on canvas, and indeed I
have seen such a picture by the theatrical designer Don Antonio Joly.
The year I was there, the Princess de la Torella was planning to give a

ball that evening at her palace on the Chiaia; but the Duke of Monteleone's death made it necessary to cancel the invitations which had already been sent out.

The miraculous statue which has made the reputation of the church of Piedigrotta is on the high altar. The devotion of the Neapolitans to this Madonna is very great, and crowds flock there, especially on Saturdays; passing ships are accustomed to fire salutes. On the Sunday of the Octave the entire church is decorated, and fireworks are set off in the streets.

[106] AN ACCOUNT OF PIEDIGROTTA, VISITED IN 1823; FROM
THE IDLER IN ITALY BY THE COUNTESS OF BLESSINGTON.

9 September. Went yesterday to see the procession of the Fête de St Maria Piedigrotto, considered to be one of the most splendid of the Neapolitan religious festivals. Balconies commanding views of the procession were in great request, and large sums were demanded for them. The Austrian troops at present occupying Naples, and amounting to about fourteen or fifteen thousand men, formed a part of the *cortège*, and added considerably to the grandeur of its effect. The royal family, followed by the ladies and officers of the court, filled about forty state coaches, drawn by eight, six, and four horses; and attended by innumerable running footmen, in quaint, but very rich liveries, wearing black velvet caps, similar to those of huntsmen. The royal *cortège* was preceded and followed by the troops, and advanced at a slow pace from the Palace, along the Ghiaja, to the Chapel of the Grotto. The streets were crowded with peasants in their richest costumes, and with lazaroni, more remarkable for the picturesqueness than neatness of theirs. The dresses of the female peasants of the various districts in the kingdom of Naples might here be seen; and presented a rich galaxy of the brightest colours, mingled with ornaments of pearl, coral, and gold. The effect was beautiful, conveying the impression of some vast *bal costumé*, rather than of the real dresses worn by peasants. As my eyes

glanced over the Chiaja, and I saw the sunbeams sparkling on the rich and picturesque groups beneath, I could have fancied them an immense moving bed of tulips; so gorgeous and various were the hues they presented. The carriage of the King was one surface of highly-burnished gilding. It was surmounted by plumes of snowy feathers, as were also the eight horses by which it was drawn. Pages, in the dresses of the olden time, walked by the side of the carriage, and outside these moved the running footmen.

[107] THE FINAL ROYAL *FESTA* AT PIEDIGROTTA; FROM SIR HAROLD ACTON'S *THE LAST BOURBONS OF NAPLES*.

The last of the Piedigrotta festivals on a majestic scale was celebrated on September 8, 1859. All the bells in the city pealed frantically on that morning when the sacred and profane were blended with traditional exuberance, and there was a vast pilgrimage towards the Queen of Neapolitan Madonnas. In the afternoon 47 battalions, 33 squadrons and 64 pieces of artillery took part in the parade before the royal palace, and such a variety of scintillating uniforms was not to be seen there again, royal guards in scarlet with bearskin caps, Calabrians in green, cuirassiers in gleaming armour, hussars in white jackets, dusky Sicilians and sturdy mariners, who lined the whole way to the church at Piedigrotta. Bands played on the square and accompanied the march with tunes grave and gay. A flotilla with a forest of little flags was moored at Mergellina. Naval guns answered those of the five castles as the royal procession advanced very slowly beside the sea: first a squadron of the guard of nobles mounted on their own fine steeds, then halberdiers from the castle garrisons on foot, then a lumbering rococo ceremonial coach quite empty with footmen behind it, followed by eight carriages with six horses to each containing court chamberlains emblazoned with insignia, then the King and Queen in a high carriage drawn by eight thoroughbreds, the King stiff with regalia, the Queen Titania-like with a diamond tiara. Two companies of bodyguards followed, and twelve more carriages containing the King's brothers, uncles and suite with another squadron of guards wound up the procession. Each carriage stopped at the church, and it was dusk when all returned after their orisons.

Thousands came in from the country for this annual event, and the gaudy costumes of the peasantry in festive mood, as well as the red-capped fishermen and street urchins in improvised fancy dress and vendors of refreshments, added colour and noise to a scene peculiarly animated even for Naples. Drums, trumpets, tambourines and fire-crackers heightened the Babel of shrill and raucous voices. The taverns adorned with trellises of foliage did a roaring trade, but there was little drunkenness as in northern cities, though censorious foreigners pretended to be shocked 'to behold a whole people, and a people professing Christianity, thus giving themselves up to all manner of ungodliness and gross indulgence'. Towards evening the street urchins ran about with paper lanterns on sticks, and there was much dancing and singing and fun in the Posillipo grotto. The garden of the [Royal] Villa was open to all and many spent the night there, with considerable damage to the flower-beds. It was essentially a popular festival, a September Saturnalia. Shorn of its official pageantry [after 1860] it languished until it was artificially revived as a festival of Neapolitan song towards 1880, when *Funiculi, Funiculà* spread its fame to the ends of the earth.

[108] THE FUTURE LADY COMPANION TO PRINCESS CHARLOTTE
OF WALES WATCHES ADMIRAL NELSON'S FLEET ARRIVING IN
THE BAY OF NAPLES IN 1798, AFTER THE BATTLE OF THE
NILE; FROM CORNELIA KNIGHT'S *AUTOBIOGRAPHY* . . .

Two ships of the line at length appeared in sight. The weather was particularly calm, and a great number of boats went out to meet them, conveying not only English residents, but many of the natives likewise. The king himself went in his barge, followed by a part of his band of music in another, and several of the foreign ministers and others joined in the glad procession. I was with Sir William and Lady Hamilton in their barge, which also was followed by another with a band of musicians on board. The shore was lined with spectators, who rent the air with joyous acclamations, while the bands played 'God save the King' and 'Rule Britannia.' . . .

The King of Naples did not go on board either of the ships, but from his barge saluted the officers on deck. His Majesty had expressed his desire to be incognito, so as not to give the trouble of paying him the usual honours. Sir William Hamilton, observing some of the seamen looking earnestly out of the portholes, said to them, 'My lads! that is the king whom you have saved, with his family and kingdom.' Several of the men answered, 'Very glad of it, sir – very glad of it.'

Two or three days later (September 22) the *Vanguard*, with the flag of Sir Horatio Nelson, came in sight; and this time the concourse of barges, boats and spectators was greater than before. The *Vanguard* was followed by two or three ships of the line, which had been in the engagement. It would be impossible to imagine a more beautiful and animated scene than the bay of Naples then presented. Bands of music played our national airs. With 'God save the King' they had long been familiar, but for the present occasion they had learned 'Rule Britannia' and 'See the conquering hero comes'. . . .

We rode out to a considerable distance, following the king, who was anxious to greet his deliverers, as he did not scruple to call them. Sir Horatio Nelson received his Majesty with respect, but without embarrassment, and conducted him over every part of the vessel, with which he seemed much pleased, and particularly so with the kindness and attention shown to the wounded seamen, of whom there were several on board. The king afterwards sat down with us to a handsome breakfast . . .

Nothing could be more gay than Naples at that period. All anxiety and fears were forgotten. Nor was the homage paid to our admiral confined to the higher classes. It was impossible for him to appear in the streets without being surrounded and followed by crowds of people, shouting out 'Viva Nelson!'

[109] ADMIRAL NELSON DESCRIBES HIS ARRIVAL AT NAPLES ON 22 SEPTEMBER 1798 AFTER THE BATTLE OF THE NILE; FROM *THE LETTERS AND DESPATCHES OF VICE-ADMIRAL LORD VISCOUNT NELSON* BY SIR HARRIS NICOLAS.

Sir William and Lady Hamilton came out to sea, attended by numerous boats with emblems etc. They, my most respectable friends, had nearly been laid up and seriously ill; first from anxiety, and then from joy. It was imprudently told Lady Hamilton in a moment, and the effect was like a shot; she fell apparently dead, and is not yet perfectly recovered from severe bruises. Alongside came my honoured friends: the scene in the boat was terribly affecting; up flew her Ladyship, and exclaiming, 'O God! is it possible?' she fell into my arm more dead than alive. Tears, however, soon set matters to rights; when alongside came the King. The scene was, in its way, as interesting; he took me by the hand, calling me his 'Deliverer and Preserver', with every other expression of kindness. In short, all Naples calls me 'Nostro Liberatore'; my greetings from the lower classes was truly affecting. I hope some day to have the pleasure of introducing you to Lady Hamilton; she is one of the very best women in this world; she is an honour to her sex. Her kindness, with Sir William's, to me, is more than I can express . . .

[110] ADMIRAL NELSON EXECUTES PRINCE FRANCESCO CARACCIOLO, FORMER COMMANDER-IN-CHIEF OF THE NAVY OF THE PARTHENOPEAN REPUBLIC, IN THE BAY OF NAPLES IN 1799; FROM ROBERT SOUTHEY'S *LIFE OF NELSON*.

(Robert Southey (1774–1843), who was made Poet Laureate in 1813, published his immensely successful biography of Nelson two years earlier.)

*　　*　　*

Caracciolo was brought on board at nine in the forenoon, and the trial
began at ten. It lasted two hours. He averred in his defence that he had
acted under compulsion, having been compelled to serve as a common
soldier till he consented to take command of the fleet. This, the apolo-
gists of Lord Nelson say, he failed in proving. They forget that the possibility of proving it was not allowed him, for he was brought to trial
within an hour after he was legally in arrest; and how, in that time, was
he to collect his witnesses? He was found guilty, and sentenced to
death; and Nelson gave orders that the sentence should be carried into
effect that evening, at five o'clock, on board the Sicilian frigate *La
Minerve*, by hanging him at the fore-yard-arm till sunset, when the body
was to be cut down and thrown into the sea. Caracciolo requested
Lieutenant Parkinson, under whose custody he was placed, to intercede with Lord Nelson for a second trial – for this, among other reasons,
that Count Thurn, who presided at the court-martial, was notoriously
his personal enemy. Nelson made answer that the prisoner had been
fairly tried by the officers of his own country, and he could not interfere, forgetting that if he felt himself justified in ordering the trial and
the execution, no human being could ever have questioned the propriety of his interfering on the side of mercy. Caracciolo then entreated
that he might be shot. 'I am an old man, sir,' said he [he was forty-
seven]; 'I leave no family to lament me, and therefore cannot be
supposed to be very anxious about prolonging my life, but the disgrace
of being hanged is dreadful to me.' When this was repeated to Nelson,
he only told the lieutenant, with much agitation, to go and attend his
duty. As a last hope Caracciolo asked the lieutenant if he thought an
application to Lady Hamilton would be beneficial. Parkinson went to
seek her. She was not to be seen on this occasion – but she was present
at the execution. She had the most devoted attachment to the
Neapolitan court; and the hatred which she felt against those whom
she regarded as its enemies made her at this time forget what was due
to the character of her sex, as well of her country. Here also a faithful
historian is called upon to pronounce a severe and unqualified

condemnation of Nelson's conduct. Had he the authority of His Sicilian
Majesty for proceeding as he did? If so, why was not that authority
produced? If not, why were the proceedings hurried on without it? . . .

The body was carried out to a considerable distance, and sunk in the
bay, with three double-headed shot, weighing two hundred and fifty
pounds, tied to its legs. Between two and three weeks afterwards, when
the king [Ferdinand IV] was on board the *Foudroyant*, a Neapolitan fisherman came to the ship, and solemnly declared that Caracciolo had
risen from the bottom of the sea, and was coming as fast as he could to
Naples, swimming half out of the water. Such an account was listened
to like a tale of idle credulity. The day being fair, Nelson, to please the
king, stood out to sea; but the ship had not proceeded far before a body
was distinctly seen, upright in the water, and approaching them. It was
soon recognized to be, indeed, the corpse of Caracciolo, which had
risen and floated, while the great weights attached to the legs kept the
body in a position like that of a living man. A fact so extraordinary
astonished the king, and perhaps excited some feeling of superstitious
fear akin to regret. He gave permission for the body to be taken on
shore and receive Christian burial.

[111] The water fête given by Ferdinand IV and
I for the ex-Empress Marie-Louise (Napoleon's
young widow) in August 1824; from *The Idler
in Italy* by the Countess of Blessington.

Last night, I witnessed one of the most beautiful scenes imaginable. It
was a sort of fête offered to Marie Louise, by the King of Naples, and
took place on the water. Never was there a more propitious night for
such a festival, for not a breeze ruffled the calm bosom of the beautiful
bay, which resembled a vast lake, reflecting on its glassy surface the
bright sky above, which was glittering with innumerable stars. Naples,
with its white colonnades, seen amidst the dark foliage of its terraced
gardens, rose like an amphitheatre from the sea; and the lights

streaming from the buildings on the water, seemed like columns of gold. The Castle of St Elmo crowned the centre of the picture; Vesuvius, like a sleeping giant in grim repose, stood on the right, flanked by Mount St Angelo, and the coast of Sorrento fading into distance; and on the left, the vine-crowned height of the Vomero, with its palaces and villas, glancing forth from the groves that surround them, was crowned by the Mount Camaldoli, with its convent spires pointing to the sky. A rich stream of music announced the coming of the royal pageant; and proceeded from a gilded barge, to which countless lamps were attached, giving it, when seen at a distance, the appearance of a vast shell of topaz, floating on a sea of sapphire. It was filled with musicians, attired in the most glittering liveries; and every stroke of the oars kept time to the music, and sent forth a silvery light from the water which they rippled. This illuminated and gilded barge was followed by another, adorned by a silken canopy, from which hung curtains of the richest texture, partly drawn back to admit the balmy air. Cleopatra, when she sailed down the Cydnus, boasted not a more beautiful vessel; and as it glided over the sea, it seemed excited into motion by the music that preceded it, so perfectly did it keep time to the delicious sounds, leaving behind it a silvery track like the memory of happiness. The King himself steered the vessel; his tall and slight figure gently curved, and his snowy locks falling over ruddy cheeks, show that age has bent but not broken him. He looked simple, though he appears like one born to command; a hoary Neptune, steering over his native element: all eyes were fixed on him; but his steadily followed the glittering barge that preceded him. Marie-Louise was the only person in the king's boat; she was richly dressed, and seemed pleased with the pageant. In-numerable vessels, filled with the lords and ladies of the court followed, but intruded not on the privacy of the regal bark, which glided before us like some gay vision or dream.

[112] THE SEAFRONT AT NAPLES, WITH WOMEN DANCING
THE TARANTELLA, IN MAY 1858; FROM FREDRIKA
BREMER'S *TWO YEARS IN SWITZERLAND AND ITALY.*

(Fredrika Bremer (1810–65) was a Swedish novelist and Lutheran
evangelist of international fame, whose particular interest was the
emancipation of women.)

Yesterday the eruption increased considerably, and the torrents of lava
have advanced. Towards evening I wandered along the shore in the
direction of Posilipo, just opposite Vesuvius. One could see the streams
of fire like fiery-hot serpents crawling down its sides, and the flames
ascended out of the hollow between the two mountains. It looked like
a burning city in the bosom of the mountain; it was magnificent but
terrible! A number of people were standing on the quay gazing on the
scene. I entered into conversation with some of them, and found all
particularly willing to communicate all they knew. The Hermitage was
said to be surrounded by the torrents of lava; the hermit had fled; many
vineyards and olive-groves were already destroyed. It was feared that
during the night the fire would advance to Barra – a village above
Portici – and the inhabitants of the surrounding farms had fled. Fears
were entertained also for Portici. Fire was seen now and then to issue
from the crater on the summit of the cone, and great devastation was
apprehended.

In the midst of this spectacle and its dangers, carriages were circling
round on the broad Chiaja, in unimpeded career and gaiety. There is
every afternoon a regular stream of carriages, greater and less, from the
Viennese carriage to the corricolo, with from twenty to five-and-twenty
persons, after one horse, and people of all classes, from princes and
princesses to girls, boys, and sailors. It is especially the equipages of the
latter, their horses adorned with feathers and finery, which you now
and then see driving madly in the endeavour the one to pass the other.
The drivers shriek and shout; the vehicles drive along three or four

abreast. Pedestrians were fewer in number and behaved quietly, all except the boys, who seem to me here to be a kind of quadruped, continually lying in the streets amidst the tumult, the wild career, or the affrays.

Another lively scene also presented itself here within view of the flames of Vesuvius. A young girl entered an open space on the Chiaja, beating the basque upon an old tambourine, to a lively and marked tune; she took her stand under a tree and began to sing as she beat her tambourine. Immediately a circle of girls was formed round her, together with children better or worse clad. Two ragged girls began to dance with castanets; two others followed their example, well-dressed and handsome, who struck the castanets extremely well, and danced well also. Many came in the same way, the castanets passing from one pair to another. Nurse-maids came up, placed their little ones in other women's arms, and went in for a dance for a moment; then resumed their infants, kissed them, and looked on whilst the others danced. The tambourine, like the castanets, went from hand to hand: they who beat the former, also sometimes sang a monotonous, unmelodious, but rhythmical song. At length the dancers amounted to above a dozen young women, who evidently were all dancing for their own hearts' joy and pleasure, whilst older and younger sailors stood smoking at some distance, without, in the slightest degree, disturbing the girls, whose dance – a kind of tarantella – they seemed to watch with pleasure, but as an every-day affair.

Very few persons, comparatively speaking, seemed to pay Vesuvius a certain fearful attention, whilst the twilight increased and lava-streams glided more brightly, and the flames tinged the clouds of smoke crimson. The carriages rolled on uninterruptedly and the girls danced.

[113] THE NEAPOLITAN SEAFRONT TWENTY-FIVE YEARS
AFTER THE BORBONI'S DEPARTURE; FROM AUGUSTUS
HARE'S *CITIES OF SOUTHERN ITALY AND SICILY*.

Travellers who have known Naples before the time of the present
government will miss many of its familiar and characteristic features,
which have been annihilated by the sea-wall along the Chiaja, and the
destruction of the greater part of the beautiful Villa Reale. The old
historic Neapolitan names have also been changed to foolish
Piedmontese appellations, which are utterly meaningless here, and
even the 'larghi, strade, vichi, calate', so characteristic of Naples, have
become 'piazze, vie, vicoli,' under the Sardinian rule. At the same time
Naples owes to the present government its magnificent drive along the
Vomero.

Many of the national characteristics of the lower classes, of which
we read so much in books of travels, have disappeared since the union
of Naples with the north Italian kingdom, but a few remain. Crowds
still listen on the quays to *Improvisatori* or to men in rags who recite
whole cantos of *Orlando Furioso* to a delighted audience, which will
adjourn afterwards to admire the antics of *Pulcinella*. The *Acquaiuoli*
still shout; *Scrivani Pubblici* or Public Letter-Writers still pursue their
avocation in the arcades near the Piazza del Municipio; the *Caprajo* still
drives his goats twice a day through the streets, and milks them under
your windows, or on your staircase; men still become frantic over *Mora*;
women still dance the *Tarantella* (but for money) to a tambourine . . .
But the *Calessini* no longer dash along the Mergellina as they did in the
time of the Bourbons, with from twenty to twenty-four passengers
inside, and a beggar or two taking the air (and the dust) for half a grano
in the net underneath, the single horse going faster the more it was
pulled, and being stopped by a hiss. The *King of the Thieves* no longer
holds his sway unmolested, and is no longer bargained with for enforc-
ing the restoration of articles stolen by his subjects. Above all, the
Lazzaroni are all but extinct, that marvellous under-population of the

Marinella and Mergellina . . . The better class of Lazzaroni were those of the port, who were for the most part hard-working and industrious, though their especial *métier* was to cheat, and they were often excessively violent. Intensely superstitious, they were always ready to take up arms in defence of their saints, if they thought that their festas or shrines were endangered; but they were also loyal subjects of their king.

The approaches to Naples

The Palace of Caserta

[114] THE BUILDING OF THE PALACE OF CASERTA
BY CHARLES III; FROM PIETRO COLLETTA'S STORIA
DEL REALME DI NAPOLI DAL 1734 AL 1825.

Charles wished to be no less magnificent than his ancestors in their palaces of Versailles and the Escorial, and to build an equally splendid palace somewhere safer than the vicinity of Vesuvius and less liable to any attack by well-armed seaborne enemies. He therefore selected a site in the plain of Caserta, some fourteen miles outside Naples. An ancient town of this name, Casa Erta, founded by the Lombards, still existed on a mountainside nearby, where a few houses amid the ruins sheltered a handful of inhabitants, who preferred the rubble of their old homes to any new city, however comfortable or imposing. Since all the famous architects had died or were too old, and Carasale was in prison, and there was no-one else in the kingdom with sufficient talent, Charles sent to Rome for a Neapolitan called Luigi Vanvitelli who was already celebrated for his work and was considered to be the best architect in Italy. The palace was designed to occupy an area of 415,939 Paris square feet, with an elevation of 106 feet [one Paris foot = 32.47 centimetres]. The outside of the building was decorated with splendid columns, massy arches, great statues and sculpture in marble, while a bronze statue of Charles on horseback was set on the façade in front.

Inside the palace there are statues and rare marbles and also paintings, all by the best artists of the time. The decorations include inlay in rare woods, plaster-work, crystal illuminations, wall-paintings, and marble and mosaic pavements in addition to precious marbles; and the building can claim to embody to perfection all the arts of its day. On three sides it is flanked by closed courtyards or wings, but on the fourth side a vast garden stretches into the distance, beautifully decorated with obelisks, statuary, marble staircases and gushing fountains which are embellished with statues. A stream, beginning as a waterfall and then gradually levelling out until it flows into a lake out of which it runs in streamlets, is to be seen flowing down the hill opposite; which is laid out like some English garden, and is a combination of truly regal art with all the benefits of a mild climate, fertile soil and seemingly never-ending spring.

The water for all this is transported from Monte Taburno along an aqueduct twenty-seven miles long, which crosses the Tifatine hills and three deep valleys, flowing through canals carved out of the rock or over tall and massive bridges. The one over the Maddaloni valley is 1,618 feet in length and rests on piers thirty-two feet thick; it is constructed in three arched tiers which rise to a height of 178 feet. Unless one knew from the inscription on the stonework, and if people had forgotten, one would think it dated from Roman times, so massive and daring is its design. After irrigating and adorning the gardens and the palace at Caserta, the water then flows underground until it mingles with that of Carmignano. It then goes on to Naples, where it provides a more than adequate water supply, however big the city.

[115] Caserta as seen by Sir Sacheverell Sitwell; from his *Southern Baroque Art*.

It is the work of slaves, some of them negro, but in great proportion European. This last great work of slave labour is heartless, as you would expect. The staircase, with its ceremonial landing, the chapel and the theatre are famed for their marbles. The stair is formed of single blocks of the Sicilian marble of Trapani, called Lumachella; on each landing are marble lions, distinctly to be known as such. On the side walls are to be seen the best breccias of Dragoni and the marbles of Vitulano *in principato ulteriore*. There are twenty-four Ionic pillars adorning the centre of the vestibule made of the red breccia of Mons Garganus, in Apulia, and sixteen of the porticoes are of the yellow breccia of the same mountain. The marbles of the theatre were, in large part, stolen from the Temple of Serapis, at Pozzuoli. The porticoes leading through the house recall drawings by Bibbiena. Beyond them lie the gardens, rising for two miles up a hill, and of such length as to necessitate a carriage. The innumerable groups of statuary on successive landings along the cascade become monotonous. The water drips down slowly past you, passing from basin to basin, between the two straight roads that border it. Arriving at last at the height of the hill, where a mere fall of water into the topmost basin precipitates this small avalanche, there awaits you the biggest and most imposing of the statue groups. But it is the view when you turn round on your ascent which is the culmination of this immense work. Very far down the avenue, just filling the space between its two arms, lies the palace, absolutely still and uninhabited.

[116] THE BORBONE KING LEAVES THE PALAZZO
REALE FOR CASERTA; FROM SIR SACHEVERELL
SITWELL'S SOUTHERN BAROQUE ART.

Long before the tail of the procession left the palace, the report of the guns would roll up the long avenues to the model town of Caserta. Great numbers of lazzaroni ran beside the King's coach, picking up the coins he threw to them and joking with him in their dialect, which he spoke like a native. Before the two hours of the journey were up, the Mayor and Corporation of Caserta were waiting some half-mile from the entrance to the palace. The Mayor would leave his tall glass coach and wait on foot, talking to the most influential of the councillors. The procession looked as if halted half-way down the avenue, so slow was their progress. But, of a sudden, they were within a hundred yards, and the rattle of wheels came louder and louder. Just before it was loud enough to drown all other sounds some white puffs of smoke jumped into the air, far away back in the bay, and the report of guns arrived very slowly and menacingly. By this time the escort of cavalry, crowing their trumpets like a farmyard, were already past, and a great many outriders and postillions pulled the King's carriage to a halt. It was just like an arrival by canal. The Mayor made an obsequious speech, thanking the Royal family for benefits conferred on the borough by their choice of a residence. The King grunted a few words in reply in the Neapolitan dialect. Then the procession moved on again. The coaches containing the Royal children and court ladies flashed along the dusty roads like raindrops rolling down a window. With an immense rumble they all arrived safely in the main courtyard of the palace. The Mayor and his attendants arrived last in their coach; they climbed out and, going through a small side door, were supplied with wine and refreshments by the King's order.

During the summer Caserta experienced great increase in population. Beside the regiment of foot and a squadron of cavalry the town was lively with the uniform, dating from Philip IV's days, of the Royal Halberdiers and the Suisse. In addition there were in residence for the summer a great many Neapolitan nobles, all of whom, without exception, spent their fortunes, great or small, on dress and entertainment. A few years before Charles [III] took possession, the one kingdom of Naples alone contained fifty princes, sixty-five dukes, one hundred and six marquises and sixty earls. Ten years before, in 1707, the numbers were, one hundred and twenty-four princes, two hundred dukes, two hundred marquises and forty-five earls. By the middle of the century, in spite of many sumptuary laws and regulations concerning the use of titles, Naples still had a large population of these needy but extravagant paragons. The almanach for each year contains long lists of the dazzling titles by which the King was surrounded. Every excuse and temptation for spending their money were given, and in this way the Royal family received entertainment, while they need never fear conspiracy. All travellers noticed the luxury and licence that obtained in Naples. Long after Venice was bankrupt the Neapolitan nobles found enough money to support the most lavishly produced opera in Europe. The immense palaces of the nobles, still inhabited, but still inaccessible, are, even now, a proof of the magnificent lives led by these ill-educated and hot-tempered fellows. Spending the summer at Caserta in attendance on the King, they obtained free lodging in the palace and could indulge in yet richer clothing.

A grand serenade was given in the evening to celebrate the arrival of these visitors. To begin with, at five o'clock the privileged were allowed in to watch the King at his dinner. Innumerable anecdotes of his family make us certain that the King acquitted himself well in this part of the entertainment. While this went on, a military string band played in a conversational undertone. Whilst the band did the talking, the brothers and sons of the King handed him the dishes. He embarked on these adventures with a Gargantuan zest. His audiences were appreciative; for a Bourbon without a nose and without an appetite would have disappointed them . . .

Here, in Naples, the Court lived in a Spanish tradition of splendour and aloofness, which they exhibited up till the very fall of the dynasty sixty years ago.

[117] A BALL AT CASERTA IN JANUARY 1770; FROM
LADY MILLER'S *LETTERS FROM ITALY*.

(Anna Riggs, Lady Miller (1741–81), was an Irish poetess and amateur of letters.)

I shall proceed to give you the history of our day at Caserta. This superb palace is not yet completed, but will certainly be finished in a shorter time than is imagined, if they continue to work upon it as they do at present. I shall only describe to you the apartments we saw and the theatre . . .

As soon as Her Majesty etc. were come into the pit, the Queen immediately danced a minuet, and to the highest perfection; both their Majesties were dressed *en Savoiarde*, the stuff was striped satin. Neither gold, silver, jewels, lace, or embroidery are permitted to be worn at these *fêtes*.

At the time I was presenting, the Queen and all the company in the box were unmasked; but when Her Majesty descended into the ball-room (the pit) she entered masked, as did the others. A small black mask which covers half the face is what everybody must wear . . .

There are three or four sets of English country dances, and when the
Queen is tired of them, minuets are danced, as many as can be at the
same time. The Queen calls out those she chooses to dance with; she
did M— the honour to order him more than once that night to dance
with her. His Majesty is not fond of this amusement; however, he
danced a country dance in a set he commanded, consisting of men only,
that he might, I suppose, dance as high and as violently as he pleased;
but he met with one young Englishman who was more than his match,
the Lord L—,who gave him such a twirl in return, as both surprised and
pleased His Majesty . . .

The stage was covered with the musicians upon benches, rising
pyramidically one above the other; the top of the pyramid is crowned
by the kettledrums. The musicians are all in a livery, their coats blue,
richly laced, their waistcoats red, and almost covered with silver, small
black hats, with long scarlet feathers stuck upright in them. Large wax
candles are placed between, so that they form a striking *coup d'oeil*
upon your entering the theatre; the whole is so artfully illuminated that
the effect is equal and seems as if the light proceeded from a brilliant
sun at the top. I imagine this may be accounted for from the reflection
of the lights by the high polished marble pillars and other ornaments,
into which the light seems even to pierce. The pit (which is more like
an antique arena) is floored with a composition coloured red, very hard
and rather slippery; here it is they dance. The boxes are appropriated to
the foreign ministers and great officers belonging to the court. At
twelve the Queen unmasks, as do all the company in the same moment:
they then adjourn to supper, those who happen to be near the door
going out first etc.; thus it may happen that their Majesties may be last,
so completely is the etiquette annihilated here. When the Queen is
near the door, all the courtiers crowd about her on their knees to kiss
her hands, which she lends on each side in the most gracious manner.

After mounting a staircase you enter several large rooms, hung and
adorned in the Italian taste with crimson damask, velvet etc. and amply
illuminated. The chairs are placed all round against the walls and each

sits down where they choose. These rooms were so full that there was a double row of chairs placed back to back down the middle. Accident placed me exactly opposite the Queen, who took the first chair she found empty. There are no tables in any of the rooms but every person being seated the supper is served thus. The best looking soldiers, chosen from the King's guards, carry about the supper with as much order, regularity and gravity as if they were performing a military manoeuvre. First appears a soldier bearing a large basket with napkins, followed by a page who unfolds and spreads them on the lap of each of the company as they happen to sit; but when it comes to the Queen's turn to be served a lord of the court presents Her Majesty's napkin. The first soldier is immediately followed by a second bearing a basket of silver plates; another carries knives and forks; then follows a fourth with a great paté composed of macaroni, cheese and butter; he is accompanied by an *écuyer trenchant* (or carver), armed with a knife a foot long, who cuts the pie and lays a large slice on the plate which has been placed on the lap of each of the company; then a fifth soldier with an empty basket to take away the dirty plates; others succeed in the same order, carrying wines, iced water etc.; the drinkables are served between the arrival of each eatable. The rest of the supper consisted of various dishes of fish, ragouts, game, fried and baked meats, Périgord pies, boars' heads etc. The dessert was formed into pyramids and carried round in the same manner; it consisted of sweetmeats, biscuits, iced chocolate and a great variety of iced fruits, creams etc. The Queen ate of two things only, which were prepared particularly for her by her German cooks; she did me the singular honour to send me some of each dish.

As soon as the Queen perceived that all the company had supped, she arose and proceeded to the coffee room, as did those of the company who chose coffee. This room is furnished like the coffee houses of Paris precisely; the walls covered with shelves on which are placed all kinds of liqueurs and Greek wines. Here are tables behind which stand young men in white waistcoats and caps, who make and serve the coffee and other refreshments, of which there are a profusion. The Queen was most gracious to me, and distressed me by her goodness, for there being a great crowd and finding a chair empty I sat down upon it, when turning my head I perceived Her Majesty close to me. I arose. She took hold of me and obliged me to sit down; and having a dish of coffee in my hand, it was with the utmost difficulty I could prevent the contents of it falling upon her clothes. I have often observed that Princes are exceeding sudden in their motions. She was so gracious as to commence a conversation, but quickly perceived how much she embarrassed me by her commands as I was sitting and Her Majesty standing close to me; she most kindly relieved me by giving me an opportunity of rising, pretending she wanted something.

The ball lasted till seven in the morning. We quitted it at four, being much fatigued with dancing. I was determined to follow the example of the Italian ladies in one instance, that of drinking iced water and iced lemonade when very warm; and what is surprising, so far from feeling any bad effect, I found myself considerably relieved from my fatigue, and not the least chilliness succeeded. We returned to Naples without any accident and slept profoundly for ten hours. We are invited to a *grand bal paré* at the French ambassador's, Monsieur de Choiseul's, and to a second at the Princess Potero's.

[118] FERDINAND II INAUGURATES HIS NEW RAILWAY TO CASERTA; FROM SIR HAROLD ACTON'S *THE LAST BOURBONS OF NAPLES*.

One of Ferdinand II's chief aims was to make his kingdom self-sufficient. He was the first Italian sovereign to take a serious interest in railways, and the line from Naples to Granatello (1839) was the first in Italy. On December 14, 1843, William Temple [the British Minister] reported: 'A Railroad which has been undertaken under the direction of His Majesty the King of Naples and the expense of which is defrayed by the Government, has been sufficiently completed to allow trains to proceed upon it as far as Caserta. This Railroad is to be carried on to

Capua in the course of the next year ... His Majesty proposes ultimately to continue this line ... to the Roman frontier and it is hoped
that the Papal Government will in the course of time be induced to
overcome the prejudice it entertains against these modern improvements, and that ultimately a communication will be established
through the Roman territory and the Tuscan States, between this country and the northern parts of Italy.

'The inauguration of the Railroad took place on the 11th instant, on
which occasion the Diplomatic Body, the Ministers of State and the
principal persons belonging to the Court and to the Magistracy of the
town of Naples were present.

'An Altar having been prepared for the occasion the ceremony of blessing the Railroad was performed, after which Their Majesties the King and
Queen accompanied by the Royal Family entered the carriage destined for
them, which had been made in England, and the rest of the party followed
into the train and proceeded at about eleven o'clock to the station at
Caserta where refreshments were served to them ... The Railroad is
about eighteen Neapolitan, or nearly twenty English miles in length, and
the journey both going and returning was performed within the hour.'

[119] FERDINAND II'S WAY OF LIFE AT CASERTA IN THE 1850S;
FROM RAFFAELE DE CESARE'S *LA FINE DI UN REGNO*.

The royal family were just like some ordinary middle-class family.
Nothing expensive was served at their meals, save on very special occasions. Normally they ate macaroni every day. Ferdinand II, a Neapolitan
to his fingertips, liked plain food and enjoyed simple Neapolitan dishes
– *baccalà* (dried cod-fish, usually fried), *soffrito* (fried onions), *caponata*
(boiled chicken), *mozzarella* (buffalo cheese), pizze and vermicelli with
tomato sauce. He was particularly fond of raw onions which he ate day
in and day out, crushing them with his fingers so that a knife would not
spoil the flavour. Queen Maria Teresa had to put up with his rather
coarse ways ...

On one occasion at Caserta when receiving the Mayor of Naples, Don Antonio Carafa, the latter had brought with him a loaf – of the sort popularly known as a 'cheat's loaf' – as a sample of what the Corporation was having specially baked for distribution during the current outbreak of cholera. Ferdinand happened to be holding one of his babies in his arms; seeing the bread it stretched a hand to grab it, unsuccessfully, and began to scream. 'Give him a piece, Don Antò,' said the King pleadingly to the Mayor, 'otherwise we shan't be able to hear ourselves speak.'

There was a special court slang for foreigners. The English were called *baccalaiuoli* (cod merchants), the French *parrucchieri* (hairdressers) and the Russians *mangiasivi* (tallow chandlers). Only the Austrians were spared, since the Queen was Austrian. Everything was said in the purest and strongest Neapolitan dialect, which Maria Teresa spoke very badly with a thick Austrian accent and a guttural pronunciation of her 'r's' . . .

The King's public audiences at Caserta were held in the ground floor drawing-room, where he listened patiently to everybody, receiving place-seekers and petitioners, walking round and asking questions, reading each petition carefully with his spectacles on, keeping some of them in his left hand and throwing others which he had decided to grant into a corner. (He was very short-sighted.) His irritation was all too plain should any petitioner refer to anything which had occurred in 1848. In the years after 1849 he used to hear up to fifty petitioners a day at Caserta.

[120] A PRIVATE AUDIENCE WITH FERDINAND II AT CASERTA IN THE 1850S; FROM *THE LEOPARD* BY GIUSEPPE DI LAMPEDUSA.

The chamberlain . . . led him towards another ante-chamber reserved for members of the Court; a little blue and silver room of the period of Charles III. After a short wait a lackey tapped at the door and they were admitted into the August Presence.

The private study was small and consciously simple; on the white-washed walls hung a portrait of King Francis I and one, with an acid ill-tempered expression, of the reigning Queen; above the mantelpiece was a Madonna by Andrea del Sarto, who looked astounded at finding herself in the company of coloured lithographs representing obscure Neapolitan saints and sanctuaries; on a side table stood a wax statuette of the Child Jesus with a votive light before it; and the modest desk was heaped with papers, white, yellow and blue; the whole administration of the kingdom here attained its final phase, that of signature by His Majesty (D.G.).

Behind this paper barricade was the King. He was already standing so as not to be seen getting up; the King with his pallid heavy face between fairish side-whiskers, with his rough cloth military jacket under which burst a purple cataract of trousers. He gave a step forward with his right hand out and bent for the hand-kiss which he would then refuse.

'Well, Salina, blessings on you!' His Neapolitan accent was far stronger than the chamberlain's.

'I must beg Your Majesty to excuse me for not wearing court dress; I am only just passing through Naples; but I did not wish to forgo paying my respects to Your Revered Person.'

'Nonsense, Salina, nonsense: you know you're always at home here at Caserta.

'At home, of course,' he repeated, sitting down behind the desk and waiting a second before indicating to his guest to sit down too.

'And how are the little girls?' The Prince realized that now was the moment to produce a play on words both salacious and edifying.

'Little girls, Your Majesty? At my age and under the sacred bonds of matrimony?'

The King's mouth laughed as his hands primly settled the papers before him. 'Those I'd never let myself refer to, Salina. I was asking about your little daughters, your little princesses. Concetta, now, that dear godchild of ours, she must be getting quite big, isn't she, almost grown up?'

From family he passed to science. 'Salina, you're an honour not only to yourself but to the whole kingdom. A fine thing, science, unless it takes to attacking religion!' After this, however, the mask of the Friend was put aside and its place assumed that of the Severe Sovereign. 'Tell me Salina, what do they think of Castelcicala down in Sicily?'

Salina had never heard a good word for the Lieutenant-General of Sicily from either Royalists or Liberals, but not wanting to let a friend down he parried and kept to generalities. 'A great gentleman, a true hero, may be a little old for the fatigues of the Lieutenant-Generalcy . . .'

The King's face darkened; Salina was refusing to act the spy. So Salina was no use to him. Leaning both hands on his desk he prepared the dismissal: 'I've so much work! The whole Kingdom rests on these shoulders of mine.' Now for a bit of sweetening: out of the drawer came the friendly mask again. 'When you pass through Naples next, Salina, come and show your Concetta to the queen. She's too young to be presented, I know, but there's nothing against our arranging a little dinner for her, is there? Sweets to the sweet, as they say. Well, Salina, 'bye and be good!'

[121] THE DEATH OF FERDINAND II AT CASERTA IN THE SPRING OF 1859; FROM SIR HAROLD ACTON'S *THE LAST BOURBONS OF NAPLES*.

Ferdinand had been given up as a hopeless case by the doctors. Among these Lanza, who had recently returned from exile, suggested ironically that he be nourished with woman's milk. Another colleague, Rosati, could not help laughing at this, which prompted Lanza to add: 'The King will die after contemplating his own corpse: there is no further remedy.' Alluding to the royal amnesty which had enabled him to come home, this amiable doctor remarked to his cronies: 'The King gave me a passport to return to Naples and I have given him one for the next world.' The gravity of Ferdinand's condition could no longer be concealed from the people. On April 12 he believed he might die at any moment and wished to receive the Blessed Sacrament. All his family except his youngest children were present at this solemn ceremony. At the cost of great effort he contrived to sit up in bed, a skeleton of his former self: he was resolved to die with dignity. To each of his brothers he made some bequest: he entrusted his fleet to Aquila, his army to Trapani. He made Generals Filangieri and Ischitella promise to assist and advise his heir. All the theatres were closed on that day. Yet he survived, and his brain remained extraordinarily lucid.

Throughout his horrible illness the Queen seldom left his sickroom; she knelt praying, beside him, she watched by him at night in an armchair or sofa, ever at his beck and call, and she tried to prevent distressing news from reaching him . . . Francis, who had hitherto been kept in the dark about his father's policy, was now given an eleventh-hour briefing about government. Ferdinand's memory was keenly retentive until he died: one by one he mentioned all the names of those who could be trusted, scrupulously distinguishing between the true and false friends of the dynasty. He warned him never to make any compromise with the revolution or take sides with Austria or Piedmont: he should wait patiently on events, regarding the Papal States as an outer bulwark. He advised him to change the ministry but not the character of the government. Above all he adjured him to maintain his zeal for the Faith and consult Cardinal Cosenza on religious matters.

When Victor Emmanuel went to Genoa to meet his ally the Emperor of the French on May 13, 'it was roses, roses all the way', as Thayer wrote. But it was rue for Ferdinand, whose plight was so desperate that he dictated his will to his heir in the presence of the Queen, the Counts of Trani and Caserta, and Monsignor Gallo, and signed it with a tremulous hand. On the 20th the pain in his left lung became excruciating: he was unable to expectorate, yet the brain was still clear and he expressed himself with precision. At mid-day he received Extreme Unction from Monsignor Gallo surrounded by his weeping family, each of whom he embraced and blessed, with a supreme effort to appear serene. Though his voice was very feeble he gathered strength for a last speech of farewell. He said he could die without remorse since he had always tried to do his duty as a Christian and a sovereign. The crown of Italy had been offered to him but he would not accept it: had he done so he would suffer remorse for injuring the rights of other sovereigns, and especially of the Pope. He thanked God for having enlightened him; he was leaving the kingdom as he had inherited it from his ancestors . . .

It was a struggle to squeeze the sentences from his throat. He was gasping for breath, and the sweat stung his glaring eyes. To quieten him the doctors begged the Princes to leave the room. The Queen came and went in a state of frantic agitation; the Hereditary Prince stood sobbing in a corner.

Ferdinand's final agony started near mid-day on May 22. Monsignor Gallo recited prayers while the royal family and household knelt weeping round the bed. At one moment the King opened his eyes and said: 'Why do you weep? I will not forget you.' Turning to the Queen, he added: 'I shall pray for you, for our children, for the Pope, for our subjects, friends, enemies and sinners.' He could speak no more. With one hand on the Crucifix of his confessor and another clutching the Queen, he expired shortly after one o'clock.

The last four months had seemed like four long years to those who had sat and stood and prayed beside the slowly disintegrating King, and they were utterly worn out and emptied of emotion. To many it was as if the kingdom had disintegrated with Ferdinand II, whose formidable will-power had kept the Two Sicilies together for twenty-nine years. It was hard to realize that he was only forty-nine. The Queen could not bear the thought of his being embalmed, but there was no alternative since his corpse had to be exposed to the public. His Spanish brother-in-law, Don Sebastian, commissioned the painter Domenico Caldara to depict his emaciated features in their final calm, and it is somewhat curious that the Queen ordered twelve copies of this ghastly record for distribution among various courtiers. Was it not better to remember him in the prime of life?

The Palace of Portici

The King and Queen, both when sailing to Castellamare in a pinnace
and during the return journey by land, were very taken with what they
saw of the charming country around Portici. Having learnt that the air
was healthy and that game abounded in not one but two seasons of the
year (quails being particularly plentiful), and that the neighbouring sea
was very well stocked with fish, Charles gave orders for a villa to be
built there. When one of the courtiers warned him that it was too near
Vesuvius, he simply replied, 'God, the Immaculate Virgin and San
Gennaro will protect us.' It was designed and built by the architect
Canovari.

[123] SIR WILLIAM HAMILTON'S ACCOUNT OF THE YOUNG
FERDINAND IV AND I AT PORTICI, FROM HISTORICAL
MEMOIRS OF MY OWN TIME BY SIR NATHANIEL WRAXALL.

No European sovereign, without exception, has been so ill educated as
the King of Naples. He is not even master of any language except
Italian, without making a painful effort, and his ordinary Italian is a
Neapolitan dialect, such as the lowest of his subjects, the Lazaroni,
speak in their intercourse with each other. It is true that he under-
stands French, and converses in it when indispensable; but he rarely
reads any French author, and still more rarely attempts to write in that
language. All the correspondence that takes place between him and
his father, the King of Spain, is carried on in the common Neapolitan
jargon ... The King's education was systematically neglected; for
Charles III, alarmed at the imbecility of his eldest son, Philip, Duke of
Calabria, who on account of his recognized debility of understanding,
was wholly set aside from the right of succession, strictly ordered at

his departure for Spain in 1759 that this, his third son, should not be compelled to apply to any severe studies, or be made to exert any close application of mind . . .

Before the present King fully attained his seventeenth year, the Marquis Tanucci, then Prime Minister, by directions issued from the Court of Madrid, provided him a wife. The Archduchess Josepha, one of the daughters of the Empress Maria Theresa, being selected for Queen of Naples, and being represented to young Ferdinand as a princess equally amiable in her mind as she was agreeable in her person, he expected her arrival with great pleasure mingled even with some impatience. So much more severely was it natural that he should feel the melancholy intelligence when it arrived from Vienna that she was dead of the smallpox. In fact, he manifested as much concern as could perhaps be expected in a prince of his disposition and at his time of life, for the death of a person whom he had never seen. But a circumstance which greatly augmented his chagrin on the occasion was its being considered indispensable for him not to take his usual diversion of hunting or fishing on the day that the account reached Naples. Ferdinand reluctantly submitted to such a painful and unusual renunciation; but having consented to it from a sense of decorum, he immediately set about endeavouring to amuse himself within doors in the best manner that circumstances would admit, an attempt in which he was aided by the noblemen in waiting about his person. They began therefore with billiards, a game which his Majesty likes, and at which he plays with skill. When they had continued it for some time, leap-frog was tried, to which succeeded various other feats of agility or gambols. At length one of the courtiers, more ingenious than the others, proposed to celebrate the funeral of the deceased Archduchess. The idea, far from shocking the King, appeared to him and to the whole company as most entertaining, and no reflections either on the indecorum or want of apparent humanity in the proceedings interposed to prevent its immediate realization. Having selected one of the chamberlains, as proper from his youth and feminine appearance to represent the Princess, they habited him in a manner suitable to the mournful occasion, laid him out on an open bier according to the Neapolitan custom at interments, and in order to render the ceremony more appropriate as well as more accurately correct, they marked his face and hands with chocolate drops, which were designed to imitate the pustules of the smallpox. All the apparatus being ready, the funeral procession began, and proceeded through the principal apartments of the palace at Portici, Ferdinand officiating as chief mourner. Having heard of the Archduchess's decease, I had gone thither on that day in order to make my condolences privately to his Majesty on the misfortune, and entering at the time, I became an eye-witness of this extraordinary scene, which, in any other country of Europe, would be considered incredible, and would not obtain belief.

The Archduchess Caroline being substituted in place of her sister, and being soon afterwards conducted from Vienna to Naples, the King advanced in person as far as the Portella, where the Neapolitan and Papal territories divide, in order to receive his new bride. She was then not sixteen years old, and though she could not by any means be esteemed handsome, yet, besides youth, she possessed many charms. Ferdinand manifested on his part neither ardour nor indifference towards the Queen. On the morning after his nuptials, which took place in the beginning of May 1768, when the weather was very warm, he rose at an early hour and went out as usual to the chase, leaving his young wife in bed. Those courtiers who accompanied him, having inquired of his Majesty how he liked her, 'Dormè com'un amazzata,' replied he, 'e suda com'un porco.' ['Sleeps as though she'd been killed and sweats like a pig.'] Such an answer would be esteemed anywhere except at Naples most indecorous; but here we are familiarized to far greater violations of propriety. Those acts and functions which are never mentioned in England, and which are there studiously concealed, even by the vulgar, here are openly performed. When the King has made a hearty meal, and feels an inclination to retire, he commonly communicates that intention to the noblemen around him in waiting, and selects the favoured individuals whom, as a mark of predilection, he chooses shall attend him. 'Sono ben pranzato,' says he, laying his hand on his belly, 'adesso bisogna una buona panciata.' ['I have dined well, now I need a good purge.'] The persons thus preferred then accompany his Majesty, stand respectfully round him, and amuse him by their conversation during the performance.

[124] FERDINAND IV AND I AT PORTICI IN JUNE
1777; FROM HENRY SWINBURNE'S *THE COURTS OF
EUROPE AT THE CLOSE OF THE LAST CENTURY*.

The weather is grown extremely hot, but the country is in high beauty, refreshed by a heavy rain. The walnut trees are good shelter, and the pomegranate flowers very ornamental to the road; the sirocco wind is oppressive. We dined at Portici, at the Maggiordomo's, and afterwards saw the king draw up a detachment of the cadets, Lipariotes and chasseurs, and hold a council of war, like a child playing *à la madame*.

At six, his majesty marched into the Boschetto, where we followed him. The advanced guards, his new Cacciatore, attacked and drove away the enemy's light troops; and after several skirmishes between the different corps, the defendants were obliged to retire into the castle; the besiegers then attacked and took by escalade a house in the woods.

At eight o'clock the company came down to the Pallone, where a large vestibule or card-room was erected for the occasion, at one end of which was a very grand theatre, at the other an immense ball-room. Though run up in such a hurry, and slightly built, they are extremely elegant and well proportioned. We had a French play, after which we all adjourned to the cardroom to take refreshments, and from thence to the ball. About twelve the king and queen retired, and soon after the assembly broke up, walking to their coaches by the light of a charming illumination through the wood and large gardens, where the fountains formed a pleasing decoration. The presence of the sovereigns in these parties, instead of causing any formality, seems to make everything more jovial and merry.

Next evening the ball was repeated, and many more English were invited. Mr Spence and Miss Snow, by their furious dancing, entertained the king prodigiously; he was in roars of laughter, bravoed, clapped his hands, and encouraged them to skip and jump about. [The lady was so fat that she was called 'Double Stout.'] Each of them was conscious how much the other was laughed at, and took care to tell it to all the company, without suspecting that their own figure and performance could be the object of merriment. There was an Italian play, great stuff . . .

Mr Spence has made quite a conquest of the king by his ridiculous dancing, which I suppose the king takes for buffoonery. He has him to play at tennis with him, and they are as great as inkleweavers.

[125] Decor, including the Capodimonte room, at the Portici palace in July 1823; from the Countess of Blessington's *The Idler in Italy*.

Went to see the Palazzo Portici to-day. The situation would have been charming were it not for its close vicinity to the road, which actually passes through its court. The view from the back of the palace, however, atones for the defect in front. It comprehends a magnificent prospect of the bay, being only divided from the sea by a garden, filled with the finest trees, plants, and flowers. No palace that I have ever seen so completely realizes the notion I had formed of an Italian one, as does this at Portici. Its close proximity to the sea, whose blue waters bathe the balustrade of the garden, and the enchanting views that on each side present themselves, render it a most delicious retreat.

This residence owes all its comfort and elegance to the good taste of Madam Murat, ex-Queen of Naples, who evinced not a little judgement in the alterations and repairs carried into effect in all the royal palaces during her brief reign here. The present sovereign and his family are said to have been hardly able to recognize their ancient abodes when they returned from Sicily; and expressed no little satisfaction at the improvements that had taken place. Ferdinand is reported to have said that Murat was an excellent upholsterer, and had furnished his palaces perfectly to his taste. The apartments at Portici continue precisely in the same state as when Madame Murat occupied them; with the exception that the portraits of the imperial family have been removed to a lumber-room on the ground floor . . .

One of the salons at Portici peculiarly attracted our attention. The ceilings and walls were covered with panels of the most beautiful china of the ancient and celebrated manufactory of Capodimonte, of which specimens are now become so rare. The panels have landscapes and groups finely painted, and are bordered with wreaths of flowers the size of Nature, of the richest and most varied dyes, in alto-rilievo; among which, birds of the gayest plumage, squirrels, and monkeys, all of china, are mingled. The chandeliers, and frames of the mirrors, are also of porcelain, and the effect is singularly beautiful. The floor was formerly covered in a similar style to the panels on the walls; but the King, when obliged to fly from Naples, intended, as it is said, to remove the decorations from this chamber, and had only detached those of the floor, when he was compelled to depart.

The portraits of the families of Napoleon and Murat are shown by the *custode*, in the small and mean apartments to which they have been consigned; and the splendour of the dresses of some of them, form a striking contrast with the rooms where they are placed; like the altered destinies of the originals, who have 'fallen from their high estate'. We were shown two portraits of Murat: one, a full-length, by Gérard, and the other a half-length, by a Neapolitan artist. Both are considered excellent resemblances; and if so, prove that the original could not have

been the handsome man he was reported to have been. An air of brag-
gadocio characterizes both portraits, conveying the impression of a
bold captain of banditti, dressed in the rich spoils he had
plundered . . .

Vesuvius and Pompeii

Eight miles from the city lies Torre del Greco, now called Torre
d'Ottavio, where Pliny, writer of the natural history and admiral of the
navy of Augustus, was near the said Tower choked with vapours, while
too curiously he desired to behold the burning of the Mountain
Vesuvius, now called Somma. This Mountain Somma is most high, and
upon the top is dreadful where is a gulf casting out flames, and while
the winds enclosed seek to break out by natural force there have been
heard horrible noises and fearful groans. The rest of the mountain
aboundeth with vines and olives, and there grows the Greek Wine,
which Pliny calls Pompei's Wine; and of this wine, they say, this place is
called Torre del Greco. The greatest burning of this mountain brake out
in the time of the Emperor Titus, the smoke thereof made the sun dark,
burnt up the next territories and consumed two cities, Pompei and
Herculaneum, and the ashes thereof covered all the fields of that territory. It brake out again in the year 1538, with great gaping of the earth
and casting down part of the mountain . . .

7th February. The next day, being Saturday, we went four miles out of
town on mules, to see that famous volcano, Mount Vesuvius. Here we
pass a fair fountain, called Labulla, which continually boils, supposed
to proceed from Vesuvius, and thence over a river and bridge, where on
a large upright stone, is engraven a notable inscription relative to the
memorable eruption in 1630.

Approaching the hill, as we are able with our mules, we alighted,
crawling up the rest of the proclivity with great difficulty, now with

our feet, now with our hands, not without many untoward slips which did much bruise us on the various coloured cinders, with which the whole mountain is covered, some like pitch, others full of perfect brimstone, others metallic, interspersed with innumerable pumices (of all which I made a collection), we at the last gained the summit of an extensive altitude. Turning our faces towards Naples, it presents one of the goodliest prospects in the world; all the Baiae, Cuma, Elysian Fields, Capreae, Ischia, Prochyta, Misenus, Puteoli, that goodly city, with a great portion of the Tyrrhene Sea, offering themselves to your view at once, and at so agreeable a distance, as nothing can be more delightful. The mountain consists of a double top, the one pointed very sharp, and commonly appearing above any cloud, the other blunt. Here, as we approached, we met many large gaping clefts and chasms, out of which issued such sulphureous blasts and smoke, that we durst not stand long near them. Having gained the very summit, I laid myself down to look over into the most frightful and terrible vorago, a stupendous pit of near three miles in circuit, and half a mile in depth, by a perpendicular hollow cliff (like that from the highest part of Dover Castle), with now and then a craggy prominency jetting out. The area at the bottom is plane, like an even floor, which seems to be made by the wind circling the ashes by its eddy blasts. In the middle and centre is a hill, shaped like a great brown loaf, appearing to consist of sulphureous matter, continually vomiting a foggy exhalation, and ejecting huge stones with an impetuous noise and roaring, like the report of many muskets discharging. This horrid barathrum engaged our attention for some hours, both for the strangeness of the spectacle, and the mention which the old histories make of it, as one of the most stupendous curiosities in nature, and which made the learned and inquisitive Pliny adventure his life to detect the causes, and to lose it in too desperate an approach. It is likewise famous for the stratagem of the rebel, Spartacus, who did so much mischief to the State, lurking amongst and protected by, these horrid caverns, when it was more accessible and less dangerous than it is now; but especially notorious it is for the last conflagration, when, in anno 1630, it burst out beyond what it had ever done in the memory of history; throwing out huge stones and fiery pumices in such quantity, as not only environed the whole mountain, but totally buried and over-whelmed divers towns and their inhabitants, scattering the ashes more than a hundred miles, and utterly devastating all those vineyards, where formerly grew the most incomparable Greco; when, bursting through the bowels of the earth, it absorbed the very sea, and, with its whirling waters, drew in diverse galleys and other vessels to their destruction, as is faithfully recorded. We descended with more ease than we climbed up, through a deep valley of pure ashes, which at the late eruption was a flowing river of melted and burning brimstone, and so came to our mules at the foot of the mountain.

[128] Dr Charles Burney visits William Hamilton
and his first wife at their villa near Vesuvius
in October 1770; from *Music, Men, and Manners
in France and Italy* by Dr Charles Burney.

Captain Forbes and I went to the Minister's in a chariot the same road as before when we visited Pompei – that is, through Portici – Resina by Herculaneum – and Torre del Greco etc. His Villa Angelica is but a small house which he fitted up himself – situated opposite and within two miles of the foot of Mount Vesuvius in a very rich and fertile spot, as everyone hereabouts is that is not covered with fresh lava. He has a large garden, or rather vineyard, with most excellent grapes. The Captain and I were received with great politeness by the Minister and his lady. After dinner we had music and chat till supper. Mr H. has two pages who play very well, one on the fiddle and the other on the violoncello. Though my companion was not invited to lie there nor did intend it, yet he was easily prevailed on to pig in the same room with me – who was – and a field bed was put up on the occasion. As soon as it was dark our musical entertainment was mixed with the sight and observations of Mount Vesuvius, then very busy. Mr H. has glasses of all sorts and every convenience of situation etc. for these observations with which he is much occupied. He favoured me with a sight of his manuscript of which he has just sent a copy to our Royal Society, in which a very ingenious hypothesis is well supported to prove that most of the mountains in this part of the world have been formed by volcanos. Though at three miles distance from the mouth of the mountain, we heard the reports of the explosion before we saw the stones and red hot matter thrown up by them, which proves, as light travels faster than sound, that they must ascend from a great depth, and we were certain that they mounted near 1000 feet above the summit of the mountain. The sight was very awful and beautiful, resembling in great [degree] the most ingenious and fine fireworks I ever saw. Mr H., who has studied very closely this mountain and all its symptoms for upwards of six years, read us very entertaining lectures upon it, and is now of opinion that it is on the eve of some great event or considerable eruption. The sound was more deep than that of thunder, which proves the cavern to be of an immense size and depth.

[129] THE POET SHELLEY VISITS VESUVIUS IN 1818;
FROM *THE LETTERS OF PERCY BYSSHE SHELLEY.*

(Percy Bysshe Shelley (1792–1822) spent the last four years of his life in Italy, and was drowned during a storm in the Mediterranean.)

Vesuvius is, after the Glaciers, the most impressive exhibition of the energies of nature I ever saw. It has not the immeasurable greatness, the overpowering magnificence, nor, above all, the radiant beauty of the glaciers; but it has all their character of tremendous and irresistible strength. From Resina to the hermitage you wind up the mountain, and cross a vast stream of hardened lava, which is an actual image of the waves of the sea, changed into hard black stone by enchantment. The lines of the boiling flood seem to hang in the air, and it is difficult to believe that the billows which seem hurrying down upon you are not actually in motion. This plain was once a sea of liquid fire. From the hermitage we crossed another vast stream of lava, and then went on foot up the cone – this is the only part of the ascent in which there is any difficulty, and that difficulty has been much exaggerated. It is composed of rocks of lava, and declivities of ashes; by ascending the former and descending the latter, there is very little fatigue. On the summit is a kind of irregular plain, the most horrible chaos that can be imagined; riven into ghastly chasms, and heaped up with tumuli of great stones and cinders, and enormous rocks blackened and calcined, which had been thrown from the volcano one upon another in terrible confusion. In the midst stands the conical hill from which volumes of smoke, and the fountains of liquid fire, are rolled forth for ever. The mountain is at present in a slight state of eruption; and a thick heavy white smoke is perpetually rolled out, interrupted by enormous columns of an impenetrable black bituminous vapour, which is hurled up, fold after fold, into the sky with a deep hollow sound, and fiery stones are rained down from its darkness, and a black shower of ashes fell even where we sat. The lava, like the glacier, creeps on perpetually, with a crackling sound as of suppressed fire. There are several springs of lava; and in one place it rushes precipitously over a high crag, rolling down the half-molten rocks and its own overhanging waves; a cataract of quivering fire. We approached the extremity of one of the rivers of lava; it is about twenty feet in breadth and ten in height; and as the inclined plane was not rapid, its motion was very slow. We saw the masses of its dark exterior surface detach themselves as it moved, and betray the depth of the liquid flame. In the day the fire is but slightly seen; you only observe a tremulous motion in the air, and streams and fountains of white sulphurous smoke.

At length we saw the sun sink between Capreae and Inarime, and, as the darkness increased, the effect of the fire became more beautiful. We were, as it were, surrounded by streams and cataracts of the red and radiant fire; and in the midst, from the column of bituminous smoke shot up into the air, fell the vast masses of rock, white with the light of their intense heat, leaving behind them through the dark vapour trains of splendour. We descended by torch-light, and I should have enjoyed the scenery on my return, but they conducted me, I know not how, to the hermitage in a state of intense bodily suffering.

[130] AN EXCURSION TO POMPEII IN 1780; FROM *DREAMS, WAKING THOUGHTS AND INCIDENTS* BY WILLIAM BECKFORD.

(William Beckford (1759–1844), a dilettante, man of letters, and the future 'Caliph of Fonthill', visited Italy on his Grand Tour in 1780.)

Nothing can be conceived more delightful than the climate and situation of this city. It stands upon a gently rising hill, which commands the bay of Naples, with the islands of Caprea and Ischia, the rich coasts of Sorrento, the tower of Castel a Mare; and on the other side, Mount Vesuvius, with the lovely country intervening. It is judged to be about an Italian mile long, and three and a half in circuit. We entered the city at the little gate which lies towards Stabiae. The first object upon entering, is a colonnade round a square court, which seems to have formed a place of arms. Behind the colonnade is a series of little rooms, destined for the soldiers' barracks. The columns are of stone, plastered with stucco and coloured. On several of them we found names, scratched in Greek and Latin; probably those of the soldiers who had been quartered there. Helmets, and armour for various parts of the body, were discovered amongst the skeletons of some soldiers, whose hard fate had compelled them to wait on duty, at the perilous moment of the city's approaching destruction. Dolphins and tridents, sculptured in relief on most of these relics of armour, seem to show that they had been fabricated for naval service. Some of the sculptures on the arms, probably belonging to officers, exhibit a greater variety of ornaments. The taking of Troy, wrought on one of the helmets, is beautifully executed; and much may be said in commendation of the work of several others.

We were next led to the remains of a temple and altar near these barracks. From thence to some rooms floored (as indeed were almost all that have been cleared from the rubbish) with tessellated mosaic pavements of various patterns, and most of them of very elegant execution. Many of these have been taken up, and now form the floors of the rooms in the Museum at Portici, whose best ornaments of every kind are furnished from the discoveries at Pompeii. From the rooms just mentioned, we descended into a subterraneous chamber, communicating with a bathing apartment. It appears to have served as a kind of office to the latter. It was probably here that the clothes used in bathing were washed. A fireplace, a capacious cauldron of bronze, and earthern vessels, proper for that purpose, found here, have given rise to the conjecture. Contiguous to this room is a small circular one with a fireplace, which was the stove to the bath. I should not forget to tell you that the skeleton of the poor laundress (for so the antiquaries will have it), who was very diligently washing the bathing clothes at the time of the eruption, was found lying in an attitude of most resigned death, not far from the washing cauldron in the office just mentioned.

We were now conducted to the temple, or rather chapel, of Isis. The chief remains are a covered cloister; the great altar on which was probably exhibited the statue of the goddess; a little edifice to protect the sacred well; the pediment of the chapel, with a symbolical vase in relief; ornaments in stucco, on the front of the main building, consisting of the lotus, the sistrum, representations of gods, Harpocrates, Anubis, and other objects of Egyptian worship. The figures on one side of this temple are Perseus with the Gorgon's head; on the other side, Mars and Venus, with Cupids bearing the arms of Mars. We next observe three altars of different sizes. On one of them is said to have been found the bones of a victim unconsumed, the last sacrifice having probably been stopped by the dreadful calamity which had occasioned it. From a niche in the temple was taken a statue of marble: a woman pressing her lips with her forefinger. Within the area is a well, where the priest threw the ashes of the sacrifices. We saw in the Museum at Portici some lovely arabesque paintings, cut from the walls of the cloister. The foliage which ran round the whole sweep of the cloister itself is in the finest taste.

Behind one of the altars we saw a small room, in which our guide informed us, a human skeleton had been discovered, with some fish bones on a plate near it, and a number of other culinary utensils. We then passed on to another apartment, almost contiguous, where nothing more remarkable had been found than an iron crow: an instrument with which perhaps the unfortunate wretch, whose skeleton I have mentioned above, had vainly endeavoured to extricate herself, this room being probably barricaded by the matter of the eruption. This temple, rebuilt, as the inscription imports by N. Popidius, had been thrown down by a terrible earthquake, that likewise destroyed a great part of the city (sixteen years before the famous eruption of Vesuvius described by Pliny, which happened in the first year of Titus, AD 79) and buried at once both Herculaneum and Pompeii. As I lingered alone in these environs sacred to Isis, some time after my companions had quitted them, I fell into one of those reveries which my imagination is so fond of indulging; and transporting myself seventeen hundred years back, fancied I was sailing with the elder Pliny, on the first day's eruption, from Misenum, towards Retina and Herculaneum; and afterwards towards the villa of his friend Pomponianus at Stabiae. The course of our galley seldom carried us out of sight of Pompeii, and as often as I could divert my attention from the tremendous spectacle of the eruption, its enormous pillar of smoke standing conically in the air, and tempests of liquid fire continually bursting out from the midst of it, then raining down the sides of the mountain, and flooding this beautiful coast with innumerable streams of red-hot lava, methought I turned my eyes upon this fair city, whose houses, villas, and gardens, with their long ranges of columned courts and porticos, were made visible through the universal cloud of ashes, by lightning from the mountain; and saw its distracted inhabitants, men, women, and children, running to and fro in despair. But in one spot, I mean the court and precincts of the temple, glared a continual light. It was the blaze of the altars; towards which I discerned a long-robed train of priests moving in solemn procession, to supplicate by prayer and sacrifice, at this destructive moment, the intervention of Isis, who had taught the first fathers of mankind the culture of the earth, and other arts of civil life. Methought I could distinguish in their hands all those paintings and images, sacred to this divinity, brought out on this portentous occasion, from the subterraneous apartments and mystic cells of the temple. There was every form of creeping thing and abominable beast, every Egyptian pollution which the true prophet had seen in vision, among the secret idolatries of the temple at Jerusalem. The priests arrived at the altars; saw them gathered round, and purifying the three at once with the sacred meal; then, all moving slowly about them, each with his right hand towards the fire: it was the office of some to seize the firebrands of the altars, with which they sprinkled holy water on the numberless bystanders. Then began the prayers, the hymns, and lustrations of the sacrifice. The priests had laid the victims with their throats downward upon the altars; were ransacking the baskets of flour and salt for the knives of slaughter, and proceeding in haste to the accomplishment of their pious ceremonies – when one of our company, who thought me lost, returned with impatience, and calling me off to some new object, put an end to my strange reverie.

[131] THE HOUSES OF POMPEII, VISITED IN MARCH 1787; FROM *ITALIÄNISCHE REISE* BY WOLFGANG GOETHE.

Since I shall not be at Naples much longer, I will first deal with the out-of-the-way matters. The more immediate, you might say, throw themselves at one. Tischbein and I have been to Pompeii. En route all those wonderful vistas we knew so well from countless landscape drawings were on each side of us, one after another, dazzling in the sheer number of them.

Pompeii astonishes one by its small scale and narrow proportions. The streets are cramped though very straight and with pavements on each side. The houses are tiny and have no windows, light entering their rooms only from the doors on to the atrium and the galleries. The very public buildings, the tomb by the gate, a temple and a nearby villa, are more like dolls' houses or models rather than the real thing. Rooms, passageways, galleries and everything else are painted in the most cheerful colours, walls always in the same shade; in the middle of the walls there were sometimes quite complicated pictures, but most of these have now been removed; borders and angles are lightly decorated, usually with charming designs of children or nymphs; occasionally wild beasts or tame animals are depicted emerging from garlands of flowers. Indeed, despite being buried by showers of fiery stone and ashes and then robbed by excavators, the city still manages to demonstrate, even in its utter desolation, that all its inhabitants had a love of painting and the arts which today's would-be *dilettante* is incapable of understanding or appreciating.

Considering how far away the city is from Vesuvius, it is obvious that the volcanic substances which buried it could not have been blown here by a sudden spasm on the part of the mountain or by a gust of wind. It is much more likely that the stone and ashes had been floating above like clouds for a considerable time before finally descending on the doomed town.

To imagine exactly what did happen, one should simply think of a mountain village being buried in the snow. Gaps in between the houses, and collapsing houses, were quickly covered up. On the other hand it is quite likely that in some places pieces of masonry still showed above the ground, and therefore attracted the attention of those who later turned the new hill into gardens and vineyards. No doubt there were many owners who made rich pickings from excavating their own plots. Some rooms were discovered to be absolutely empty, while in the corner of one of them a pile of ornaments and other goods had been deliberately hidden by heaping ashes over them.

We had to rid ourselves of the odd, and in some ways unpleasant, sensations which this mummified city left on our minds. We did so in the garden of a little inn on the edge of the sea, where we ate a simple meal and exulted in the blue sky, the sea waves and the cheerful sunshine. We found ourselves hoping that we might make a second visit together to the hill, when it is once more disguised by vine leaves.

[132] A DESCRIPTION OF POMPEII IN 1818; FROM
THE LETTERS OF PERCY BYSSHE SHELLEY.

I was astonished at the remains of this city; I had no conception of anything so perfect yet remaining. My idea of the mode of its destruction was this: First, an earthquake shattered it, and unroofed almost all its temples, and split its columns; then a rain of light small pumice-stones fell; then torrents of boiling water, mixed with ashes, filled up all its crevices. A wide, flat hill, from which the city was excavated, is now covered by thick woods, and you see the tombs and the theatres, the temples and the houses, surrounded by the uninhabited wilderness. We entered the town from the side towards the sea, and first saw two theatres; one more magnificent than the other, strewn with the ruins of the white marble which formed their seats and cornices, wrought with deep, bold sculpture. In the front, between the stage and the seats, is the circular space, occasionally occupied by the chorus. The stage is very narrow, but long, and divided from this space by a narrow enclosure parallel to it, I suppose for the orchestra. On each side are the consuls' boxes, and below in the theatre at Herculaneum, were found two equestrian statues of admirable workmanship, occupying the same place as the great bronze lamps did at Drury Lane. The smallest of the theatres is said to have been comic, though I should doubt. From both you see, as you sit on the seats, a prospect of the most wonderful beauty.

You then pass through the ancient streets; they are very narrow, and the houses rather small, but all constructed on an admirable plan, especially for this climate. The rooms are built round a court, or sometimes two, according to the extent of the house. In the midst is a fountain, sometimes surrounded by a portico, supported on fluted columns of white stucco; the floor is paved with mosaic, sometimes wrought in imitation of vine leaves, sometimes in quaint figures, and more or less beautiful, according to the rank of the inhabitant. There were paintings on all, but most of them have been removed to decorate the royal museums. Little winged figures, and small ornaments of exquisite elegance, yet remain. There is an ideal life in the form of these paintings of an incomparable loveliness, though most are evidently the work of very inferior artists. It seems as if, from the atmosphere of mental beauty which surrounded them, every human being caught a splendour not his own. In one house you see how the bed-rooms were managed: a small sofa was built up, where the cushions were placed; two pictures, one representing Diana and Endymion, the other Venus and Mars, decorate the chamber, and a little niche, which contains the statue of a domestic god. The floor is composed of a rich mosaic of the rarest marbles, agate, jasper, and porphyry; it looks to the marble fountain and the snow-white columns, whose entablatures strew the floor of the portico they supported. The houses have only one storey, and the apartments, though not large, are very lofty. A great advantage results from this, wholly unknown in our cities. The public buildings, whose ruins are now forests, as it were, of white fluted columns, and which then supported entablatures loaded with sculptures, were seen on all sides over the roofs of the houses. This was the excellence of the ancients. Their private expenses were comparatively moderate; the dwelling of one of the chief senators of Pompeii is elegant indeed, and adorned with most beautiful specimens of art, but small. But their public buildings are everywhere marked by the bold and grand designs of an unsparing magnificence. In the little town of Pompeii (it contained almost twenty thousand inhabitants), it is wonderful to see the number and the grandeur of their public buildings. Another advantage, too, is that in the present case, the glorious scenery around is not shut out, and that, unlike the inhabitants of the Cimmerian ravines of modern cities, the ancient Pompeians could contemplate the clouds and the lamps of heaven; could see the moon rise high behind Vesuvius, and the sun set in the sea, tremulous with an atmosphere of golden vapour, between Inarime and Misenum.

We next saw the temples. Of the temple of Aesculapius little remains but an altar of black stone, adorned with a cornice imitating the scales of a serpent. His statue in terra-cotta, was found in the cell. The temple of Isis is more perfect. It is surrounded by a portico of fluted columns, and in the area around it are two altars, and many ceppi for statues; and a little chapel of white stucco, as hard as stone, of the most exquisite proportion; its panels are adorned with figures in bas-relief, slightly indicated, but of a workmanship the most delicate and perfect that can be conceived. They are Egyptian subjects, executed by a Greek artist, who has harmonized all the unnatural extravagances of the original conception into the supernatural loveliness of his country's genius. They scarcely touch the ground with their feet, and their wind-uplifted robes seem in the place of wings. The temple in the midst, raised on a high platform, and approached by steps, was decorated with exquisite paintings, some of which we saw in the museum at Portici. It is small, of the same materials as the chapel, with a pavement of mosaic, and fluted Ionic columns of white stucco, so white that it dazzles you to look at it.

Thence through other porticos and labyrinths of walls and columns (for I cannot hope to detail everything to you), we came to the Forum. This is a large square, surrounded by lofty porticos of fluted columns, some broken, some entire, their entablatures strewed under them. The temple of Jupiter, of Venus, and another temple, the Tribunal, and the Hall of Public Justice, with their forests of lofty columns, surround the Forum. Two pedestals or altars of an enormous size (for, whether they supported equestrian statues, or were the altars of the temple of Venus, before which they stand, the guide could not tell), occupy the lower end of the Forum. At the upper end, supported on an elevated platform, stands the temple of Jupiter. Under the colonnade of its portico we sat, and pulled out our oranges, and figs, and bread, and medlars (sorry fare, you will say), and rested to eat. Here was a magnificent spectacle. Above and between the multitudinous shafts of the sun-shining columns was seen the sea, reflecting the purple noon of heaven above it, and supporting, as it were, on its line the dark lofty mountains of Sorrento, of a blue inexpressibly deep, and tinged towards their summits with streaks of new-fallen snow. Between was one small green island. To the right was Capreae, Inarime, Prochyta, and Misenum. Behind was the single summit of Vesuvius, rolling forth volumes of thick white smoke, whose foam-like column was sometimes darted into the clear sky, and fell in little streaks along the wind. Between Vesuvius and the nearer mountains, as through a chasm, was seen the main line of the loftiest Appennines, to the east. The day was radiant and warm. Every now and then we heard the subterranean thunder of Vesuvius; its distant deep peals seemed to shake the very air and light of day, which interpenetrated our frames, with the sullen and tremendous sound. This scene was what the Greeks beheld (Pompeii, you know, was a Greek city). They lived in harmony with nature; and the interstices of their incomparable columns were portals, as it were, to admit the spirit of beauty which animates this glorious universe to visit those whom it inspired. If such is Pompeii, what was Athens? What scene was exhibited from the Acropolis, the Parthenon, and the temples of Hercules, and Theseus, and the Winds? The islands and the Aegean sea, the mountains of Argolis, and the peaks of Pindus and Olympus, and the darkness of the Boeotian forest interspersed?

From the Forum we went to another public place; a triangular portico, half enclosing the ruins of an enormous temple. It is built on the edge of the hill overlooking the sea. That black point is the temple. In the apex of the triangle stands an altar and a fountain, and before the altar once stood the statue of the builder of the portico. Returning hence, and following the consular road, we came to the eastern gate of the city. The walls are of enormous strength, and inclose a space of three miles. On each side of the road beyond the gates are built the tombs. How unlike ours! They seem not so much hiding-places for that which must decay, as voluptuous chambers for immortal spirits. They are of marble, radiantly white; and two, especially beautiful, are loaded with exquisite bas-reliefs. On the stucco-wall that incloses them are little emblematic figures, of a relief exceedingly low, of dead and dying animals, and little winged genii, and female forms bending in groups in some funereal office. The higher reliefs represent, one a nautical subject, and the other a Bacchanalian. Within the cell stand the cinerary urns, sometimes one, sometimes more. It is said that paintings were found within; which are now, as has been everything movable in Pompeii, removed, and scattered about in royal museums. These tombs were the most impressive things of all. The wild woods surround them on either side; and along the broad stones of the paved road which divides them, you hear the late leaves of autumn shiver and rustle in the stream of the inconstant wind, as it were, like the steps of ghosts. The radiance and magnificence of these dwellings of the dead, the white freshness of the scarcely finished marble, the impassioned or imaginative life of the figures which adorn them, contrast strangely with the simplicity of the houses of those who were living when Vesuvius overwhelmed them.

I have forgotten the amphitheatre, which is of great magnificence, though much inferior to the Coliseum. I now understand why the

Greeks were such great poets; and, above all, I can account, it seems to me, for the harmony, the unity, the perfection, the uniform excellence, of all their works of art. They lived in a perpetual commerce with external nature, and nourished themselves upon the spirit of its forms. Their theatres were all open to the mountains and the sky. Their columns, the ideal types of a sacred forest, with its roof of interwoven tracery, admitted the light and wind; the odour and freshness of the country penetrated the cities. Their temples were most upaithric [open to the sky]; and the flying clouds, the stars, or the deep sky, were seen above.

Life, Customs and Morals in Naples

[133] THE EARLIEST ENGLISH DESCRIPTION OF NAPLES AND THE NEAPOLITANS, FROM *THE HISTORIE OF ITALY* BY WILLIAM THOMAS.

(William Thomas was once Clerk of the Privy Council to Edward VI, and his *Historie of Italie* was published in 1549. He was hanged, drawn and quartered at Tyburn in 1554 for rebellion against Queen Mary.)

The city of Naples (sometimes called Parthenope) is one of the fairest cities of the world for goodly streets and beautiful building of temples and houses, specially the Castel Nuovo wherein the kings were wont (as the Viceroy now is) to be most commonly resident, being one of the rarest buildings for greatness and strength that anywhere is likely to be found.

The country about is so pleasant that in manner every village deserveth to be spoken of, as well for sumptuous buildings and number of commodities, namely, abundance of delicate fruits, as also for the wholesome air. For in most places it seemeth always (yea, at the deadest of the winter) to be continual springtime. Indeed, the heat of summer doth somewhat grieve them, but they are so provided of large and open buildings that it doth not much annoy them . . .

The Neapolitan for his good entertainment [is] reckoned to be the very courtesy of the world, though most men repute him to be a great flatterer and full of craft. What will you more? They are rich, for almost every gentleman is lord and king within himself; they have very fair women and the world at will, insomuch as Naples contendeth with Venice whether [it] should be preferred for sumptuous dames.

[134] SPANISH CUSTOMS INTRODUCED TO NAPLES
UNDER THE VICEROYS; FROM L. COLLISON-
MORLEY'S *NAPLES THROUGH THE CENTURIES*.

The outlook of the Spaniards under Gonzalvo de Cordova [the first viceroy, 1503–7] was quite different from that of Alfonso's Catalans. The latter came to learn, with a profound respect for a superior civilization. The Cinquecento Spaniards were military adventurers, who despised culture as unworthy of a hidalgo. They were conquerors, flattered and imitated by a people that looked up to them. The penniless, proud Spanish soldier, whose one object was to line his pockets, became a well-known figure in Naples, the headquarters of the Spanish garrison in Italy. Pontanus tells of the Spaniard who asked to be allowed to dine with some Italians off a duck at an inn; but when they heard him roll out his four long names, they exclaimed, 'God have mercy on us! One poor duck will never be enough for four such great gentlemen, and Spaniards to boot.'

He is the braggart Captain of the Mask Comedy under many names – Matamoros, Coccodrillo and the like. He is also the dismal lover, Don Diego, with his sighs and his 'mi vida', 'mi corazón'. But he set the fashion as a conqueror. 'They greatly affect the Spanish gravity in their habit,' says Evelyn of the Neapolitans. The Spaniard brought with him the black clothes which he had been taught to wear by Charles V . . . With him too came his love of ceremony and elaborate courtesy, not a little of which he has left behind him – the handkissing, the taking off the hat by way of salute, the obsequious endings of letters, 'I kiss your hands and feet', 'Your most humble servant', and the like; even the habit of addressing your equals in the third person, which so distressed Annibal Caro, since we must talk to someone as if he were someone else, and in any case in the abstract, as though we were talking to the idea of a man and not to the man himself.

He also brought his sports, the Moorish game of darts and the bull-ring. Toledo himself was a skilled *torero*, taking part in a *corrida* in honour of Charles V's visit, though bull-fighting never became popular in Italy.

[135] THE GROWTH OF NAPLES' POPULATION IN THE SEVENTEENTH
CENTURY UNDER THE SPANISH VICEROYS; FROM 'SOCIETY
IN NAPLES IN THE SEICENTO' BY GIUSEPPE GALASSO, IN
PAINTING IN NAPLES FROM CARAVAGGIO TO GIORDANO.

How many inhabitants were there in Naples at the end of the sixteenth and the beginning of the seventeenth century? Giulio Cesare Capaccio, well-informed on Neapolitan matters and long secretary of the city's administration, said there were 300,000 people, distributed in 44,000 families and 20,000 dwellings. The general impression was that there were many more. But these were enough to make it by far the largest Italian city (Rome, Milan, Venice, Florence and Genoa had between 80,000 and 170,000 inhabitants) and the second largest in Europe after Paris. Moreover, the city must have been far larger halfway through the seventeenth century after three decades of tumultuous and dramatic events which attracted more immigrants from the southern regions.

The extraordinary size of the city was due to constant immigration from the countryside and from the smaller centres of the Kingdom of the Two Sicilies, of which Naples had unexpectedly become the capital in 1266. This role increased its population from some 30,000 to 100,000 inhabitants at the beginning of the sixteenth century. To understand this growth it is necessary to look more closely at the structure and physiognomy which Naples had acquired. Her function as capital had been the cause of the growth by which Naples had first drawn close to the size of the other great Italian cities and then, from the beginning of the seventeenth century, outstripped them. Economic reasons had been less important in this than political, institutional and social ones.

From the mid-fifteenth century the monarchy had gradually concentrated in Naples the administration of the Kingdom, which covered most of southern Italy. In 1503 the Kingdom had passed to the House of Aragon and thus, in 1516, became a part of the Habsburg patrimony. The Spanish Habsburgs, from Charles V (1516–56), Philip II (1556–98), Philip III (1598–1621), Philip IV (1621–65) to Charles II (1665–1700), reigned over Naples for two centuries. Their power rested on great military forces, both on land and at sea, that were stationed in Naples. It was powerful enough to deny the feudal lords the possibility of local resistance which they had offered the rulers of the Houses of Anjou and Aragon in the past, often reducing the royal power to a shadow. Now the barons had to renounce their claim to act as semi-autonomous rulers on their own estates. They had to accept their role as courtiers, subjects who were privileged and titled, but still subservient. The power that in theory was supposed to be delegated to them by the sovereign, and which they had traditionally used as a platform for their antagonism to the sovereign himself, was far more firmly controlled.

Under the new regime most of the barons were induced to abandon their residences in the provinces and live in the capital. Power games now revolved around the royal government in Naples. The obligations of loyalty imposed by the new balance of power, the etiquette and demands of a culture that had changed profoundly since medieval times and the elements of city life that at this date made it more refined and attractive than the provinces, induced the most powerful and wealthy families to migrate *en masse* to Naples. Transformed into modern gentlefolk, they formed a circle round the court of the viceroy, the *alter ego* of the King, giving an unprecedented worldliness to the social life of the capital.

Neapolitan feudalism evolved into a modern monarchy on French lines, rather than the anarchy that resulted from the ruinous predominance of the nobility over the monarchy, as, for instance, in Poland. The French model led to the pre-eminence of royal power, to the modern authoritarian State, where the capital was both a product and an image of power: a great bureaucratic metropolis that supported its nobles, courtiers and law-courts, while the lower orders remained poverty-stricken. The same pattern was repeated in Madrid, Vienna, Rome, Berlin and Paris. In an age of absolutism, Naples was one of the largest such centres in Europe, marked by the exceptional colour and individuality of Neapolitan life.

The vast population was concentrated in a restricted area, within a circumference of eight miles – twelve including the suburbs. The population density cannot therefore have been less than 7,000 to the square kilometre. However, the very spacious religious, civic and military buildings, the vast green spaces still present here and there in the central zones as well as in many outlying areas, the grandiose administrative buildings and embassies and the scale of the great houses of the aristocracy and the bourgeoisie, all combined to reduce considerably the area available for the mass of the population and so to increase the density of inhabitants in the dwelling quarters.

This soon led to frenetic building, with space being intensively exploited. Most of the houses in Naples had four to six stories while in other cities they rarely exceeded three. The effect was enhanced by the fact that the city plan was still, with very few alterations, that of the Greek settlers who had founded it around the seventh century BC: a checkerboard of long and narrow streets, overshadowed by continuous high buildings removing air and light from the lower stories and the street, but giving welcome cool shade in hot weather and an overall impression of metropolitan grandeur.

The crowding was, and still remains, everyone's first impression of Naples. 'I see in every street, every alley, at every corner so many people who jostle me and tread on me, and I have difficulty in getting away from them', wrote Gapaccio. 'I go into churches, of which there are so many, and I find them full of people; yet they are all there outside, not to mention all those who are at work, at home or in the offices and other buildings; one sees the streets, not just one or ten, but all of them full of people on foot, on horseback, in carriages'. With the crowds went noise, another characteristic immediately noted in modern Naples, 'a murmuring everywhere as if it were the buzzing of bees'. And with the crowds and the noise, 'Nothing', concluded Capaccio, 'is more difficult than getting about in Naples, wherever I go and at whatever time of day.'

The height of the buildings was possible because of the solid local stone and mortar. But Capaccio, although a great admirer of his city, recognized that this height and bulk was not matched by aesthetic and monumental qualities, and he found Naples inferior in this respect to cities like Rome, Florence or Venice. But this did not mean that there was a lack of great palaces worthy of aesthetic appreciation. Indeed, in the sixteenth and seventeenth centuries there was a resurgence of palace building. It was then that the historic centre assumed the aspect which it still preserves; for decades it was a great and ceaselessly busy building-site. Building became perhaps the greatest economic activity in Naples, and rent from properties the biggest item in the income of many social groups. Overcrowding led to the occupation of grottoes, courtyards, warehouses, attics and mezzanines as make-shift homes, in precarious conditions and devoid of any comfort. Many slept in the streets, on or by their stalls, under porticoes or in open lobbies, wherever some shelter could be found . . .

Against a background of congested streets and constant building, the political, administrative, judicial, military and financial workings of the city took place. The influx into Naples had been stimulated by the possibilities of work there, although this soon became more of a myth than a reality. Many arrived in the entourage of their lords, or to be employed by the religious institutions or the army. The great court of the viceroy, dozens of smaller courts in noble houses, the innumerable churches and religious centres, the civil and military offices of all kinds, and extensive wholesale and retail trade, a myriad of workshops and the extensive building trade, all demanded a work force. The sea also played an important part in the life of the city; apart from military and commercial considerations, there were thousands of fishermen, fish-sellers and boatmen, and the fish market was one of the most important in the city. The merchant fleet of Naples was not large, but its commercial maritime importance was nevertheless great, because the port of Naples was in practice the only great port in the country and the trade of a large part of the kingdom therefore converged upon it . . .

Some chroniclers said that from this time the physical appearance of Neapolitans changed: they were shorter in height, had more swarthy skins and less gentle features. But physique was also affected by the foodstuffs available in the city. In the sixteenth century, pasta replaced vegetables as the staple food and the Neapolitans passed from being 'leaf-eaters' to being 'macaroni-eaters' . . .

Moreover, in 1656 it was struck by a plague of unprecedented violence; one can reckon that sixty per cent of the population were killed by it. Although, once again, a high rate of immigration and a rapid growth in the birthrate immediately afterwards quickly repopulated Naples, at the end of the seventeenth century it still had roughly twenty-five per cent less inhabitants than in 1656 while other European cities, including London and Vienna rapidly outstripped it. The economic and social recovery was slow . . .

By way of recompense, intellectual activity and the political and civil conscience underwent a renaissance during this period of recession in the second half of the seventeenth century. It was to constitute the basis for a great attempt at alliance between monarchy and intellectuals in the eighteenth century. But above all, it allowed Naples to reach a new level of cultural achievement and prestige that would mark perhaps the finest moment of its modern history.

[136] LIFE IN NAPLES IN 1645 AS SEEN BY AN ENGLISH TRAVELLER
ON THE GRAND TOUR; FROM *THE DIARY OF JOHN EVELYN*.

We went by coach to take the air and see the diversions, or rather madness, of the Carnival; the courtesans (who swarm in this city to the number, as we are told, of 30,000, registered and paying a tax to the State) flinging eggs of sweet water into our coach as we passed by the houses and windows. Indeed the town is so pestered with these cattle that there needs no small mortification to preserve one from their enchantment whilst they display all their natural and artificial beauty, play, sing, feign compliment and by a thousand studied devices seek to inveigle foolish young men . . .

The building of the city is for the size the most magnificent of any in Europe, the streets exceeding large, well paved, having many vaults and conveyances under them for the sulliage, which renders them very sweet and clean even in the midst of winter. To it belongeth more than 3000 [sic] churches and monasteries, and these the best built and adorned of any in Italy. They greatly affect the Spanish gravity in their habit, delight in good horses – the streets are full of gallants on horseback, in coaches and sedans (from hence brought first into England by Sir Sanders Duncomb). The women are generally well-featured but excessively libidinous. The country people [are] so jovial and addicted to music that the very husbandmen almost universally play on the guitar, singing and composing songs in praise of their sweethearts, and will commonly go to the field with their fiddle. They are merry, witty and genial, all of which I much attribute to the excellent quality of the air.

[137] THE NEAPOLITAN LOVE OF OSTENTATION, IN
1739; FROM *LETTRES HISTORIQUES ET CRITIQUES
SUR L'ITALIE* BY CHARLES DE BROSSES.

To my way of thinking Naples is the only city in Italy which really feels like a capital. Hustle and bustle, crowds, an enormous number of jostling carriages, a Court which is a proper Court and a glittering one at that, the attendants and the air of magnificence of the great nobles, all these help to create the same busy and lively atmosphere one finds in Paris or London and which does not even exist in Rome. The lower orders are turbulent, the bourgeoisie pretentious. The higher nobility is ostentatious, the lesser is greedy for splendid-sounding titles – of which it certainly had enough to satisfy it when the House of Austria ruled here. The Emperor sold titles to anyone who wanted one, whence comes the saying '*E veramente duca, ma non cavaliere*', and the butcher who supplies us only does business through his shop-assistants since he became a duke. A tradesman's wife will not leave her house in her carriage unless she has another carriage in attendance, probably without a single person in it, but this always makes a good impression and gets talked about everywhere . . .

Let us return to Neapolitan *grands seigneurs*. They live more in the Spanish than the Italian style. They may be visited in their palaces and receive foreigners most graciously, keeping open house and frequently an open table as well. The Duke of Monteleone (of the Pignatelli family) does not quite keep an open table at his palace, but he nonetheless holds a reception there every day which is the finest and most magnificent in the entire city, it being rumoured that each one costs him more than 50,000 francs for candles, ices and refreshments, etc. He is the richest man in the country. We received a no less hospitable welcome from the Marquis of Montalegre, the first minister; from the very plump Carafa duke; from the Abbé Galiani, one of the realm's most distinguished intellects; from Prince Jaci; and from Don Michele Reggio, General of the Galleys, whom I hold in particular esteem on account of the good cheer he so often gave us.

[135] The Neapolitan way of life in 1779–80; from *Reminiscences* by the Irish singer Michael Kelly.

It is remarkable, that notwithstanding the vices of these people [the *lazzaroni*], and the extraordinary cheapness of wine in Naples, I never, during my sojourn there, witnessed a single instance of intoxication. The Neapolitans in general hold drunkenness in abhorrence. A story is told there of a nobleman, who, having murdered another in a fit of jealousy, was condemned to death. His life was offered to him on the sole condition of his saying, that when he committed the deed, he was intoxicated. He received the offer with disdain, and exclaimed, 'I would rather suffer a thousand deaths than bring eternal disgrace on my family, by confessing the disgraceful crime of intoxication.' He persisted, and was executed . . .

The mode of living of the Neapolitans at first was disagreeable to me. They are very early risers; and at noon flock to the coffee houses, shops, promenades, &c; the streets are crowded with monks, abbés, mountebanks, and lawyers. (It is calculated that in the kingdom of Naples only, there are twenty thousand lawyers, most of them younger branches of the nobility, whom poverty condemns to the bar. There is no nation, however large, in which so many lawsuits are carried on.) Twelve o'clock is their usual hour of dinner, after which they take the siesta, rising usually an hour or two before sunset, and repairing again to the coffee houses to eat ice, which is in Italy beyond conception fine. Their chocolate, melon, grape, peach, &c. are delicious; my favourite was the harlequin, which is a mixture of all, served up in a silver cup, piled like a pagoda, which cost then only two-pence English.

Even the Lazzaroni have their cooling luxuries; at the corner of every street, there are stalls, belonging to vendors of water melons, iced and lemonade water, crying out, 'Bella cosa è l'acqua fresca~' (What a beautiful thing is fresh water). For a novo callo (half a farthing), a man, at the time I am speaking of, could get a large glass of iced water, with the juice of a lemon, and a slice of water melon in it.

The favourite drives of the nobility are the Molo, and along the shore to Posilipo; there they enjoy the sea breeze in their carriages. It is only the very commonest people who go on foot; a Neapolitan gentleman would be branded with disgrace, if he were caught committing the hideous misdemeanour of using his own legs . . .

Calashes are to be found at the corners of all the principal streets in Naples. A calash is a small narrow gilt chair, set between two wheels, and without springs, drawn by one horse, which is guided by a cord tied round his nose, without bridle or bit. The driver, who usually wears his hair in a net, sometimes sports his night-cap, with a gold-laced hat over it, gets up behind, and, to do you honour, endangers your neck, driving helter-skelter through the streets, even through the Toledo Street, the longest and most populous one in all Naples, I think as long as Oxford Street, and actually swarming with friars, lawyers and Lazzaroni. All the time he bellows, with the lungs of a stentor, 'Make way there for my Lord Anglais!'

[139] NEAPOLITAN EXTRAVAGANCE IN THE LATE EIGHTEENTH CENTURY; FROM *TRAVELS IN THE TWO SICILIES* BY HENRY SWINBURNE.

Citizens and lawyers are plain enough in their apparel, but the female part of their family vies with the first court ladies in expensive dress, and all the vanities of modish fopperies. Luxury has of late advanced with gigantic strides in Naples. Forty years ago, the Neapolitan ladies wore nets and ribbons on their heads, as the Spanish women do to this day, and not twenty of them were possessed of a cap: but hair plainly dressed is a mode now confined to the lowest order of inhabitants, and all distinction of dress between the wife of a nobleman and that of a citizen is entirely laid aside. Expense and extravagance are here in the extreme. The great families are oppressed with a load of debt; the working part of the community always spend the price of their labour before they receive it; and the citizen is reduced to great parsimony, and almost penury, in his housekeeping in order to answer these demands of external show; short commons at home whet his appetite when invited out to dinner; and it is scarce credible what quantities of victuals he will devour. The nobility in general are well served, and live comfortably, but it is not their custom to admit strangers to their table; the number of poor dependants who dine with them, and cannot properly be introduced into company, prevents the great families from inviting foreigners: another reason may be their sleeping after dinner in so regular a manner as to undress and go to bed: no ladies or gentlemen finish their toilet till the afternoon, on which account they dine at twelve or one o'clock. The great officers of state, and ministers, live in a different manner, and keep sumptuous tables, to which strangers and others have frequent invitations.

The establishment of a Neapolitan grandee's household is upon a very expensive plan; the number of servants, carriages, and horses, would suffice for a sovereign prince; and the wardrobe of their wives is formed upon the same magnificent scale; yet it is a fixed rule, that all ladies whatever be the circumstance of their husbands, affluent or circumscribed, have an hundred ducats a month, and no more, allowed them for pinmoney. [There were forty-nine ducats to the English pound.] At the birth of every child, the husband makes his wife a present of an hundred ounces, and some valuable trinkets, according to his fortune. [An *oncia d' oro* was a gold coin worth three ducats.] Marriage portions are not very great in general; it does not cost a noble-man more to marry a daughter than it does to make her a nun; for a thousand pounds will not defray the expense of the ceremonies at her reception and profession: she must have a pension settled upon her, and reserves, besides, a power over her inheritance, in case she shall arrive at any dignity in the convent, and wish to enrich it with build-ings, plate, or vestments.

Servants and artificers of the city give from forty to an hundred ducats with their daughters; peasants and country workmen go as far as three hundred. Females at and near Naples are esteemed helpless and indolent, and therefore have always twice or thrice as much fortune as their brothers, who have greater resources in their strength and activity. A girl would scarce get a husband, if her lover did not expect to be reimbursed by her portion the sum he had paid away with his own sisters. In the plains, it is customary for a peasant, on the birth of a daughter, to plant a row of poplar trees, which are cut down and sold at the end of seventeen years, to make up a fortune for her. The proverbial benediction of *Figlii maschi*, 'Male children', which a Neapolitan gives a woman when she sneezes, is founded on the great facility with which the common people provide for their sons: as soon as they can run about they are able to earn their bread, while their sisters remain idle.

[140] The Neapolitan temperament; from *Travels in the Two Sicilies* by Henry Swinburne.

The women are always fighting and scolding, but never resist their husbands' authority, when he comes to separate the combatants, and carry home his dishevelled spouse, who seems to stand as much in awe of her consort, as the Russian wives do of theirs, and suffers herself to be beaten by him with a little murmuring. I was shewn a woman here, who, during the life of her first husband, was a pattern of modesty and evenness of temper to the whole parish; but upon contracting a second marriage, surprised and scandalized the neighbourhood with her perpetual riots and obstreperousness. On being reprimanded for her behaviour by the curate, she very frankly acknowledged that her former husband understood the management of a wife, and used to check her intemperate bursts of passion by timely correction; but that her present helpmate was too mild, to apply the proper chastisement which every wife requires more or less. Men seldom interfere in feminine brawls; and if they do, generally content themselves with abusing, threatening, or shaking a cudgel or pitchfork at their antagonist, till the crowd comes in to part them. Sometimes a man is stabbed, but this is a rare event among the fishermen, the class of inhabitants I have had most constantly under my eye. Manners vary with the districts; in some they engage with bludgeons, and those are the true lazaroni of Massaniello; in others the attack is made with knives and other deadly weapons; but the Neapolitans are by no means so bloody and revengeful a people as they are represented by many travellers. It requires more than a slight provocation to lead them to extremities. During the prodigious hurry and confusion of the races in carnival, not the least tumult or quarrel was heard of; and even in the cruel famine of 1764, the only act of violence committed by a hungry populace, increased to double its number by the concourse of peasants from the provinces, where all crops had failed, was to break open and pillage a single baker's shop. Can as much be said for the temper of the mobs at London and Edinburgh? Drunkenness is not a common vice at Naples, and therefore quarrels, its usual consequences, are rare; besides, the Neapolitan rabble allow each other a great latitude of abuse and scolding before they are wound up to a fighting pitch. It is also uncommon to see anything in public like gallantry among the people; no soldiers are met leading their doxies, or girls going about in quest of lovers; all of which are, in other countries, sources of riot and bloodshed. At Naples there is nothing but a mere nominal police; yet burglaries are unknown, riots still more so, and the number of assassinations inconsiderable.

[141] THE SLUMS OF NAPLES IN THE EIGHTEENTH CENTURY;
FROM *LES STRUCTURES DU QUOTIDIEN* BY FERNAND BRAUDEL.

(Fernand Braudel (born 1902) is one of the most original and influential of modern historians, and has received extraordinary international acclaim.)

Both sordid and beautiful, abjectly poor and very rich, certainly gay and lively, Naples counted 400,000, probably 500,000 inhabitants on the eve of the French Revolution. It was the fourth town in Europe, coming equal with Madrid after London, Paris and Istanbul. A major breakthrough after 1695 extended it in the direction of Borgo di Chiaja, facing the second bay of Naples (the first being Marinella). Only the rich benefited, as authorization to build outside the walls, granted in 1717, almost exclusively concerned them.

As for the poor, their district stretched out from the vast Largo del Castello, where the burlesque quarrels over the free distribution of victuals took place, to the Mercato, their fief, facing the Paludi plain that began outside the ramparts. They were so crowded that their life encroached and overflowed on to the streets. As today, washing was strung out to dry between the windows. 'The majority of beggars do not have houses; they find nocturnal asylum in a few caves, stables or ruined houses, or (not very different from the last) in houses run by one of their number, with a lantern and a little straw as their sole equipment, entry being obtained in exchange for a *grano* [a small Neapolitan coin] or slightly more, per night.' 'They are to be seen there,' continued the Prince of Strongoli (1783), 'lying like filthy animals, with no distinction of age or sex; all the ugliness and all the offspring which result from this can be imagined.' These ragged poor numbered at the lowest estimate 100,000 people at the end of the century. 'They proliferate, without families, having no relationship with the state except through the gallows, and living in such chaos that only God could get his bearings among them.' During the long famine of 1763–4 people died in the streets.

The fault lay in their excessive numbers. Naples drew them but could not feed them all. They barely survived and some not even that. Next to them an undeveloped petty-bourgeoisie of half-starved artisans scraped a bare living. The great Giovanni Battista Vico (1668–1741), one of the last universal minds of the West capable of speaking *de omni re scibili*, was paid a hundred ducats a year as professor at the University of Naples and only managed to live by private lessons, condemned 'to go up and down other people's staircases'.

Above this totally deprived mass let us imagine a supersociety of courtiers, great landed nobility, high-ranking ecclesiastics, obstructive officials, judges, advocates, and litigants. One of the foulest areas of the town, the Castel Capuano, was situated in the legal district. It contained the *Vicaria*, a sort of *Parlement* of Naples where justice was bought and sold and 'where pick-pockets lie in wait for pockets and purses'. How was it, asked a rational Frenchman, that the social structure remained standing when it was 'laden with an excessive population, numerous beggars, a prodigious body of servants, considerable secular and regular clergy, a military force of over 20,000 men, a multitude of nobles, and an army of 30,000 lawyers'?

But the system held as it always had, as it held elsewhere and at small cost. In the first place, these privileged people did not always receive rich livings. A little money was enough to move a man into the ranks of the nobles. 'Our former butcher no longer practises his trade except through his assistants since becoming a duke,' meaning since he bought a title to the nobility. But we are not forced to take Président de Brosses literally. Above all, thanks to State, Church, nobility and goods, the town attracted all the surplus from the Kingdom of Naples, where there were many peasants, shepherds, sailors, miners, craftsmen and carriers inured to hardship. The town had always fed on this hardship outside its boundaries since Frederick II, the Angevins and the Spaniards. The Church – which the historian Giannone attacked in his weighty pamphlet, *Istoria Civile del Regno di Napoli* in 1723 – owned at the lowest estimate two-thirds of the landed property in the kingdom, the nobility two-ninths. This was what restored the balance of Naples. It is true that only one-ninth was left to the *gente piu bassa di campagna*.

When Ferdinand, King of Naples, and his wife Maria Carolina visited Grand Duke Leopold and 'Enlightened' Tuscany in 1785, the unhappy King of Naples, more *lazzarone* than enlightened prince, grew irritated by the lessons set before him and the reforms held up for his admiration. 'Really,' he said one day to his brother-in-law, Grand Duke Leopold, 'I cannot understand what use all your science is to you; you read incessantly, your people do as you do, and your towns, your capital, your court, everything here is dismal and gloomy. As for me, I know nothing, and my people are still the liveliest people of all.' But then his capital city, Naples, could draw on the whole Kingdom of Naples, together with Sicily. In comparison little Tuscany could be held in the palm of the hand.

[142] THE CAMORRA IN THE BORBONE PERIOD; FROM L.
COLLISON-MORLEY'S NAPLES THROUGH THE CENTURIES.

What exactly was the Camorra? It was 'an association of men of the
people, corrupt and violent, which levied tribute by intimidation from
the vicious and cowardly'. As to its origin, it dates almost certainly from
the period of Spanish rule, from the days of the hired 'bravi'. The word
means a short jacket, such as was worn by them. During the revolutionary period the Camorra adopted some of the characteristics of the
Carbonari and other secret societies, with an elaborate ceremonial of
initiation, which was gradually discarded. The 'head of the Lazzerony
an old friend' with whom Emma Hamilton had dealings on behalf of
Ferdinand was probably the Head of the Camorra, and it was to him
that Ferdinand applied when Madame de Genlis was in Naples with the
Duchesse de Chartres and their panniers were stolen as they entered
the city. They were returned gratis, thanks to Ferdinand's intervention,
but they had to pay for their servants' liveries as they had not been
included in their application to the King.

The Camorra was first organized in the prisons and it was there
that it lingered longest and had the greatest power. Indeed, according
to Monnier, it was not till 1830 that it really left them and began to
obtain a hold on the life of the city as a whole. Ultimately it was
organized in twelve divisions corresponding to the twelve quarters of
the city, each with its own head. During the early part of the nineteenth century the prisons were entirely ruled by the Camorra, which
was openly recognized by the authorities. The Camorristi alone could
give and refuse the right to carry arms and it was they who superin-
tended the distribution of food and clothing. If they were at times
insolent and disorderly, they at least prevented disorder among the
other prisoners, while they used their authority to protect those who
submitted to them and to make it hot for those who did not. As usual
they began by levying contributions. The new-comer was at once met
by the Camorrista and asked for something 'for the oil of the Madonna',

i.e. for the oil for the lamp in front of the shrine of the Madonna, which was always kept burning . . .

The Camorristi had a special cult for the Madonna del Carmine and the Souls in Purgatory. The chief of the [Piazza del] Mercato Camorra possessed a picture of these Souls warding off the blows of the adversary whom he had killed in the duel that gave him his rank as a 'picciotto di sgarro', which he showed the liberal historian Niccola Nisco in prison. One of their superstitions was that, if you cut your arm and placed a consecrated wafer upon it, you became invulnerable.

It went ill with the unfortunate prisoner who failed to comply with this demand. The poorer prisoners would sell half their food, their blankets and the clothes distributed free to them twice a year, to the Camorrista, who shared the profits with the gaolers, for the right to drink, smoke or gamble, and for other indulgences, and the profits, even in prisons, were considerable. Each room had its Camorrista, who would collect every morning the fee for the extra bedding the richer prisoners hired from him. At Avellino, where the prison was cold and the air fresh, the prisoners were allowed by the Governor an extra loaf a day, but the Camorra never permitted them to receive it. Some of them were driven to chew straw and stray pieces of cotton to appease their ravenous craving for food. In fact, the Camorra robbed the prisoners in every conceivable way.

Sometimes, however, they met their match. A burly Calabrian priest, sent to prison for a scandalous love adventure, was met at the door, as usual, by the Camorrista who asked him for money for the oil of the Madonna. When he said he was penniless, the Camorrista threatened him with a stick. The priest, being a Calabrian, was no coward and said that if he had been armed, the Camorrista would never have dared to insult him in such a way. The Camorrista at once went to the secret store of arms belonging to the society and came back with two daggers, one of which he offered the priest, doubtless expecting him to refuse to fight. But he had mistaken his man. The priest had him stretched dead on the floor in a moment. He fully expected to expiate the murder with his life, but not only was nothing more heard of it – the authorities systematically winked at such little accidents where the Camorra was concerned – but on waking the next morning he found a comfortable sum by his bed, the share of a fully fledged Camorrista in the week's takes (*barattolo*) . . .

Naturally, when the Camorra began to extend its activities outside the prisons it retained its criminal character. The Camorrista, we are told, is a do-nothing on principal, a thief, a pick-pocket, a cheat, a stabber, anything. His object is to live by sponging on someone else, and he is merciless to anyone who stands in his way. The Camorra was thus the controlling and organizing power among the forces of evil inside the city, which supported it because of the protection it gave them. Every article stolen in Naples was instantly brought to Headquarters. A refusal to do so might mean the forfeit of his life by the offender. Hence those who knew how to go to work could always recover an article stolen by paying a reasonable price, from the King downwards, as we have seen, whereas an application to the police would have been worse than useless . . .

The Camorra had its regular grades. The lowest rank, the apprentices, if we may so call them, were the 'giovani onorati' or the 'garzoni di malavita', among whom the aspirant was enrolled only after the most careful inquiries had been made. As a rule he had been in trouble with the police, or had shown himself to be a youth of dash and spirit in some not very desirable way. The hilly region round S. Maria della Sanità, below Capodimonte – 'o monte', as it is called – was said to furnish many recruits to the Camorra, as its inhabitants were quarrelsome and unruly. The next stage was the 'picciotto di sgarro', the class of whom we hear most, and finally the full Camorrista. Promotion to the rank of 'picciotto di sgarro' was secured not merely by diligence and obedience, but also by bribery of the superiors. All the work and the danger fell to the lot of the lower grades, especially the 'picciotto', and it is generally a 'picciotto' that is meant when a Camorrista is mentioned. A defaulter in the lower ranks was punished much more severely than a full Camorrista, since absolute obedience was the first essential in such a society. Sentence of death was not uncommon and often carried out amid the greatest difficulties even in prison. Marc Monnier gives a number of interesting cases. The 'sfregio', the slashing of the face with a razor, was not unusual, but it was a punishment more often inflicted on women by jealous lovers, especially on prostitutes by their bullies, and the girls were frequently proud of it as a sign of love and devotion. It was always almost impossible to get evidence against the Camorristi, and in any case you could arrest only the Camorrista, never the Camorra. So long as it was securely rooted in the support of public opinion and looked up to by the people of Naples as a whole, no power on earth could put it down.

The full Camorrista only directed or received and divided the profits. He rarely fell into the hands of the police because, should he commit a crime, a junior would be ordered to take it upon himself and bear the full penalty and would be delighted with the honour thus conferred upon him. The position of a Camorrista was, in fact, ideal. He was a real gentleman, living at ease without work, universally respected and looked up to by the whole populace of Naples as a hero and a great man. A Capo-Camorrista such as the notorious Salvatore de Crescenzo was a power in the land.

But this position was not easily reached. The 'picciotto di sgarro' who had shown promise was first obliged to fight a duel with another Camorrista with knives, taking care to wound only in the arm, not in the breast. The duel was carefully umpired by someone in authority, similarly armed, who might even kill either of the combatants if they showed signs of turning it into a serious duel by aiming at the breast. The winner sucked the blood from the wound he had given and then embraced his opponent. If the 'picciotto' lost, he had to fight another duel. If he was beaten three times, he was suspended till he had won a serious duel, fought in earnest.

[143] CHARITABLE HELP FOR THE NEAPOLITAN POOR AT
THE START OF THE NINETEENTH CENTURY; FROM *A TOUR
THROUGH ITALY* BY JOHN CHETWODE EUSTACE.

(John Chetwode Eustace (1762–1815) was an English Catholic priest,
an antiquary, and a friend of Edmund Burke.)

To almost every hospital is attached one and sometimes more confraternities or pious associations, formed for the purpose of relieving
some particular species of distress, or averting or remedying some evil.
These confraternities though founded upon the basis of equality, and
of course open to all ranks, generally contain a very considerable
proportion of noble persons, who make it a point to fulfill the duties of
the association with an exactness as honourable to themselves, as it is
exemplary and beneficial to the public. These persons visit the respective hospitals almost daily, inquire into the situation and circumstances of every patient, and oftentimes attend on them personally,
and render them the most humble services. They perform these duties
in disguise, and generally in the dress or uniform worn by the
confraternity . . .

Of charitable foundations in Naples, the number is above sixty. Of
these seven are hospitals properly so called; thirty at least are conservatories or receptacles for helpless orphans, foundlings etc.; five are
banks for the relief of such industrious poor as are distressed by the
occasional want of small sums of money: the others are either schools
or confraternities . . . The two principal hospitals are that called *Degli
Incurabili*, which notwithstanding its title is open to sick persons of
all descriptions, and constantly relieves more than eighteen hundred;
and that *of Delia Santissima Annunziata*, which is immensely rich, and
destined to receive foundlings, penitent females etc. and is said sometimes to harbour two thousand. To each belong in the first place a
villa, and in the second a cemetery . . . When a patient has recovered
his health and strength and is about to return to his usual

occupations, he receives from the establishment a sum of money sufficient to compensate for the loss of time and labour unavoidable during his illness . . .

Of the numberless confraternities I shall only specify such as have some unusual and very singular object: such as that whose motto is *Succurre Miseris*, the members of which make it their duty to visit condemned criminals, prepare them for death, accompany them to execution, and give them a decent burial. They carry their charitable attentions still further, and provide for the widows and children of these unhappy wretches . . .

The congregation *De S. Ivone* consists of lawyers, who undertake to plead the causes of the poor gratis, and furnish all the expenses necessary to carry their suits through the courts with effect. To be entitled to the assistance and support of this association, no recommendation or introduction is required; the person applying has only to prove his poverty, and give in a full and fair statement of his case.

Congregations della Croce, composed principally of nobility, to relieve the poor and imprisoned, and particularly to bury the bodies of such distressed and foresaken persons when dead . . .

The Congregation of Nobles for the Relief of the Bashful Poor. The object of this association is to discover and relieve such industrious persons as are reduced to poverty by misfortune, and have too much spirit, or too much modesty, to solicit public assistance . . .

All these confraternities have halls, churches and hospitals.

[144] THE *LAZZARONI*, POOREST OF THE POOR, IN
1820; FROM *ITALY* BY LADY MORGAN.

Their poverty scarcely leaves them a home to shelter in; and their climate renders a domicile rather a luxury, than a necessity. The roof that screens them from the inclemency of the night, is the only roof they seek or know. The refuse of the people, with their common name of Lazzaroni, require not even this: – a bench, or a boat, pillows their slumbers, and the sky is their canopy, except in those transient and violent gusts of bad weather to which Naples is subject; when the portico of a palace, or the colonnade of a church, affords them all the temporary shelter they require.

The weather was occasionally very severe while we were at Naples; and it frequently happened, that on returning late from the opera, or from *Soirées*, we found the filthy portico of our old palace strewn with Lazzaroni. Some lay upon the earth, others were flung over a cask, or gathered round a brazier of hot embers, just sufficiently bright to glare upon their marked and grotesque features. Nothing could be more courteous or cordial than their manner: they all jumped up to make way for us, welcomed us home, wished us a good night's rest; and one or two of them, who had got up some English phrases, applied them at random, by way of being particularly polite . . .

The Mola on these occasions [Sundays] generally presented several circles, each two or three deep; they were composed of the lowest orders and the Lazzaroni; sometimes seated on wooden benches, sometimes on the ground, according to the price paid to some peripatetic philosopher, or READER, who occupied the centre, and who read aloud – Tasso or Mastrillo, stories from 'La Bibbia', or legends of much less edifying character. The image of one of these *academicians* will not readily escape my memory, as it never failed, during the Sundays of successive weeks, to fix my eye: he was a short square grotesque figure, with a face moulded on the model of the French polichinel – all nose, chin, and bushy eyebrows; he wore an immense wig, a large but torn cocked hat, the jacket, or the fragments of a jacket, of an Italian courier, and a pair of bright yellow buckskin small-clothes, from the cast-off wardrobe of some English groom. He was without shoes or stockings; his spectacles were immense; and he held a filthy tattered Tasso in one hand, and a stick or wand in the other, which he moved with great dignity and variety of gesture. For every line he recited he gave a commentary of his own, that might fill a page: sometimes pathetic, sometimes humorous, and always with an air so proudly oracular, as to excite the strongest disposition to laughter. Such however was not the effect produced on his auditors: never were countenances more concentrated, or more intensely expressive of the deepest interest – eyebrows were knit, lips distended, cheeks glowed, and heads shook, at the feats and fêtes of the 'Goffredo' and the 'Rinaldo', against whom, in vain,

'S'armò d'Asia e di Libia il popol misto.'

Some half-rose in their emotion – others uttered a deep ejaculation; and the murmured 'Bravo!' circulated with all the restrained emotion of those who feared to interrupt, by their applause, strains that commanded the most enthusiastic admiration! . . .

The two 'grani' that purchased their daily ration of maccaroni, the two more that went for ice-water and a puppet-show, were surely and easily earned; and a little surplus of ingenuity and industry procured a few yards of canvass, which made up their whole wardrobe (a shirt and trowsers), allowing even something for the superfluity of their red-worsted sash and cap. These wants supplied, nothing remained but the delicious far niente – the lounge in the sun or the shade – the laugh raised indiscriminately at friend or foe – a prayer offered at a shrine – or curses given to the scrivano [police magistrate], who mulcts some crime which poverty cannot redeem by a bribe . . .

[145] THE HIGH SPIRITS OF THE NEAPOLITAN WORKING-CLASSES IN 1823; FROM THE COUNTESS OF BLESSINGTON'S THE IDLER IN ITALY.

The more I see of the Neapolitans, the better I like them. I have not detected among the individuals of the lower class that have fallen in my way, a single instance of the rapaciousness so generally, and I am inclined to think so unjustly, attributed to them by strangers. Their politeness has nothing in it of servility; and their good humour is neither coarse nor boisterous. The gardeners, and their wives and families, appertaining to the Palazzo Belvedere, seem actuated by an unceasing desire to please us. Fresh flowers are sent in by them, every morning, for the apartments; the finest figs, and grapes, are offered for our acceptance; and smiling faces and courteous enquiries about the health of every individual of the family meet us, whenever we encounter any of them. They sing, and not inharmoniously, while at work in the garden; occasionally duos and trios, and at other times, one begins a song descriptive of rural occupations, and his companions answer it. There is something inexpressibly charming to me, in these wild airs; but perhaps they owe much of the attraction to the delicious atmosphere in which I hear them, which disposes the mind to be pleased. No night passes in which these good people, joined by the *custode* and his family, do not dance the *tarantella* in the court yard, to the music of their own voices, accompanied by the *tambour de basque*. Old and young all join in this national dance, with a gaiety it is quite exhilarating to witness . . .

The streets of Naples present daily the appearance of a fête. The animation and gay dresses of the lower classes of the people, and the crowds who flock about, convey this impression. Nowhere does the stream of life seem to flow so rapidly as here; not like the dense arid turbid flood that rushes along Fleet Street and the Strand in London; but a current that sparkles while hurrying on. The lower classes of Naples observe no medium between the slumber of exhaustion and the fever of excitement; and, to my thinking, expend more of vitality in one day than the same class in our colder regions do in three. They are never calm or quiet. Their conversation, no matter on what topic, is carried on with an animation and gesticulation unknown to us. Their friendly salutations might, by a stranger, be mistaken for the commencement of a quarrel, so vehement and loud are their exclamations, and their disagreements are conducted with a fiery wrath which reminds one that they belong to a land in whose volcanic nature they strongly participate. Quickly excited to anger, they are as quickly propitiated; and are not prone to indulge rancorous feelings.

It is fortunate that this sensitive people are not, like ours, disposed to habits of intoxication. Lemonade here is sought with the same avidity that ardent spirits are in England; and this cooling beverage, joined to the universal use of macaroni, is happily calculated to allay the fire of their temperaments.

[146] CARNIVAL IN NAPLES; FROM *THE IDLER IN ITALY* BY THE COUNTESS OF BLESSINGTON.

The Neapolitans, high and low, rich and poor, enter into the spirit of the carnival, with a reckless love of pleasure and zest, that appertains only to children in other countries. Even the old seem to enjoy the general hilarity produced by the heterogeneous *mélange* of Neptunes, Hercules, Cupids, shepherdesses, sailors, Spanish grandees, and a hundred other absurd masks. Innumerable carriages, filled with these votaries of pleasure, pass and repass in the Strada Toledo, playing their antics, and hurling at the persons they encounter, showers of bon-bons and bouquets of flowers. The dress of English sailors seems to be a favourite one with the maskers at the carnival, for we saw several worn by persons whose equipages indicated that they were of the aristocracy. The lower class substitute a composition of plaster of Paris for bon-bons, and often throw them with a violence that occasions accidents. Large are the sums expended by the gay Neapolitan gallants, in the purchase of the most delicate bon-bons and fragrant bouquets, which they throw into the carriages or windows, where they recognize their female acquaintances. A party of the *noblesse* a year ago, during the carnival, passed through the Strada Toledo, in a ship, placed on wheels, and fired from the guns at each side, volleys of bon-bons. Never were broadsides so amicably received, or so agreeably remembered, for they still form the topic of conversation, whenever a carnival is mentioned.

[147] The King of Thieves; from *The Story
of my Life* by Augustus Hare.

While we were at Naples [in 1858] my mother lost her gold watch. We
believed it to have been stolen as we were entering the Museo
Borbonico, and gave notice to the police. They said they could do nothing unless we went to the King of the Thieves, who could easily get it
back for us: it would be necessary to make terms with him. So a *raga-
zaccio* (or young rascal) was sent to guide us through one of the labyrin-
thian alleys on the hill of St Elmo to a house where we were presented
to the King of Thieves. He mentioned his terms, which we agreed to,
and he then said, 'If the watch has been stolen anywhere within twelve
miles round Naples, you shall have it in twenty-hour hours.' Meanwhile
the watch was found by one of the custodes of the Museo at the bottom
of that bronze vase in which you are supposed to hear the roaring of the
sea; my mother had been stooping down to listen, and the watch had
fallen in.

[148] Neapolitan life before 1860; from
Naples: a Palimpsest by Peter Gunn.

(Peter Gunn was born in Melbourne in 1914. *Naples: a Palimpsest*,
published in 1961, is probably the best general study of the city – an
Italian translation appeared in 1971.)

These were the last great days of Neapolitan society; members of the
diplomatic corps and distinguished foreign visitors and residents joined
the aristocracy in functions which were considered at the time to be
the most brilliant in Europe. The Tsar's brother, the Grand Duke
Constantine and his wife, and the King and Queen of Prussia, travelling
incognito as the Count and Countess of Zollern, visited Naples in
Ferdinand II's last days. The club of the Accademia Reale, who only
admitted members who could show four quarterings, had its

headquarters over the Caffè di Europa in Piazza San Ferdinando, and gave splendid balls at San Carlo. Cosmopolitan society met at the Palazzo Torella, where the old Princess received every evening. Receptions, balls, theatrical performances in private theatres provided a round of amusement for the aristocracy. The Palazzi Scalafani, Bivona, Sant'Antimo, Santa Teodora and Bovino were the scenes of magnificent entertainments. In the Palazzo di' Angri during the summer they danced on the terrace in the open air, and the Largo dello Spirito Santo was crowded with waiting carriages.

The Count of Syracuse, Ferdinand's brother, was often seen at these houses. He was an openly avowed liberal, and had won a gold medal at the Exhibition of 1859 as a sculptor – the statue of G.B. Vico seen today in the Villa Communale is his work; he was a leader of the gayer, more cosmopolitan set, in strong contrast to the asceticism of Ferdinand and his Court. It was in the private theatre at his palace on the Riviera di Chiaia that a verse drama, written especially by the Duke Proto, was put on in March 1858. On this occasion the King and Court were present; indeed the young Duke of Calabria was said to have looked uncomfortable, overawed by the sight of so much magnificence and attractive femininity. The theme was an edifying one: that beauty has the power not only to lead perverted hearts to virtue but also to cure ancient hates. The parts were played by members of the nobility; 'the Duchess Ravaschieri was splendid, dressed all in white, with a diadem of brilliants on her head; and when, in the fourth scene she appeared on the stage, coming out of a star, there was a chorus of admiration and applause' . . .

The upper middle class, too, led a life that often was cultivated and gay. There were receptions where music was heard, poetry read, and history and literature discussed. To read de Cesare's *La Fine di un Regno* is to understand how much was lost to Naples with the gain of its vaunted liberty. In the houses of the lower middle classes the customary Neapolitan good nature prevailed: '*Nuie simme gente' e bon core*' ('We are good-hearted people', almost 'Take us as you find us') was the cue for bountiful hospitality, especially if the guests were in a position to assist their hosts in obtaining some favour. And it was the same *piccoli borghesi* – removed, as they were, but little either in rank or in sentiment from the 'people' – who contributed so much to the rich spontaneity, colour and charm of Neapolitan culture in the nineteenth century. The songs of the period are peculiarly theirs; in the words and the music are found all the warmth, aspiration and sadness of their popular philosophy.

It was the period of the crinoline and sleeves *à gigot*, of ribbons and little jackets trimmed with fur, of large straw hats covered with flowers for the summer, and parasols of lace-edged taffeta. Madame Cardon and Madame Giroux were the names of the fashionable *couturières*, and Madame Fass showed off the elegance of Parisian *haute mode* in her shop in the Palazzo Calabritto. The colourful dress of the lower classes can be seen in de Bourcard's *Usi e Costumi di Napoli*. On days of *festa* when Naples was filled with peasants from the countryside, the scene was still little different from what it was earlier in the century, when it was said to have resembled a gorgeous bed of tulips. The popular songs at this time were *Santa Lucia, Palummella Janca, Scetete Scè, U Cardillo*, Donizetti's charming *Io te Voglio Ben' Assai* and Bellini's *Fenesta ca Lucive*. These songs were known and sung by all classes; a young fisherman would serenade his *innamorata*, in the strong throbbing lilt of:

> *Io te voglio ben' assai,*
> *E tu non pienza' a me.*
> (I want you very much,
> And you don't think of me.)

In November 1857, Verdi was in Naples for the production of his opera *Il Trovatore* at San Carlo, which had the greatest success. For the beginning of the winter season his *Leonello*, as *Rigoletto* was then called, had an unfortunate opening. One of the leading singers,

Coletti, was hoarse, and to save his voice, the middle of the opera, from the end of the first act to the quartette in the last, was omitted, causing scenes of the greatest indignation. In the ballet which followed la Tedeschi, the prima ballerina, came on the stage to the shouts and hisses of the furious audience. The operas of Bellini, Donizetti and Rossini were still much in vogue at this time. Performances of military bands in public were very popular, especially with the *lazzaroni* and the young ladies . . .

Men of fashion favoured mostly the English style of tailoring. Lennon Taylor and Mackenzie were the best known of these, but Plassenell, who cut in the French manner, was also patronized. Diaco, too, a Neapolitan, was said to have adapted 'French grace with England's good taste' to the local style. After the Crimean war the Raglan became fashionable for winter. Later the English firm of Gutteridge was established on the Toledo. Shops were both elegant and varied. The brothers Savarese had a famous establishment, where Gambrinus now is; there they sold all manner of *objets d'art* and gifts from bronzes to expensive dolls. On Good Friday, after taking part in *lo struscio* (the traditional walk down the Toledo), the King would shop and accept refreshment from the Savarese. The most elegant shop for English goods was Peirce, on the Toledo; for articles from France, Monsieur Germain, in the Piazza San Ferdinando . . .

Although the great age of the cafés did not begin in Naples until the 'sixties, the Caffè di Europa was at this period the meeting-place of fashionable Neapolitans of the aristocracy and richer middle class. In small rooms on the mezzanine floor distinguished foreigners used to lunch; and after the opera at San Carlo the *habitués* of the theatre would stroll across the square, and in the mirrored rooms of the café would meet the *dilettanti* of the arts, the pungent epigrammatists of the day, and the *jeunesse dorée*. It was said that the Caffè di Europa was regarded as a kind of Jerusalem by those Neapolitans who were not noble or elegant or amusing. At Benvenuto's in the Via Chiaia the upper classes went to take their ices; Benvenuto was regarded as making an ice which was the last word in perfection. Matthew Arnold, a discriminating critic, wrote of these, 'In England, no-one knows what ices are – the water-ices of Naples.' And not far away from Benvenuto's was a much patronized *patisserie française*, and also that of Spiller, the Swiss, who opened his shop in 1858 and gained a high reputation for exquisite cakes and pastries. Of the Neapolitan pastrycooks, Pintauro is said to have borne the palm with his traditional *sfogliatelle*. The well-known firm of Caflisch was established as early as 1825.

Indeed, with the beautiful veal from Sorrento, the fish and oysters, fresh vegetables, fruits and nuts, and a number of French cooks (called by local corruption '*monsù*' to add distinction to the *cuisine*, there was no lack of 'viands of the rarest and choicest quality', as Mr Gunter would have said, in Naples at this time. For those who could afford it. Then there were the *pizzerie*, like those in the Via di Pietro il Pizzaiuolo; by the sea at Santa Lucia the stalls of the vendors of *zuppa di vongole*; and in every piazza, on *bancarelle* and trays, roasted chestnuts, oranges, delicious wild strawberries, biscuits and aqua-vita were displayed; there were the sellers of cooked snails, the *maruzzaro*, or the soup of *polpi* and *pepperoni*; and in summer the *melonaro* who claimed that his melons refreshed you and washed your face at one and the same time; and everywhere the purveyors of sulphurated water from the spring at Santa Lucia, and of the *spremute* of oranges and lemons.

Among this gay Neapolitan crowd the noise was deafening – both Lady Blessington and Nietzsche had cause to complain of it: the clack of horses' hooves on the *piperno* paving-stones and the grating of carriage wheels, the raucous cries of street vendors, the shouts of the *lazzaroni* who seemed unable to carry on a conversation except at the top of their voices; the music that was heard everywhere, from wandering mandolins and guitars or from street and military bands; and the clamour of bells from a hundred churches and convents. It was only in the early hours of the morning, when the last carriage had put down at their palazzi those returning from the ball at San Carlo, and the late walker paused to avoid treading on a bundle of rags curled up by the steps of a church, that one could say with Shelley:

'The city's voice is soft, like Solitude's.'

[149] THE LAST ARMY OF THE TWO SICILIES; FROM
TRUFFLE HUNT BY SIR SACHEVERELL SITWELL.

The musuem in the Certosa di San Martino, above Naples, has many fascinating memorials of the Bourbon Kingdom of the Two Sicilies. Not least of them is a series of water colours of the new uniforms for the Neapolitan army. I used to be greatly intrigued by these, and to my delight I found they had been published in a volume. It was not long before I bought a copy of this book from Detken and Rocholl, the bookseller in the square in front of the Royal Palace, flanking the equestrian statues of Kings of Naples by Canova. My copy was sent to me in England. It is bound in rose-coloured velvet and the bookseller alleged that this was King 'Bomba', Ferdinand II's own copy.

Here is a brief description of this precious item in my library. *Tipi Militari dei differenti Corpi che compongono Il Reale Esercito e l'Armata di Mare di S. M. il Re del Regno delle Due Sicilie*, Napoli, 1850, per Antonio Zezon. It opens, in splendour, with the above engraved title on a label, in midst of a perfect arsenal of weapons, bristling with banners, spears and halberds, with artillery at the foot, but, it is to be noted, with the real emphasis given to all the different instruments of a full military brass band, drums, kettledrums, and so forth, lying upon the ground, and one or two footsoldiers and mounted hussars to guard them. You turn the page, and find Ferdinand II as Captain-General, in buckskin breeches and tunic covered with orders; and on the next page a dear old gentleman, in crimson trousers with a blue stripe and blue tailcoat covered with orders, suffering obviously from gout and leaning heavily on a stick, the King's uncle, Leopoldo di Borbone, Principe di Salerno. Born in 1790, he was the son of Ferdinand I and Maria-Carolina, sister of Marie Antoinette.

Reluctantly, I heighten the pace, passing a Field-Marshal in full gallop before the Royal Palace, and come to another prince, King 'Bomba's' younger brother, Don Francesco di Borbone, Conte di Trapani. On a further page, three officers of the general staff, or Stato Maggiore, are arguing furiously with a wealth of Neapolitan gesture by a table and a curtain, and at the side there is the 15th Century Porta Capuana. The book becomes more exciting. On a black horse there is a damson-coloured Hussar, that is to say, he rides on a damson-coloured saddle-cloth and has damson froggings on his chest and slung jacket, scarlet trousers, and a busby with a red plume. Next, two Guides, like the Guides of the French army, in white duck trousers, blue tails, and high bearskins with rose-coloured plumes. A Guardia del Corpo à Cavallo, a very small man, on horseback, in white buckskin breeches and high boots, and a blue tunic with red facings, a carbine on his saddle, and an enormous classical helmet, with leopard-skin visor, and crest of a horse's tail; and the Guardie del Corpo on foot, in the Royal Palace, in ordinary dress, *tenuta giornaliera*, and in *gran tenuta*; ordinary dress like that of the Carabiniere of our own day, but the uniform is blue instead of black, and the *gran tenuta* is buckskin breeches and a blue tight-fitting tail coat with broad white facings. This more imposing figure has his white gauntleted hand upon his sword hilt. Next, a pair of Guardie del Corpo, dismounted; white trousers, in *tenuta giornaliera* and blue tail coat with red epaulettes; and in *gran tenuta*, white breeches, a tail coat with white facings, and an enormous bearskin with red cording and white plume. This gorgeous pair are on duty with rifle and bayonet. And a page of Guardie d'Onore, young men in the favourite damson colour who, the text tells us, have 'implored the Royal grace' to be allowed to form themselves into squadrons to attend the King upon his 'munificent journeys in the provinces' on occasions of *solennita e gala*, and have been assigned into eight squadrons in the different provinces.

Now come the two regiments of Grenadiers of the Royal Guard, a white-trousered officer wearing a bearskin, of which the loose ends mingle with his moustache and whiskers, and he has a remarkably dreary expression of face. The next page is one of the highlights of the whole volume; a sapper of the Grenadiers in a long white apron nearly down to his ankles, damson trousers and a bearskin which must have been appallingly hot to wear in the sun of Naples; and two bandsmen, a drummer and a bugler, the latter in damson, with blue tail coat, and hat of extraordinary invention, like a small bearksin 'worked' onto a helmet, and then folded over with a scarlet and white wrapping, and graced, finally, with an enormous tent-shaped plume. All this, on a quay in Naples harbour, with the Castello dell'Ovo in the distance. The ordinary guardsman of the Grenadiers, on the next page, looks undersized and disagreeable in his blue coat, red trousers, and bearskin with enormous dangling tassel.

Passing rapidly over plates of lesser interest, the Ussari della Guardia Reale look dashing enough in their scarlet and blue uniforms on damson saddle-cloths, particularly because in the background, in front of a crowd of *lazzaroni*, the mounted band is marching past a corner pavilion of the Royal Palace, and in another moment you would see Vesuvius across the bay. But a plate of a dismounted hussar has a melancholy expression and drooping moustache of enormous proportions which flows down in two waves and touches on his shoulders. The moustache is auburn, and he has a damson képi. I turn over some dozen plates of little interest . . . and come to a halt again at the Carabinieri à Piedi, wearing bearskins and the inevitable dark damson plumes and trousers. For the whole background of this plate is a view of Naples, with the harbour, and the Certosa di San Martino on the hill of Vomero, above the town. This is nostalgic to those who know Naples. In the very next plate, which is of no interest, there is Vesuvius smoking in the distance.

A *guastatore* [pioneer] of the 8th Battaglione Cacciatori wears dark blue and sombre black apron. He is one of the sappers of the regiment and he, again, wears a heavy bearskin which must have been insupportable in the heat, and has a bushy black beard to match. And we come to

the Swiss Regiments. There were three of these Regiments, who by
contract with the Swiss government came from the different cantons.
The first was of Grenadiers; and, as well, a battalion of Swiss Cacciatori
(Chasseurs) was formed on March 20, 1850, by 'Real Decreto di Sua
Maestà il Re N.S.'. . . And the first part of the book ends in a blaze of
glory with Carabinieri à Cavallo in blue and scarlet, with helms carrying the plume and horsetails, and long white cloaks; Dragoni-Re, or the
first regiment of Dragoons; and a dashing regiment of Lancers. All
these wear blue tunics, and trousers and saddlecloth of that peculiar
damson red which seems to have been the insignia of the Neapolitan
Army . . .

The last lithograph of the book carries the date 1856, so it was six
years in preparation. Upon the appearance of Garibaldi, four years
later, the Bourbon Army in their new uniforms fled in disorder, except
for a few regiments who held out at Gaeta from November 1860 until
February 13, 1861, with Francesco II, the last King, and his nineteen-
year-old wife Marie of Bavaria, a younger sister of the Empress Elizabeth
of Austria . . . Her husband died in 1894, but Queen Marie of the Two
Sicilies survived until 1925, and was to be seen staying at the Continental
Hotel in Munich.

[*In fact not just 'a few regiments' but well over 50,000 troops under General
Giosuè Ritucci rallied to Francis II at Gaeta, many of them having travelled
long distances barefoot and in rags. Of these 40,000 were defeated during
the battles around the Volturno river in October 1860 only because of unin-
spiring commanders, though it was a very close-run thing. The next month
another 9,000, hopelessly outnumbered, were overwhelmed at Capua by
Piedmontese invaders. Even then more than 900 officers – including the
heroic General Ferdinando Bosco – and 12,000 men chose to make a final
stand at Gaeta with their King and Queen.*]

[150] A LAMENT IN 1863 FOR THE PASSING OF THE TWO SICILIES,
BY AN EXILED SUPPORTER OF THE BORBONI; FROM GIACINTO
DE SIVO'S *STORIA DELLE DUE SICILIE DAL 1847 AL 1861.*

I don't say the old *Regno* was faultless, that it was a paradise. Wherever
men govern each other there is always bound to be some discontent,
whatever the country. Human good is relative – everything cannot be
quite the same for everybody. Some nations are warlike, others consists
of farmers, or of merchants, artists or manufacturers; what suits them
is for them to decide. Only bad judges omit to weigh good against evil,
since as many blessings as possible and as few ills are the real measure
of a country's prosperity. Political bias magnifies a government's failings without taking the times and the circumstances into account, and
crudely simplistic judgements obscure anything else worthwhile – as if
perfection were attainable by human endeavours. Closing one's eyes to
all that is good makes everything else look bad and raises countless
questions. Naples had fewer troops than France, fewer ships than
London, less liberty than America, not so much of the fine arts as Rome,
and less polish than Paris, though those are not the only things which
make for happiness. Nonetheless, in relation to its size and status the
country had enough of them to be second to none. Commerce, arts and
letters, morality, religion, security, comfort, industry, civil rights, all
these it had in plenty. People lived pleasantly and inexpensively, with
an abundance of entertainment and amusements; anybody who
avoided subversive politics enjoyed complete freedom and could do
what he liked. In short the realm was the happiest in the world.
Countless foreigners who came to it prospered so much that they
settled.

During the last forty years the population increased by a quarter.
There was a wealth of public buildings, of good roads, aqueducts, warehouses, free hospitals, bridges of stone, brick or iron, arsenals, arms
factories, barracks, foundries, high schools, academies, universities,
churches, royal palaces, convents, monasteries, harbours, docks,

shipping, fortresses, prisons, orphanages, flourishing industries, scientific farming, prize herds, reclaimed marshes, reservoirs, rivers harnessed for irrigation, botanical gardens, pawnshops, corn exchanges, stock markets and finance houses, freeports, arts and crafts institutes, funded charities, savings banks, insurance agencies, shipping brokers, merchant banks, railways, electric and submarine telegraphs, and every other amenity of civilized life. As for crime, murder was rare. Paupers were few and hunger practically unknown, since there was provision by religious, private, municipal and government charities. There was no paper money, only gold and silver. Taxes were light and expenses small – one lived very well on a modest income. Work was plentiful, prices low and holidays many. There was respect for the gentry, for the law, for authority, safety and order for everyone everywhere.

Then Gladstone came and called the regime 'the negation of God,' fed with lies by the opposition who wanted to bring in their 'God', and ruined us . . . almost unbelievable calumnies were repeated in newspapers all over the world.

Appendix A:
List of the Sovereigns who reigned at Naples

House of Anjou

Charles I	1266–1285
Charles II	1285–1309
Robert	1309–1343
Giovanna I	1343–1382
Charles III	1382–1386
Ladislaus	1386–1414
Giovanna II	1414–1435
René	1435–1442

House of Aragon

Alfonso I	1442–1458
Ferrante	1458–1494
Alfonso II	1494–1495
Ferrantino	1495–1496
Federigo	1496–1503

From 1503 to 1713 Naples was governed by Spanish viceroys and from 1713 to 1734 by Austrian viceroys.

House of Borbone

Charles VII	1734–1759
Ferdinand IV and I	1759–1825
Francis I	1825–1830
Ferdinand II	1830–1859
Francis II	1859–1860

Charles VII is generally known as Charles III after his title as King of Spain. Ferdinand IV adopted the title Ferdinand I instead in 1816 to mark the administrative union of Sicily with the mainland kingdom.

Appendix B: Chronology

1268   Charles I executes Conradin in what is now the Piazza del Mercato.

1279   Charles I begins to build the Castel Nuovo.

1282   Charles I loses half his kingdom in the Sicilian Vespers – Naples becomes a capital.

1294   Pope St Celestine V abdicates the Papacy – the only pontiff to do so – at the Castel Nuovo.

1310   King Robert the Wise begins the church of Santa Chiara.

1340   King Robert the Wise entertains Petrarch at the Castle Nuovo.

1345   Murder of the first husband of Queen Giovanna I, Andreas of Hungary.

1348   Hungarian occupation of Naples, followed by plague.

1348   Queen Giovanni I regains Naples.

1372   St Bridget, Queen of Sweden, visits Naples.

1382   Queen Giovanna I is deposed and murdered by Charles of Durazzo.

1385   Charles III – Charles of Durazzo – becomes King of Hungary as well.

1386   Charles III is murdered in Hungary.

1435   Death of Queen Giovanna II, the last unopposed Angevin sovereign.

1442   King René of Anjou is besieged and driven out of Naples by Alfonso of Aragon, who becomes the first King of The Two Sicilies.

1452   The Holy Roman Emperor Frederick III (of Habsburg) visits Naples.

1464   Ferrante of Aragon wins the battle of Ischia and defeats the last Angevins.

1479   Lorenzo de' Medici visits King Ferrante at Naples.

1484   Revolt of the barons against King Ferrante.

1486   King Ferrante arrests and kills the barons at the Castel Nuovo.

1487 Work begun on the Porta Capuana.

1495 The French occupy Naples.

1495 King Ferrantino recaptures Naples.

1503 The Spanish armies capture Naples. Federigo, the last King of the House of Aragon, goes into exile. Naples ruled from Spain for the next two centuries.

1528 Naples is besieged unsuccessfully by the French.

1532 The great viceroy, Don Pedro de Toledo, begins his reign of twenty-two years.

1536 The Emperor Charles V – Charles IV of The Two Sicilies – visits Naples.

1536 Construction of Via Toledo begins.

1540 The Vicaria – or High Court of Justice – is installed in the Castel Capuano.

1547 Successful rebellion against introduction of the Spanish Inquisition.

1586 Construction of the Gesù Nuovo begins.

1600 Construction of the Royal Palace begins.

1606 The painter Caravaggio comes to work in Naples.

1616 The painter Ribera (*Il Spagnoletto*) begins more than thirty years' work in Naples.

1623 Cosimo Fanzago appointed master of works at the Certosa di San Martino.

1630 The painter Domenichino comes to Naples to work there until his death in 1641.

1647 Masaniello's Revolt.

1656 The great plague – 60 per cent of Neapolitans die.

1656 The painter Mattia Preti (*Il Cavaliere Calabrese*) comes to Naples.

1685 First performance of Domenico Scarlatti's first opera, *Pompeo*.

1688 Severe earthquakes damage the city.

1692 Carlo Celano publishes his guide to Naples

1697 Laying out of the Riviera di Chiaia.

1707   Austrian occupation of Naples.

1713   Emperor Charles VI (Habsburg) recognized as Charles VI of The Two Sicilies – Naples is ruled by Austrian viceroys for the next twenty-one years.

1723   Publication of Pietro Giannone's *Historia Civile del Regno di Napoli*.

1725   Publication of Giambattista Vico's *Scienza Nuova*.

1733   Production of Pergolesi's *La Serva Padrona*, the first *opera buffa*.

1734   Charles VII (the future Charles III of Spain) becomes the first Borbone King of The Two Sicilies – return of the monarchy to Naples.

1737   Building and opening of the Teatro San Carlo.

1738   Construction of the royal palaces of Capodimonte and Portici begun.

1743   Establishment of the royal porcelain factory at Capodimonte.

1744   King Charles defeats the Austrians at the battle of Veletri.

1745   Death of Francesco Solimena, last great painter of the Neapolitan Baroque.

1751   King Charles commissions Ferdinando Fuga to build the Albergo dei Poverei.

1752   King Charles lays the first stone of the palace of Caserta.

1755   Bernardo Tanucci becomes Minister for Foreign Affairs as well as for Justice and for the Royal Household.

1757   Luigi Vanvitelli begins work on the Foro Carolino (Piazza Dante).

1759   King Charles abdicates and leaves Naples to become King of Spain – he is succeeded by his son, the eight-year-old Ferdinand IV.

1764   Sir William Hamilton becomes British Minister at Naples.

1768   Ferdinand IV marries the Archduchess Maria Carolina of Austria.

1776   Bernardo Tanucci is dismissed from his ministerial posts.

1777   Foundation of the Museo Borbonico (now the Museo Archeologico).

1780–88   Publication of Gaetano Filangieri's *La Scienza della Legislazione*.

1787   Goethe visits Naples.

1789   Sir John Acton becomes Prime Minister of The Two Sicilies.

1798   Triumphant reception of Admiral Nelson after the Battle of the Nile.

1799   French invasion. The royal family flees to Sicily. Establishment of the Parthenopean Republic.

1799   Cardinal Ruffo and his Calabrian peasants overthrow the Parthenopean Republic and drive out the French with English assistance.

1802   Ferdinand IV returns to Naples.

1806   French invasion. The royal family again flees to Sicily. Joseph Bonaparte is installed at Naples as 'King Joseph Napoleon'.

1808   Joseph Bonaparte is given the Spanish throne and replaced at Naples by Marshal Murat, 'King Joachim Napoleon'.

1815   Murat defeated by the Austrians at Tolentino – Ferdinand IV returns to Naples – Murat lands secretly in Calabria but is caught and shot.

1816   King Ferdinand IV begins building the church of San Francesco di Paola and its colonnade opposite the Royal Palace. He adopts the style 'Ferdinand I' to commemorate Sicily's administrative union with the mainland. The San Carlo is burnt down.

1817   San Carlo rebuilt and reopened.

1818   First performance of Rossini's *Mosè in Egitto* at the San Carlo.

1818   Naples launches the first steamship in the Mediterranean.

1819   First performance of Rossini's *La Donna del Lago* at the San Carlo.

1820   Carbonari revolution of 1820. Ferdinand I grants a constitution. Anarchy – and flight of the King.

1821   Austrian troops occupy Naples; the King returns.

1825   Death of Ferdinand I and accession of Francis I.

1826   First performance of Bellini's *Bianca e Gernando* at the San Carlo.

1827   Austrian troops withdraw from Naples.

1830	Death of Francis I and accession of Ferdinand II.
1835	First performance of Donizetti's *Lucia di Lammermoor* at the San Carlo.
1837	Royal Palace partly destroyed by fire, and rebuilt.
1839	Opening of railway from Naples to Granatello, the first in Italy.
1840	Gas lighting installed in all main streets in Naples.
1840	Lenticular lighthouse at Naples, the first in continental Europe.
1840	'Sulphur war' between The Two Sicilies and Britain.
1845	All Italy Scientific Congress at Naples.
1845	First performance of Verdi's *Alzira* at the San Carlo.
1848	Revolution and granting of a constitution. Sicily secedes. Ferdinand II puts down armed rising in Naples; constitution in abeyance.
1849	Ferdinand II regains Sicily. The exiled Pope Pius IX visits Naples. First performance of Verdi's *Luisa Miller* at the San Carlo.
1851	Gladstone publishes his *Letters to Lord Aberdeen*.
1852	Opening of the new dockyard and dry dock at Naples. Electromagnetic telegraph cable to Naples, the first in Italy.
1856	Undersea electric magnetic telegraph cable to Naples, the first in Italy.
1859	Death of Ferdinand II and accession of Francis II.
1860	Garibaldi overruns Sicily and invades the southern mainland. Francis II withdraws to Gaeta. Naples ceases to be a royal capital.

Bibliography

ACTON, SIR HAROLD, *The Bourbons of Naples*, London, 1956.

—, *The Last Bourbons of Naples*, London, 1961.

—, Preface to *Painting in Naples from Caravaggio to Giordano*, London, 1982.

Almanack de Gotha, Gotha, 1859.

ATTERIDGE, A. HILLIARD, *Marshal Murat*, London, 1911.

BADDELEY, W. ST CLAIR, *Queen Joanna I*, London, 1893.

BECKFORD, WILLIAM, *Dreams, Waking Thoughts and Incidents*, in *The Travel-Diaries of William Beckford of Fonthill*, ed. G. Chapman, London, 1928.

BLESSINGTON, COUNTESS OF, *The Idler in Italy*, London, 1839.

BLUNT, ANTHONY, *Neapolitan Baroque and Rococo Architecture*, London, 1975.

BRAUDEL, FERNAND, *Les Structures du Quotidien* – translated as *The structures of everyday life* by M. Kochan, London, 1981.

BREMER, FREDRIKA, *Two Years in Switzerland and Italy*, London, 1861.

BROSSES, CHARLES DE, *Lettres Historiques et Critiques sur l'Italie*, Paris, 1799.

BURCKHARDT, JACOB, *Civilisation of the Renaissance in Italy*, London, 1929.

BURNEY, DR CHARLES, *Music, Men and Manners in France and Italy in 1770*, London, 1969.

BUTLER, ALBAN, *The Lives of the Fathers, Martyrs and other Principal Saints*, Dublin, 1756–59.

CELANO, CARLO, *Notizie del Bella, dell' Antico e del Curioso della città di Napoli*, Naples, 1692.

CESARE, RAFFAELE DE, *La Fine di un Regno*, Città di Castello, 1909.

COMMYNES, PHILLIPE DE, *Mémoires*, ed. J. Calmette and G. Durville, Paris, 1924–5.

COLLETTA, PIETRO, *Storia del Realme di Napoli dal 1734. al 1825*, Florence, 1848.

COLLISON-MORLEY, L., *Naples through the Centuries*, London, 1925.

CRAVEN, HON. KEPPEL, *A Tour through the Southern Provinces of the Kingdom of Naples*, London, 1821.

CROCE, BENEDETTO, *Un Calvinista Italiano, il Marchese di Vico Galeazzo Caracciolo*, Bari, 1933.

DOMINICI, BERNARDO DE, *Vite dei Pittori, Scultori ed Architetti Napoletani*, Naples, 1742.

DORIA, GINO, *Storia di una Capitale*, Naples, 1935.

EUSTACE, JOHN CHETWODE, *A Tour through Italy*, London, 1813–19.

EVELYN, JOHN, *The Diary of John Evelyn*, London, 1907.

GALASSO, GIUSEPPE, 'Society in Naples in the Seicento' in *Painting in Naples from Caravaggio to Giordano*, London, 1982.

GIANNONE, PIETRO, *Istoria Civile del Regno di Napoli*, Naples, 1723.

GIGLIOLI, CONSTANCE, *Naples in 1799*, London, 1903.

GOETHE, WOLFGANG, *Italiänische Reise*, Berlin, 1885.

GUICCIARDINI, FRANCESCO, *Istoria di Italia*, Pisa, 1819.

GUNN, PETER, *Naples: a Palimpsest*, London, 1961.

HAMILTON, SIR WILLIAM, *Campi Phlegraei*, Naples, 1776.

HARE, AUGUSTUS, *Cities of Southern Italy and Sicily*, London, 1883.

—, *The Story of My Life*, London, 1896–1900.

HUGHES, S., *Great Opera Houses*, London, 1966.

HUTTON, EDWARD, *Giovanni Boccaccio*, London, 1910.

JAEGER, PIER GIUSTO, *Francesco II di Borbone, L'ultimo re di Napoli*, Milan, 1982.

KELLY, MICHAEL, *Reminiscences*, London, 1826.

KNIGHT, E.C., *Autobiography of Miss Cornelia Knight, Lady companion to the Princess Charlotte of Wales*, London, 1861.

LALANDE, JOSEPH LEFRANÇAIS DE, *Voyage d'un François en Italie*, Paris, 1769.

LAMPEDUSA, GIUSEPPE DI, *Il Gattopardo*, translated as *The Leopard* by Archibald Colquhoun, London, 1961.

LECOY DE LA MARCHE, R.A., *Le Roi René*, Paris, 1875.

MANN, H.K., *Lives of the Popes in the Middle Ages*, London, 1929.

MILLER, LADY [ANNE], *Letters from Italy*, London, 1776.

MISSON, MAXIMILIEN, *Nouveau Voyage d'Italie*, London, 1691.

MORGAN, LADY, *The Life and Times of Salvator Rosa*, London, 1824.

—, *Italy*, London, 1821.

MORYSON, FYNES, *An Itinerary containing His Ten Yeeres Travell through the Twelve Dominions of Germany, Bohmerland, Sweitzerland, Netherland, Denmarke, Poland, Italy, Turky, France, England, Scotland & Ireland, written by Fynes Moryson, Gent.*, London, 1617.

NICOLAS, SIR HARRIS, *The Letters and Despatches of Vice-Admiral Lord Viscount Nelson*, London, 1845.

Painting in Naples 1606–1705 from Caravaggio to Giordano, catalogue, Weidenfeld and Nicolson, and Royal Academy of Arts, London, 1982.

PEPE, GUGLIELMO, *Narrative of Scenes and Events in Italy from 1847 to 1849*, London, 1850.

PERKINS, CHARLES, *Italian Sculptors*, London, 1868.

PETRARCH, F., *Epistolae de rebus familiaribus et variae*, 3 vols, Florence, 1859–63.

PIUS II, POPE, *Memoirs of a Renaissance Pope*, translated by F.A. Gragg, London, 1960.

REUMONT, ALFRED VON, *Die Carafa von Maddaloni. Neapel unter spanischer Herrschaft*, Berlin, 1851.

RUNGIMAN, SIR STEVEN, *The Sicilian Vespers*, Cambridge, 1958.

SHELLEY, P.B., *The Letters of Percy Bysshe Shelley*, ed. F.L. Jones, Oxford, 1964.

SHORTHOUSE, J.H., *John Inglesant*, London, 1881.

SISMONDI, J.C.L., *Histoire des Républiques Italiennes du Moyen Age*, Paris, 1809–26.

SITWELL, SIR SACHEVERELL, *Southern Baroque Art*, London, 1924

—, *Truffle Hunt*, London, 1953.

SIVO, GIACINTO DE, *Storia delle Due Sicilie dal 1847 al 1861*, Trieste, 1868.

SOUTHEY, ROBERT, *Life of Nelson*, London, 1813.

STENDHAL, *Rome, Naples et Florence*, Paris, 1826.

—, *La Vie de Rossini*, Paris, 1824.

SUMMONTE, PIETRO, *Lettera di P. Summonte a M.A. Michiel*, ed. G.B. Nicolini, Naples, 1925.

SWINBURNE, HENRY, *Travels in The Two Sicilies*, London, 1783.

—, *The Courts of Europe at the Close of the Last Century*, London, 1841.

TATHAM, EDWARD, *Francesco Petrarca*, London, 1925.

THOMAS, WILLIAM, *The Historie of Italy*, London, 1549.

TREVELYAN, G.M., *Garibaldi and the Making of Italy*. Greenwood Press, USA.

VIGÉE-LEBRUN, MME, *Souvenirs*, Paris, 1835.

VILLANI, GIOVANNI, *Croniche Fiorentine*, Florence, 1823.

WARD, WILFRID, *Life of Cardinal Newman*, London, 1897.

WEINSTOCK, HERBERT, *Vincenzo Bellini*, London, 1972.

WRAXALL, SIR NATHANIEL, *Historical Memoirs of my own time*, London, 1904.

Index